50 VOICES
of
HCA HEALTHCARE

Copyright © 2018 HCA Healthcare

All rights reserved.

No part of this book may be reproduced, stored in a retrieval system or transmitted in any form or by any means without the prior written consent of the publisher, except by a reviewer who may quote brief passages in a review to be printed in a newspaper, magazine, online article, blog, or journal.

Publisher: Word of Mouth Conversations

Writer: Lily C. Hansen
Editor: Jennifer Chesak
Photographer: Ron Manville
Contributing Photographer: Olivia Weetch
Designer: Benjamin Rumble

HCA Healthcare
One Park Plaza
Nashville, TN 37203

Word of Mouth Conversations
100 Middleton St. No. 211
Nashville, TN 37210

ISBN: 978-0-9997512-2-0

First Edition

50 VOICES
of
HCA HEALTHCARE

by LILY CLAYTON HANSEN

PHOTOGRAPHY *by* RON MANVILLE

THE VOICES

1) **Foreword**
   by Lily Clayton Hansen

2) **Let me tell you a quick story.**
   by Dr. Karl VanDevender

4) **Milton Johnson**
   {Chairman and CEO, *HCA Healthcare*}

8) **Joyce Burns, RN**
   {Consulting Product Analyst, *HCA Healthcare*}

12) **Ruselle Cimeni, RN**
    {Direct Care Nurse, *Park Plaza Hospital*}

16) **Bob Ingram, RN**
    {Direct Care Nurse, *South Atlanite Division*}

20) **Arnold Lemay**
    {Director of Engineering, *Frankfort Regional Medical Center*}

24) **Jane Englebright, PhD, RN**
    {SVP and Chief Nurse Executive, *HCA Healthcare*}

28) **Imelda Guzman/Palmira Arellano/ Ariel Blanchard**
    {VP of Marketing and Public Relations, *San Antonio Division*, VP of Public Relations, *San Antonio Division* & Human Resources Coordinator, *San Antonio Division*}

32) **Kathryn Beechinor, RGN, RM**
    {Nurse Midwife, *The Portland Hospital*}

36) **Bud Reed/Jeff Reed**
    {Past Maintenance Supervisor & Maintenance Specialist, *HCA Healthcare*}

40) **Ann Nguyen, MSN, RN**
    {Clinical Nurse Manager, *Regional Medical Center Of San Jose*}

44) **Sam Hazen**
    {President and COO, *HCA Healthcare*}

48) **Alonzo Smith**
    {Sergeant, Security Officer, *Wesley Medical Center*}

52) **Sandra Osmond, BSN, RN**
    {CNO, *St. Mark's Hospital*}

56) **Eric Ward & Ryann Schneider**
    {President and CEO, *Parallon Business Performance Group* & Legal Counsel, *Parallon Business Performance Group*}

60) **Devon Moore, RN, CCRN**
    {Direct Care Nurse, *Metropolitan Methodist Hospital*}

64) **Dr. Jon Perlin**
    {CMO and President Clinical Services Group, *HCA Healthcare*}

68) **Lenora Everett-Gayle, RN**
    {Direct Care Nurse, *Ocala Regional Medical Center*}

72) **Bill Rutherford**
    {CFO, *HCA Healthcare*}

76) **Kristin Baker, RN**
    {Direct Care Nurse, *Oak Hill Hospital*}

8) **Dr. Fernando Triana**
    {Cardiologist, Chief Officer for Strategy and Innovation, *Cardiology Clinic of San Antonio*}

84) **Tina Billberry, RN**
    {Transfer Center Coordinator, *Rapides Regional Medical Center*}

88) **Dr. Lara M. Lane**
    {OBGYN, *Women's Care of Colorado*}

92) **Freddie Woods**
    {Manager of Network Engineering, *HCA Healthcare*}

96) **Noel Williams**
    {SVP and CIO (retired), *HCA Healthcare*}

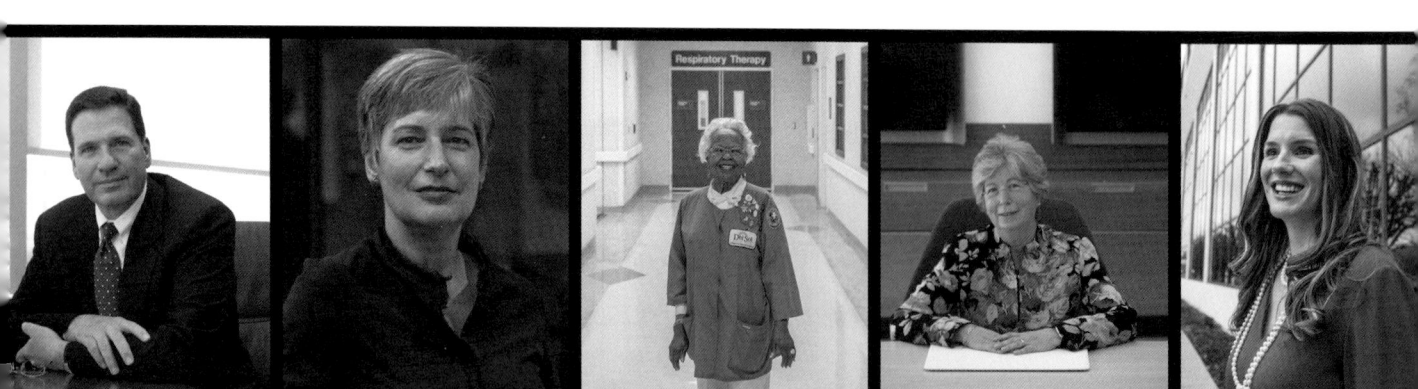

100) **Heather J. Rohan**
{President, *TriStar Division*}

104) **Louis Joseph**
{Group VP of Physician Services Group, *HCA Healthcare*}

108) **Baby Ruth Boswell**
{Volunteer, *Del Sol Medical Center*}

112) **Edward T. Jones**
{President and CEO, *HealthTrust*}

116) **Diane McNealy**
{EVS Director, *Parkland Medical Center*}

120) **Dr. Stanley Wang**
{Cardiologist & Sleep Specialist, *Austin Heart*}

124) **Liz Harms, RN, CMSRN**
{Direct Care Nurse, *Rose Medical Center*}

128) **Bruce Moore**
{President of Operations & Service Lines Group, *HCA Healthcare*}

132) **Elizabeth Baumgarten**
{Director Service Line Solutions, *Sarah Cannon*}

136) **Vic Campbell**
{SVP Investor Relations and Government Affairs, *HCA Healthcare*}

140) **Natashia Floyd**
{Utilization Coordinator, *TriStar Division*}

144) **Jack O. Bovender Jr.**
{Past Chairman and CEO, *HCA Healthcare*}

148) **Karen Giovengo, DNP, RN, CNL/ Hazel Antiola, RN**
{Director of Medicine/Surgery/Oncology/Pediatrics, *St. Lucie Medical Center* & Charge Nurse and Supervisor, *St. Lucie Medical Center*}

152) **Jill Fainter**
{VP of Clinical Standards Clinical Services Group (retired), *HCA Healthcare*}

156) **Marty Paslick**
{SVP and CIO, *HCA Healthcare*}

160) **Joann Ettien**
{COO/Administrator, *Centennial Women's and Children's*}

164) **Richard Bracken**
{Chairman and CEO (retired), *HCA Healthcare*}

168) **Sharn Barbarin, FACHE**
{CEO, *Medical City Lewisville*}

172) **Maurice "Mel" Lagarde III**
{President, *MidAmerica Division*}

176) **Jennifer Buford**
{Executive Recruiter, *HCA Healthcare*}

180) **Gabriel O. Perez**
{Director Application Development, *East Florida Division*}

184) **Beverly Wallace**
{President (retired), *Parallon*}

188) **Christina Hux, RN**
{Direct Care Nurse, *Tulane University Hospital and Clinic*}

192) **Marcus Thomas**
{EVS Supervisor, *Sunrise Hospital and Medical Center*}

196) **Mary Greer**
{IT&S Voice Services Supervisor, *HCA Healthcare*}

200) **Dr. Thomas Frist, Jr.**
{Co-founder, *HCA Healthcare*}

FOREWORD
by Lily Clayton Hansen

Welcome to 50 Voices of HCA Healthcare, a series of interviews and portraits that document, highlight, and celebrate the culture of this 50-year-old institution. HCA is a company that cares deeply for its people, and in turn, its employees express their loyalty by remaining at HCA for decades. The HCA family members see the value of building their careers within a supportive environment, being seen by their supervisors as whole people, and developing strong bonds with their co-workers. This 250,000-person Fortune 100 company has flourished for decades by allowing its locally driven hospitals to become integrated into their communities and treating its employees like family.

HCA's success endures because its mission and values fall in line with its employees' own. May this book honor those who contributed to HCA's first 50 years and welcome the next generations who will carry on the company's culture. Everyone who has contributed to HCA's mission—above all else, we are committed to the care and improvement of human life—has created history.

Dr. Karl VanDevender, cofounder of The Frist Clinic and HCA historian, has been one of those history-makers. An academic, public speaker, and son of a civil rights activist, Dr. VanDevender has spread the culture of HCA around the world. The much-admired physician, who at one point in his life wanted to become a minister, has applied a spiritual overlay to his medical career by giving eulogies at many of his patients' funerals—including the joint memorial service for HCA co-founder Dr. Thomas F. Frist, Sr. and his wife, Dorothy Cate Frist.

For Dr. VanDevender, medicine is an amalgam of art, science, and business, but the most important element is culture, the glue that bonds the staff of every medical facility together. HCA's culture, as Dr. VanDevender explains, is one of a "can do" attitude combined with kindness and respect.

Dr. VanDevender grew up in Meridian, Mississippi, home to a number of cultural game changers, including Dr. Frist, Sr. After attending the University of Mississippi on a full scholarship, earning his graduate degree at Oxford University in England, and completing his internship and residency at Vanderbilt University Medical Center, Dr. VanDevender found himself working with the HCA founder in 1982. It would forever change his perspective on the practice of medicine.

On his very first day, as he was about to enter a patient's room, Dr. Frist, Sr. pulled him aside to offer his observations of the four key dynamics that govern a physician-patient relationship: the need to respect the inherent dignity all humans possess and deserve; an appreciation for suffering, which is simply a part of the human condition; a person's need for independence, which encourages the patient to be an active part of treatment; and a fear of dependence, which is the natural worry that one day we may all become a burden to society and those we love. These ideals, rooted in kindness and empathy, shaped Dr. VanDevender's interactions from that day forward. They are foundational tenets of his practice that he continues to share with young physicians today.

LET ME TELL YOU A QUICK STORY.
by Dr. Karl VanDevender

When I started my practice at Centennial Medical Center in 1982, HCA was 14 years old. It *felt* like a 14-year-old. The hospital and the company were energetic and ambitious, full of promise and big ideas. It was growing in every direction. It's hard for me to realize that the organization I signed on with is now 50 years old and that the new kid on the block is now the elder statesman of the industry.

We live in a present that is layered on top of the past. I never walk into the Sarah Cannon Cancer Center without remembering the old Park View hospital or without thinking about a time when a patient had to make an appointment to go to the emergency room, when we now have three emergency rooms to walk into: adult, children, and obstetrics. I joined Centennial in the "dark ages" before cell phones and texting. Doctors still had answering services, and pagers were only starting to catch on. Back then, the most reliable way to get ahold of a doctor who wasn't in the hospital was to call Mrs. Frist, the wife of Dr. Frist, Sr. and the mother of Tommy Frist. She spent her weekends sitting by the phone like a sentry, and she knew where everyone was and how to get ahold of them.

I show my age when I take new doctors around the hospital and tell them stories of what used to be where, but that's the nature of having lived through history. In this book we're paying tribute to where we've come from, celebrating the remarkable healthcare we're providing now, and looking ahead to more growth in the future. The proof of HCA's vitality is best found in how we continue to change and grow. New areas are being added onto the hospital as I write this.

I like to tell my patients that age is just a number, that what matters is how you take care of yourself, how you feel. But the milestone numbers offer us a chance for reflection. It's the moment to write history down before it's lost, and to assess both our progress and ambition. That's why this book was put together. To say that this is a company built around doctors and patients is to only tell half the story. Any business that has grown and thrived for fifty years is filled with visionaries and risk-takers, architects and accountants. But so much of the success of our hospitals comes from the kind attention of the housekeeping staff and the nurses who know how to tell a joke and when to hold a hand. It comes from the good cheer of the people who are there to check a patient in for surgery at five in the morning, the chaplains who sit with the families through hard times, and the men and women who roll the patients to their cars when the stay is over. What I've seen in my years at HCA is that no one person is ever the whole story, and that the health of the industry is really the health of our HCA family, everyone working together for our main purpose: the health of the patient.

So it stands to reason that this would be a book of interviews, many voices all reporting on the HCA of which they've been a part. Hopefully, by reading these stories together, a larger picture will start to unfold and keep unfolding into the future.

MILTON JOHNSON

{Chairman and CEO, *HCA Healthcare*}

Upbeat and unbelievably driven, HCA Healthcare CEO Milton Johnson wakes up every morning convinced his day is going to be great. Connecting every one of his decisions to HCA's mission keeps Johnson on top of his game personally and professionally. He understands the responsibility that comes along with running HCA and living up to those who led the way before him. Since joining the company as a trained CPA in 1982, Johnson has been groomed by some industry greats. From them, he learned that values and culture are as central as strategy to the success of an organization. Johnson, who aims for HCA to be a community asset, takes patient safety, experience, and outcomes into account every time he makes a decision. Once Johnson makes up his mind, he keeps on moving. Over 34 years, he has learned to balance the many dimensions of his role and plan for an industry that is perpetually in flux. Though he leads a $70-billion enterprise value integrated healthcare system, Johnson's humble beginnings keep him grounded. The Nashville native credits his mother for his strong moral compass and the ethical people in his life for never letting him lose sight of what it's all about.

How did your upbringing influence your demeanor in the workplace?

My father passed away when I was four years old, and I grew up in a single-parent home. My mother was an incredible woman who grew up on a tobacco farm in Tennessee. In those days, if you were a woman and had an eighth-grade graduation, which she did, you were considered fully educated. After the farm, she moved to Nashville at age 17. She set an incredible example through her hard work and self-sacrifices. My mom was incredibly honest, value-driven, and had high expectations of me to reflect those principles. While we were a low-income family, as she worked at a garment factory and in childcare, money wasn't something she put a lot of emphasis on in terms of measuring success. Everything came down to who you were as a person. She instilled in me the importance of hard work and respecting people for their character and integrity. That contributed greatly to how I operate in my personal and professional life.

Did the instability of your childhood serve as a driving force for your success?

Definitely. My mother always made it clear that education was the key to having an opportunity to reach my potential. I was the first in my immediate family to go to college, which opened all sorts of doors that I never imagined. I wanted success—maybe more than others, due to the way that I grew up—and was willing to put in the work to earn it. My first job, at age 14, was at a mom-and-pop local grocery store. By 18, I was self-sufficient. In college, I worked from 6 a.m. to 6 p.m. Friday, Saturday, and Sunday in computer operations to support myself as I attended college. I have always had a drive to achieve in order to improve the circumstances that I faced in childhood.

What attracted you to an accounting and business major at Belmont University?

I wanted to earn money, quite frankly. Prior to attending Belmont, I was pursuing an associate degree at Nashville Tech, studying computer programming. There, a retired CPA who was one of my teachers at the time suggested that I explore accounting. He recognized my knack for numbers, logical mind, and potential. I was encouraged to pursue accounting and business as a profession and transferred to Belmont to do so.

How were you first introduced to HCA and why did you want to work here?

After completing college, I began working at Ernst & Young and was assigned to the HCA account. I recognized through meeting employees of the company that they were smart, high-quality people. At E&Y, HCA was known for having an incredibly positive work environment, and with its growth there were high expectations for the future. HCA was in a rapid growth phase at the time, and after making a large acquisition, they offered me an opportunity to join the company. So in 1982, I joined HCA's tax department.

What is your secret sauce in terms of your discipline and work ethic?

I have always believed one must earn their opportunities in life. I also enjoy my work and the purpose of HCA, which motivates me to be the best that I can. Every day, I enter the building prepared and try to remain curious. Always trying to understand why things work the way they do helps me to maintain a focus on improving them.

CEOS DON'T SUCCEED AS INDIVIDUALS BUT RATHER BY LEADING A SUCCESSFUL TEAM.

Which HCA mentors helped you move up within the company?
There have been several over the past 35 years, but the influence, guidance, and support of Dr. Tommy Frist, Jr. has been a constant in my career. His confidence helped me to believe in myself as my career progressed. I want to earn and keep his trust.

What qualities do you believe connect HCA's leaders throughout its history?
I think back to the founding of the company and how all three men set the tone for HCA because they shared the same values. Past leaders led with authentic passion and kept the patients' well-being as their top priority. Each had a deep desire to win in the right way. Valuing our history and culture is a key connector in this organization.

What qualities did you pick up from former CEOs?
What I learned from them is to have an exceptional sense of accountability when it comes to serving our patients. Solid relationships are key for effective leadership. One must also be decisive, as leaders must make difficult decisions.

What does it feel like to be the CEO of HCA?
It is a humbling experience to run HCA because of my respect for those who preceded me. Most days it's an incredibly rewarding job that I feel very blessed to experience.

Good times are great. How do you get through the tough moments?
You're never as good as your best day or as bad as your worst. Life experiences have taught me that we all will have disappointments and hurdles to overcome, and managing a company naturally presents challenges. Having a strong counsel around me is valuable. I try to address challenges with a sense of urgency but never panic.

How do you stay connected to what is happening on the ground to continuously improve clinical quality?
Our clinical performance is a top priority for the company. We have invested heavily in technology and people to constantly improve clinical quality. I routinely meet with our clinical and operational teams to review our performance at hospital, market, and corporate levels. It's the core of what we do.

How do you cut through communication filters?
Because I am CEO, a lot of information is filtered by the time it reaches my office. It's human nature not to want to give someone, and especially a leader, bad news. However, I encourage what I call "straight talk." You don't shoot the messenger. If we have a problem, let's fix it. It's also important to get out of your office. You can learn a lot by walking down the hallway and asking a few questions.

What is the biggest lesson you've learned as CEO?
The pace of play is fast, and decision-making is critical, but I cannot overstate the importance of taking the time to listen to others. CEOs don't succeed as individuals but rather by leading a successful team.

Why do you feel company culture is so critical to HCA's success?
It keeps me grounded and focused on providing healthcare at our best. We have a culture of caring, a culture of putting the patient first, and a culture of providing an engaging environment for physicians, nurses, and staff.

What does HCA's mission mean to you?
If we achieve our mission as an organization, then we improve the lives of millions of patients. I am passionate about our mission and know HCA as a whole is too.

What keeps you engaged in your passion for healthcare?
Visiting one of our hospitals recharges my batteries. I wish I could do it more often. HCA was tested this year with three major disasters: Hurricanes Harvey and Irma and the tragic mass shooting in Las Vegas. In those moments you see the true dedication of your team. Those events are inspirational because of the sacrifices so many colleagues made for others. Seeing our mission carried out during these disasters while under intense pressure inspires all of us at HCA.

How would you like to cement your legacy at HCA?
I would like to be known as a passionate leader who improved the quality and service of healthcare. I hope to do this by continuing HCA's investments in clinical capabilities and therefore improving our patient experience. Lastly, I want to continue HCA's long tradition of internal leadership development. This will ensure that our values and culture are passed on to future generations.

JOYCE BURNS, RN

{Consulting Product Analyst, *HCA Healthcare*}

"Once a nurse, always a nurse," says Joyce Burns. The Consulting Product Analyst, whose nickname is "Mama Joyce," embraces technology as a means of giving nurses more time with their patients. In her childhood, vocational options were limited. As a fourth-grader, Burns fell down and broke her arm. Wowed by the tenderness with which the medical team treated her during her trauma, she vowed to become a nurse. Shortly after high school graduation in 1965, she lucked upon Park View Hospital's first licensed practical nurse course. The education opened up opportunity and gave Burns an outlet for her natural caretaking disposition. By the 1990s, Burns transitioned into a role at IT&S to spearhead the development and implementation of MEDITECH. Her medical background and analytical mind unified in such a way that Burns could teach her colleagues about cutting-edge technology. In 2015, Burns was nominated for the Noel Williams Award in Excellence. Her co-workers applaud her for her easygoing attitude, forward-thinking strategies, and her ability to troubleshoot any problem. Decades later, she is just as driven to make IT&S the best department it can be.

How did your upbringing influence your character in the workplace?
My mother left my father with six children when I was in the third grade. We had nothing to eat and nowhere to go. Daddy packed us in the car and drove down to Nashville where his family lived. I was then sent to an orphanage for two years. It was a tragic, impoverished situation, which I got out of through my nursing career.

How were you able to pursue your nursing education?
On our street there was a neighbor who was paralyzed from her chest down. Her mother worked at Park View Hospital in the cafeteria. One day she told me that Park View was hosting their very first licensed practical nurse class, which I immediately applied for. My father did not approve, which was crushing, so I went to live at the neighbor's house. I gave her a bath and cleaned the house for my room and board. I was an LPN for nine years, and with the help of HCA tuition reimbursement, went back to school and became a registered nurse.

What is it like to have witnessed the growth of HCA?
It is phenomenal how fast this organization has grown. Back then HCA was a little four-story hospital and a tiny house. Yet, we've always had the most up-to-date treatment modalities and given the patient whatever they needed. Patients want the best care possible, and we got it here.

In your eyes, what makes someone a great nurse?
Having the perceptiveness to assess what a patient needs at all times. You have to be able to communicate well with physicians so they can understand your insights in regards to the patient. As a nurse, I always said things the way I saw them, which is how you save lives. In the medical world, you can't sugarcoat information.

How did you transfer from working on the hospital floor to IT&S?
"Computer land" had just launched at HCA when I was working as the Director of Surgical Nursing at Park View. I was sent over to corporate to learn a new technology system for nursing administration. Soon after, the nurse who was supposed to look after IT&S quit. I guess she didn't want all that responsibility. (Laughs) I believed those computers could help nurses, so I got out my books, studied, and taught myself the program. The next thing I know, I get a phone call saying, "You're the Director of Staffing and Scheduling."

Were you excited?
Not really! But every time they had to roll out a new documentation system I was nominated for the position. Nursing was the last department to have automated paperwork, and I was motivated to help my colleagues get a handle on the programs. I saw my role as necessary and the next phase in my career. I thought, *Take it or leave it*.

What was it like to educate others about an entirely new way of doing things?
It was hard. The typical nurse was not open to new programs, and I listened to people complain most of the time. My unofficial role was to encourage them to see the good points in the system. My go-to line was, "You're gonna like it."

What does it feel like to be one of the first people in IT&S?
All the people that started along with me are gone. And here I still am. (Laughs) I like that we've come a long way and now have a huge team helping with the work. Like it or not, technology had to happen because that was the way the industry was going.

PATIENTS WANT THE BEST CARE POSSIBLE, AND WE GOT IT HERE.

What was your reaction when you were nominated for the Noel Williams Award?
It did my heart good. For so long I had to be the tough guy who said, "No, we can't do that!" I tell things straight up. So many people try to make things seem better than they are, which isn't something that I'm capable of. People respect that. My heart is with the nurse because I know what it's like to be in the trenches.

What technology do you wish you'd had access to as a nurse?
Everything! Back in my day, they used to call you on the intercom system, and now the nurses and physicians connect through their cell phones. I also love the interactive TVs, which educate patients about their condition. Every time a nurse says, "This is so much better than what we had before," I feel very happy.

What is your expertise?
Finding a solution when something goes wrong. I dig in the corners and don't take the most obvious route. I also have a pretty good memory, which means I can take a computer problem and say, "If this happened, then maybe that's why it's happening now."

Has this job kept the pep in your step?
At age 70, I believe a purpose keeps you vibrant. If you just sit in a chair, you die. This job keeps me alert and productive, which provides joy. When I came over to IT&S, I was only going to be here for five years, and now I've been here 25! They can't get rid of me!

What's kept you at HCA so long?
Feeling worthwhile and respected. You can go as far as you want at HCA with all of the help you need at your fingertips. That's a gift.

How do you continue to grow in your current role?
The work changes constantly because the industry is always evolving. You have to learn new computer skills and software all of the time, which keeps you stimulated. I'm not sure if that's growth. Maybe that's maintenance. (Laughs)

Since you've worked on both ends of the clinical spectrum, as a nurse and also on the supportive IT&S level, how do you hope your work has impacted patients?
I hope patients and their families say that the initiatives I've led at HCA have provided them with the best care possible without any strings attached.

Has mentoring others been important in your career?
I would consider myself more of a role model than a mentor because I don't often give others advice. Hopefully those on my team can just follow in my footsteps.

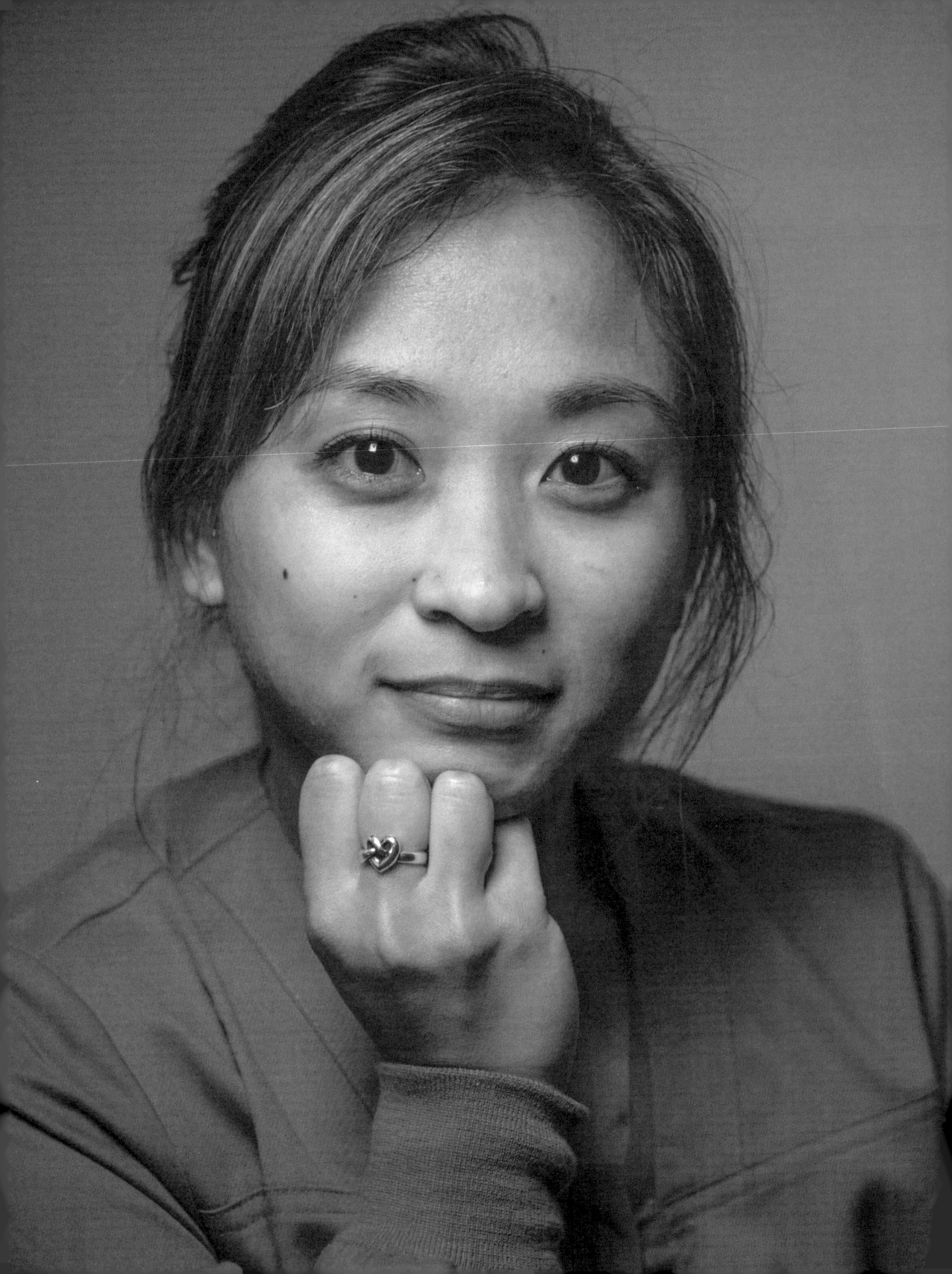

RUSELLE CIMENI, RN

{Direct Care Nurse, *Park Plaza Hospital*}

Ruselle Cimeni enjoys brightening her patients' darker days. Perhaps it is her peppy voice or naturally optimistic outlook, but the 24-year-old nurse has a mysterious knack for bringing patients' blood pressures down. She treats every patient like a best friend. Cimeni always knew she would become a nurse. Many members of her family, all from the Philippines, work in the medical industry. Born in New York, yet a Texan most of her life, Cimeni became a post-surgical staff nurse at Bayshore Medical Center in Pasadena, Texas, before transferring to Park Plaza Hospital in Houston. When she began her career in nursing nearly four years ago, she immediately found the profession to be rewarding not only because she was able to care for patients but also because they gave something back in the form of a shared smile or kind word. In spite of being naturally shy, Cimeni finds it easy to engage on the floor. She feels lucky to be in a line of work that keeps her intellectually, emotionally, and socially stimulated.

What is one fun fact about Ruselle?
Everyone asks about my name! (Laughs) It's a great conversation starter

What were your first experiences like as a nurse?
The first time I was ever on the floor, I found the job to be very overwhelming. Fast forward, and my daily reaction is, *This is awesome.* However, it is nerve-racking to be in a hospital for the first time because you are literally responsible for people's lives. It took me a minute to embrace and convince myself that I could do that. I also worried that patients wouldn't take me seriously because of my age. Fortunately, my youth was never an issue, and I gained my confidence through experience, like anything in life. I love helping people so every day is a good one.

Can you describe what you do and how you feel about what you do?
Every day is new and will never go as planned. I hope for the best but also make room for the unexpected. No experience is the same in nursing, which is what makes it such an exciting profession. As a charge nurse, I write reports, do my daily audits, assign beds, round, attend meetings, and help out wherever I am needed. You are everyone's resource and first point of contact, which is thrilling and slightly terrifying. (Laughs) I want to give everyone everything I've got!

Did you have any mentors who were particularly influential?
From the beginning, a charge nurse named Noreen took me under her wing. She encouraged me constantly and is someone I credit for a lot of my knowledge. Everyone at both of my hospital jobs has been so welcoming and willing go out of their way to help me figure out the answers to my questions. Whatever I needed, my fellow nurses took it upon themselves to give to me. That support system shaped me to embrace my fellow staff members and new nurses in the same way. When you are treated with such kindness, you want to give it back.

Why are you driven to be a great nurse?
It's an honor to be witness to other people's lives. The connections that I make with my patients are heartwarming. While it's hard to put into words, my job makes my spirit and soul feel really good. Touching other people in a positive way keeps me going and gives my life purpose. I am excited to see my second home and family every week, which makes for an enjoyable existence.

What is most satisfying about your job?
I get what I give back. In what other industry do you find that?

How did you learn to connect with patients?
Outside of work I am not a social butterfly; however, in a hospital setting, it feels very natural to make small talk with my patients. This job has helped me to become a more open person. Finding a common ground with your patients gives them faith in your caretaking abilities. That in turn gives me confidence. Asking my patients questions in order to find out what makes them tick is one of the most fun parts of the job. It's fascinating to learn about their lives.

Do you find that social interaction is healing for patients?
Absolutely! I had a patient once who was really sad because his family didn't visit very often. When I learned that he played guitar professionally, which I've pursued myself as a hobby, I would encourage him to play for me. "I would love to hear your music as I walk down the hallway," is what I would say, which cheered him up a great deal. As a nurse, we are the patient's support system.

How do you turn a tough shift around?
It feels so good when a patient says, "I appreciate everything that you do." As we care for patients they care for us, too. It's a two-way street.

How do you go above and beyond in your role?
I am what I call "spongey," which means I want to take in as much as I can while I can. Perhaps that's because of my age. With my patients, I try to be the best version of myself because they are often having their worst day. Most importantly, I let them know that I care, will always make time to listen to them, and treat them as a unique individual. I create a safe space in which I can be their caretaker, surrogate family member, and friend. We're here for 12 hours at a time, so we might as well have an enjoyable day together.

What about your personality makes you good at your job?
As a child, I was very timid, and that may have made me more empathetic. It's natural for me to look at a patient and think, *What if that were my family or me?* Every patient is one-of-a-kind and must be treated in a compassionate, individualized manner. If nurses ever start to label patients, then they need to rely on their listening skills more.

In your opinion, what makes for a really great team?
People who are willing to stop what they're doing and help another member if they need help. A great team member looks around the unit and asks their coworkers, "Can I do anything to assist you?" Nurses care for patients and should, therefore, look after their coworkers, too. This is a full-circle job.

What are the benefits of being a team player?
You feel like you have a life jacket on and aren't in danger of drowning. Teamwork makes for a smoother shift. Our work is about the patient, and great care should be given in a positive environment. Strength is found in numbers.

Do you have any guidance for your fellow nurses?
Be curious, ask questions, and try new things. I used to be afraid to ask patients about their illness for fear they would think I was dumb. However, sometimes they know more about their disease processes than we do because they live with it. Staying humble and open-minded is how you constantly learn. Our job is not about being a superhero but rather stepping up to the situation at hand. If you put in the effort and look to your team for support then you can overcome any fear.

TOUCHING OTHER PEOPLE IN A POSITIVE WAY KEEPS ME GOING AND GIVES MY LIFE PURPOSE.

How do you care for yourself while taking care of others?
I am really good at compartmentalizing, which means that I rarely talk about work at home. Keeping the two separate helps me a lot. Positive self-talk and a great support system are also critical to getting through those days where you feel like you can't catch a break. While it's tough, I also try to not take the way others treat me personally. Patients are in pain, and by making their situation better it benefits everyone involved. The way most people act has nothing to do with you.

How would you describe the HCA company culture?
The environment is family-like, from the nurses who look after me to the CEOs who know everyone's names. Our hospital's leaders are the best of the best. They are involved rather than a mysterious face behind a curtain. They are committed to the company, hospital, and value system. When leadership knows you on a personal level, you feel respected and valued as an employee.

How do you feel about the rapidly changing medical landscape?
Technology is all I know as a nurse. I think a computerized system makes our job easier in many ways. Other times I worry that our patients think we don't spend enough time with them. Documentation and spending quality time with our patients is a constant balancing act and common struggle amongst nurses.

What does the HCA mission mean to you?
The mission is simple and straightforward, which is why I think it makes such a great impact. It exemplifies my own devotion to caretaking, which comes down to treating every patient whom I come into contact with compassionately. At one point in time I wondered, *What would I do if I weren't a nurse?* For days, my best friend and I racked our brains and made lists of various jobs. We couldn't think of any industry that mattered or was more meaningful than healthcare. I honestly would never want to be anything else.

BOB INGRAM, RN

{Direct Care Nurse, *South Atlantic Division*}

Robert "Bob" Ingram is a former United States Navy Hospital Corpsman Third Class and a recipient of the highest military decoration, the Medal of Honor, for his courage in the Vietnam War. Today, at Memorial Family Medicine in Jacksonville, Florida, Ingram, a nurse of 47 years, still believes in putting his team first. Originally from Clearwater, Florida, Ingram enlisted in the Navy because of limited career options. In boot camp, Ingram caught pneumonia and was treated by corpsmen whose dedication woke him up to his own purpose. From there, he promptly enrolled in the Navy's Hospital Corps School and studied around the clock so he could become certified. Ingram earned his Medal of Honor for actions on March 28, 1966, during an intense battle against dozens of North Vietnamese troops. After hearing cries for a corpsman, Petty Officer Ingram, only 21 years old, exhibited bravery beyond what most can comprehend. He endured four gunshot wounds, including one to the head, as he crept across the terrain collecting ammunition from the dead and aiding the wounded. When Ingram accepted his Medal of Honor several decades later, he humbly referred to it as a symbol for all of the men he had fought alongside. Today, Ingram, who supervised Memorial Family Medicine for 37 years and still works at the facility part time as a nurse, educates others about how to engage with Vietnam vets. People fear what they don't understand, which is why Ingram wants to shed light on the invisible emotional wounds veterans carry. The goal is for everyone to work together by communicating effectively and efficiently.

Why did you want to become a corpsman?
While in boot camp, I got sick and was sent to a dispensary. I was beyond inspired by the commitment of the corpsmen. I wanted what they had.

How would you describe the Marine mentality?
The Marine Corps training eliminates any thoughts you ever had and ingrains their philosophies. When a Marine comes out of boot camp, he will follow the order that he is given, without question, to the point of death. I made it my responsibility to learn why these guys acted and reacted the way that they did. Upon entering the Marines, I needed to comprehend their unique mindset in order to meet their needs.

What goes through your mind before you go into combat?
The enemy wants to take out the corpsman and officers first. The team does not function well without medical presence. When the war started, most of the corpsmen quit, retired, you name it. No one wants to die. Fortunately, most of the guys on my team had been in the Marines for three years, which is an extremely long time, by the time we hit Vietnam. The noncommissioned officers had a good amount of time in the service and therefore an idea of what transpires in battle. The high-ranking officers had been there on many wars. They were good leaders and, most importantly, understood how one another functioned. When we entered Vietnam, we were hit with most of the action. The day on which I earned my medal, only 112 men were left out of 242.

What do you think makes for a successful team?
Preparation, experience, leadership, and communication are what make a team function. Everything starts at the top, which is why your leaders must be strong.

How would you describe your relationship with your teammates?
We worked, ate, and slept together. It is the most intense relationship you can imagine. You depend on and would die for one another—similar to a good marriage. When I saw my team 32 years later, our bond was still that tight. That type of trust is born out of circumstance and getting through the crucible of combat together.

How is a corpsman viewed within the team dynamic?
You are their medical professional, mother, and occasional pastor. A great corpsman treats his teammates to a deeper degree than most medical professionals because of the unfamiliar environment you are in and intense pressure. You can't crumble because your team depends on you. You immediately assess the situation and do what needs to be done to the best of your ability.

What would most people not know about being in a war setting?
At times I was the only corpsman on our team. I went on every patrol, which meant I was running two to three times as much combat as most Marines. A corpsman isn't supposed to carry a rifle, but it became evident that I needed to be armed. Otherwise, I would have been a moving target. I adapted to my circumstances and became a part of the team. I had to be just like my men in order to survive. Every day you think, *My life could be over tomorrow*, which is an unbelievable thing to experience with other human beings.

Did you think you would survive?
I had no intentions of coming back to the States, which is why I didn't communicate with my family while I was in combat. They wouldn't have understood. I believe I was spared because it wasn't my time. God makes those decisions and didn't want me to go. Coming back home was like stepping out of a nightmare. I gave my 100 percent during every moment of Vietnam. It was the only way I could stay sane in the midst of the chaos. Ever since, I've had to compartmentalize those memories in order to function in the real world.

How did being in combat change your perspective of life?
You begin asking yourself questions like, *Where are you in this big world?* Well, you're just you. *Are you better than anyone else?* No. *Are you lower than anyone else?* No! War changes your perspective on what is and isn't important.

What advice do you have for other veterans post-combat?
Veterans don't have the same tools as everyone else. Our mindset is to eliminate the enemy, which is why we experience a tremendous amount of frustration. The people above, alongside, and behind you don't understand the way that you view the world. Intuition and introspection are what veterans must rely upon in order to function. They have to be self-aware enough in order to constantly assess their actions. Hopefully, they are in a work environment, like I was, where their supervisors and coworkers can do the same. I am very fortunate that my supervisors did all they could to help me post-combat rather than get in my way. When I eventually became a supervisor, I was disciplined and consistent in my expectations. As a leader, I hit the floor with my employees as opposed to sitting in my office. Working alongside your team and asserting that you have their best interest at heart goes a long way.

I KNOW I WAS PUT HERE TO TAKE CARE OF PEOPLE AS A CORPSMAN, NURSE, AND LEADER.

Can you describe your passion for caregiving?
I have taken care of many men who have lived and died. A lot didn't know my last name, but what does that matter? I was their corpsman, and they were grateful for my service. It's an indescribable bond, which is why when I saw my men many years later at the Medal of Honor reception I still recognized their voices and the way they walked. If that's not love, then what is?

What does courage mean to you?
The Marine Corps motto is "honor, courage, and commitment," which underscores everything we do. You can't have one without the other, because they are all intrinsically linked. Every situation must be assessed by asking the question, *What is the right thing to do right now?* In my mind, that always came back to taking care of my men. There are probably 30 or 40 men who deserved the medal more than I did. Everyone's actions on my team were above and beyond the call of duty.

What has been the most satisfying thing about your medical career?
I know I was put here to take care of people as a corpsman, nurse, and leader. My purpose was to help develop the Memorial Family Medicine practice, patients, and clientele. I like to think of myself as the peacemaker between different departments, spokesman for the hospital, and someone who makes others think.

What do you think makes someone a great leader?
I don't believe in telling others what to do but rather sitting them down, providing an array of options, and allowing them time to think about it. People should think for themselves. Every decision I've made in my medical career has been about the family practice. Putting others before your own interests is courage in my eyes.

ARNOLD LEMAY

{Director of Engineering, *Frankfort Regional Medical Center*}

From fixing patient monitors to room thermostats, Arnold "Arnie" LeMay keeps everything functioning properly to allow physicians to focus 100 percent on their patients. The Director of Engineering at Frankfort Regional Medical Center loves the constant change and learning curve of his job. While growing up in Central Kentucky, LeMay realized the ability to fix things fascinated him. In high school, he became enamored by medical equipment, which he saw as an opportunity to heal others by means of his technical abilities. The 34-year veteran of HCA and humble hero who leads with his heart refers to the organization as one where "being exceptional is acceptable." LeMay, known as a symbol of compassion by his coworkers, brings a humanitarian approach to every action. In addition to doing his work as an engineer, LeMay is a hands-on philanthropist who has been honored by the Frist Humanitarian Award at the local and national levels. LeMay is the cofounder of Water with Blessings, an organization that empowers women around the world to provide clean water for their families and communities and embodies LeMay's personal philosophy: small acts of kindness can result in huge ripples.

How did your upbringing influence your personality in the workplace?
I've always been pathologically curious and, as a child, took everything apart and put it back together. I wanted to know why and how it all worked. I was a typical nerd before it had the cool factor. (Laughs)

When was the first time you were introduced to your current field?
I was taken on a field trip to tour our local hospital, which is the first time I saw an SMA 12/60, also known as an auto analyzer. Right then and there I decided that this would be my career path. Next, I worked for the state government in the Instrumentation and Chemistry Section, where the laboratories for air and water quality were housed. One day, one of the fundamental analysis machines went down, and the lab technician freaked because she couldn't finish her work. I figured out what was wrong with her machine, and afterwards she made the suggestion that I sign up for a vocational school electronics program and helped me to get in there.

What happened next?
I attended school during the day and worked in a factory at night, which basically meant that I had no life. (Laughs) After I graduated, I moved over to the pre-engineering program at the University of Kentucky. While I was in school, a drunk driver killed my mom, so I never finished. After I took some time off, I cold-called a medical repair company one day that hired me on for a field-service position. In that job, I traveled quite a lot, and when I got tired of that, I started at Frankfort Regional Medical Center in 1983. After working in the shared service medical maintenance program, I moved over to the engineering department in 1988.

Did tragedy fuel your drive at all?
Like many, my childhood was difficult at times and gave me the predisposition to help others as a result. I never liked how people sometimes took advantage of women, and even as a little guy, I would stand up for my mother, a single parent.

What is your personal philosophy in terms of healthcare?
Care is incomplete without human connection. Patients may not understand the lab results or the machines in their rooms, but they do recognize when people slow down enough to engage. Fortunately, compassion is not only a core value but also honored, respected, and expected at HCA. It's the right way to do things.

Does face-to-face connection motivate you?
Yes. Helping others gives me joy, which is different from happiness, because joy is of the divine. The first time I made a distinction between the two was in my humanitarian work, which is always a very spiritual experience for me. In regards to a fast-paced clinical environment, any caregiver must be detached enough to deal with what needs to be done but also attached enough to perhaps weep for their patients if they are moved to do so. Making those human connections with patients a priority is incredibly healing for both parties.

COMPASSION IS NOT ONLY A CORE VALUE BUT ALSO HONORED, RESPECTED, AND EXPECTED AT HCA. IT'S THE RIGHT WAY TO DO THINGS.

Tell me about your own humanitarian work with Water with Blessings.
I unexpectedly entered into humanitarian work in regards to water safety. During the first mission trip I went on, myself and the other cofounders, Jim Burris and Sister Larraine Lauter, realized if we could find a way to give residents clean water then we could eliminate at least half of the illnesses we treated. I was attracted to helping the invisible neighborhoods around the world which most people tend to avoid.

Is your humanitarian work ever emotionally difficult?
Sometimes. I try to accept that burden and bring in prayer, patience, and perseverance to get past it. Do what you can to move through the painful moments in small steps. When we first started Water with Blessings, I thought, *What are we doing?* I am a country kid from Central Kentucky who is trying to solve a problem that has plagued the world forever. The real turning point was in the creation of our programming, which was fine-tuned by our community of women through their feedback. We equip, empower, and entrust women to provide clean water for themselves and their community. Their deep appreciation for safe drinking water is something most of the Western world could not comprehend.

What is it about safe water that you are so passionate about?
I am passionate about helping women to become agents of change within their communities. There is no better feeling in the world than putting clean water in the hands of a child.

How would you describe the community of HCA?
HCA's philosophy and method of operation inspires compassionate care. There is no unimportant work in a hospital. Even if my team is doing a technical job, they engage with each patient in a way that respects their human dignity and makes them feel special.

What did it feel like to be honored by the Frist Humanitarian Award?
I felt surprised, humbled, and honored at first, and by the time I got to the national level, I was absolutely stunned. I've just been doing the work and trying to help.

What advice would you give to others who want to do humanitarian work?
God doesn't work with superheroes. God works through you. Everyone has the same opportunity to improve the world through his or her actions. The real power lies in small deeds done with great love. It has been said that once you really see something you can't turn away. Listen to others, persevere, and figure out what needs to be done. This work, whether at home or abroad, is our obligation and can be very restorative.

What does it feel like to find your calling?
My work is interesting and educational, but it isn't finished yet. I don't spend that much time looking back but rather trying to help others in ways that are sustainable.

What do you like most about working in hospitals?
I find the unique vibrations of each department to be quite fascinating. I also love that it takes so many types of intelligence and compassion to keep a hospital operating well. We all trust and rely upon one another, which leads to a robust, resilient, and caring community that can tackle almost anything.

What does the HCA mission mean to you?
HCA has steadfastly improved its culture of integrity, compassion, and clinical excellence and kept it aimed in the right direction. It's a rare thing to have a culture that is so powerful and widely understood throughout the organization. Every day, I work with intelligent, caring people who are engaged in their work. There is an energy that comes out of that type of environment, which is one of the many reasons I've committed myself to this company.

JANE ENGLEBRIGHT, PHD, RN

{SVP and Chief Nurse Executive, *HCA Healthcare*}

Jane Englebright, PhD, RN, CENP, FAAN, HCA's first Senior Vice President and Chief Nurse Executive, believes she has the best job in the world. From the start of her nursing career as a bedside nurse to her various roles as a nurse leader, she has always found the field to be challenging and rewarding. Englebright, a Bowling Green, Kentucky, native, began her HCA career as a critical care nurse at Lewisville Medical Center. In 1999, she joined HCA's corporate quality department. Today, she guides the organization's strategic nursing agenda along with nursing leaders throughout HCA, including a team of chief nursing officers and more than 87,000 nurses. While she enjoys her executive role, she maintains a focus on supporting direct care nurses. Through the founding of HCA's patient safety program and developing a strategic approach to nursing, Englebright has found true fulfillment.

How did your upbringing influence your character in the workplace?
My dad was a college professor and my mother a graduate admissions officer. I grew up at Western Kentucky University, where I also got my first degrees in nursing and education. My parents gave me a love for learning that continues to this day.

What are the characteristics of a great nurse?
There are so many varieties of nursing. You just have to find the right spot for your particular gifts and approach. If you are relationship-focused, rehab is perfect because you can form long-term relationships with your patients. If you like technology, the ICU is great. I think there is a place for any type of person. At HCA we encourage nurses to move between different departments, facilities, and locations. Matching people with their passion is one of our core competencies.

What did your time as a direct care nurse teach you?
My clinical practice was primarily critical care and rehabilitation. In both of those areas, you have to work as a team, be thoughtful, have a strong attention to detail and follow-through. Critical care taught me how to stay calm in the midst of a crisis. You learn to keep your wits about you in order to direct your team, which is a handy skill in a leadership role.

What did it feel like to step into a leadership role?
My first leadership position was an assistant manager in ICU. My supervisor recommended me for the position because she felt I had the skills to advance practice and solve problems. While I always found taking care of patients to be rewarding, I realized that I could have more influence on patient care through leadership. That became a great motivator. While some of my leadership roles were challenging, I would always go back to what my dad said, which is, "The chair you are sitting in should always feel a little too big."

How would you describe your position as Chief Nurse Executive?
My main responsibility is to design, develop, and deliver a plan for nursing at HCA that advances patient outcomes, professional practice, and our organization's performance. First and foremost, we want to create an engaging, empowering work environment in which nurses can thrive. That elicits the best clinical outcomes, patient experience, and physician confidence. HCA has many community physicians who make their rounds and then leave the unit. It's imperative that they trust the nurses to continue the advancement of each patient's care. That relationship makes the system work.

How do you create an inspiring, productive nursing culture?
The HCA mission resonates with nurses, and they find it easy to rally around because it speaks to their motivation and calling. Nurses have an unwavering focus on caring for patients and working in teams. As a leader, I build upon that focus by designing strategies and looking for the most important problems to solve on behalf of our nurses so they can better care for our patients.

What does your problem-solving process look like?
I take data and evidence into account when I am making a decision. In an enterprise of this size and scale, nothing will ever come down to just my opinion. I call upon input from experts who are closer to the action or know more about the issue's aspects than I ever could.

How do you find those experts?
We have the best of the best working inside of HCA who can advise me on anything from finance to logistics. I also rely on those who are doing the day-to-day work; they can tell us what is effective or not. By combining different perspectives, we create a better analysis and plan. We have councils of leaders and subject-matter experts that provide input. At times we might make a special effort to gain information around a specific topic. In 2013, we did the Call for Innovation, in which 800 nurses examined their workflow and frustrations and identified ways that technology could help solve their problems. Their feedback indicated that they needed more mobility, better technology, and less documentation. Out of that came our technology roadmap.

easier. Patients invite us into their bedrooms at the most vulnerable times of their lives. That sacred trust, as Jack Bovender calls it, is why it is important to bring our best selves to patient care every day.

What do you find interesting about healthcare?
Healthcare is an incredibly complex industry that continues to grow and transition. I love problem-solving and tackling challenges, and there are always new challenges and problems to solve in this industry. It's meaningful work. It's important and intellectually challenging.

What is your proudest achievement in your HCA tenure?
Throughout my 25 years I've had the opportunity to learn, be exposed to amazing leaders, and constantly have access to new ideas. I've been fortunate to be a part of several technology initiatives that advanced the practice of nursing such as barcode medication administration (BCMA) and evidence-based clinical documentation (EBCD). However, developing a nursing strategy and moving our leaders in the same direction is my proudest achievement. Our new

FIRST AND FOREMOST, WE WANT TO CREATE AN ENGAGING, EMPOWERING WORK ENVIRONMENT IN WHICH NURSES CAN THRIVE.

That's great that your team feels comfortable giving you feedback.
Nurses usually tell it like it is. (Laughs) In order to work with patients and physicians, you have to be clear and direct. You can't leave things up to interpretation.

What is it like to lead 87,000 people?
My role humbles, excites, and energizes me. When we change practice at HCA, we change 5 percent of U.S. healthcare. Having that kind of impact is incredibly rewarding.

What would you like your 87,000 nurses to know?
A nurse's work matters. I have so much respect for what nurses do, and I see it as a huge honor to support, develop, and make their lives

framework has four components: advocacy and leadership, performance and visibility, consistency in care and operations, and shared services. With 87,000 nurses working in concert, there's no limit to what we can accomplish.

What does the HCA mission mean to you?
It is the guidepost by which we make all of our decisions. Every single action at HCA begins with one question: *Will this further the mission for our patients or not?* By following those strongly ingrained values every single day, without fail, our nurses are able to take great care of patients.

IMELDA GUZMAN, PALMIRA ARELLANO & ARIEL BLANCHARD

{VP of Human Resources, *San Antonio Division*, VP of Marketing and Public Relations, *San Antonio Division* & Human Resources Coordinator, *San Antonio Division*}

Imelda Guzman's, Palmira Arellano's, and Ariel Blanchard's confidence stems from their championing of others inside and outside of the HCA community. The Methodist Healthcare System colleagues have a fire inside of them to fight for justice and create power through female solidarity. Close-knit as can be, they are proof that altruism creates allies in the workplace. Guzman, Vice President of Human Resources and a San Antonio native, grew up in a charitable family who instilled in her the importance of having a social conscience. Arellano, Vice President of Marketing and Public Relations and a fellow Alamo City original, was drawn to Methodist 20 years ago because of the organization's spiritual principles. Blanchard, an HR Coordinator raised in Houston, chose the medical ecosystem so she could lend a hand to those who helped others. What struck a chord in all three was using their administrative roles to help Methodist meet the needs of their beloved city. In their mentor-mentee relationships, the trio teaches one another through real-life experience. They illustrate how one generation can always learn something new from the next. Through humanitarianism, they honor God, one another, and their organization.

How did you wind up in the Methodist Healthcare System?
Palmira: To raise scholarship money to help cover college expenses, I participated in beauty pageants. After participating in Miss Hispanic San Antonio, a woman on the judging panel called to ask if I wanted to work for her advertising agency. There, I gained my first experiences in marketing and public relations. Then I moved on to a national Hispanic advertising agency, working for high-profile clients like Coca-Cola, Burger King, and Proctor and Gamble. During that time, my Uncle Rudy became ill and was taken to Metropolitan Methodist Hospital. I will never forget the compassion and patience the ER staff had with my family when Rudy arrived to the ER without a pulse or heartbeat. I remember looking up at one point and reading the hospital's mission statement and thinking that the staff was following it to a tee. In that moment everything crystallized. I wanted to do more in my career. A few months later, a recruiter from Methodist called to tell me they were hiring. It was fate.

Imelda: Prior to this role, I worked in HR for two major hotel chains. It was busy and fun; however, I wasn't quite satisfied. Since I began working at Methodist eight years ago, I have found great contentment in ensuring that all of the behind-the-scenes action runs smoothly so our team members can take care of patients.

Can you describe in your own words what you do every day?
Palmira: I never know what I am walking into, which is exciting. On any given day, I could deal with a lobbying issue or rolling out information about a new robot. Even though I don't touch patients directly, I feel privileged to make others aware, through internal and external campaigns, of what is happening at Methodist.

Imelda: The other Methodist leaders and I communicate frequently to make sure all of the departments are on the same path. The goal is to create a joint plan to move our individual agendas forward, increase staff retention, and build a culture of accountability. Any problems that arise are evaluated collectively.

Palmira, how did you become a mentor to Imelda?
Palmira: While Imelda was pursuing her master's degree, her boss introduced us. "You two are very similar and need to know one another," he said. Imelda wanted to learn about marketing and PR and was willing to work on weekends in order to gain those skills. I saw a spark in Imelda from day one that made me want to be around her and help however I could.

Ariel, how did you become Imelda's mentee?
Ariel: I met Imelda after she was transferred to my facility. Shortly after, she took me under her wing. She has a beautiful spirit and is one of the most strong-minded women I've ever met. She is active in the community, gives great advice, and is constantly thinking about the bigger picture. She's been a game changer.

every way that I can. Volunteering is fun, easy to incorporate into your schedule, and a great way to spend time with your friends and mentors.

Ariel: There are so many options when it comes to volunteering, which allows you to find one that appeals to your personality.

Imelda: No matter how many people show up, I always consider it a success.

Palmira: I think it's important to connect volunteering activities to purpose. The amount of people who need help is endless, so you just have to find your niche.

THE MISSION REMINDS ME OF WHY I GOT INTO HR IN THE FIRST PLACE, WHICH IS TO STAND UP FOR OTHERS. WE ARE A VOICE FOR METHODIST EMPLOYEES. MY PERSONAL GOALS AND THIS ORGANIZATION'S VALUES COMPLETELY ALIGN, WHICH IS A GREAT FEELING.

Imelda: I am so moved right now! My entire life I've felt as though I have something to say. My family is very strong and always encouraged me to shoot for the stars. I feel very fortunate to have experienced that kind of support and therefore want to help others achieve whatever it is that they want.

What advice would you like to give to other women in your industry?
Imelda: Go after the seat that you want and don't allow it to be cold. Speak your mind and be confident in yourself. Leave a mark on whomever you touch.

Palmira: Once you have obtained some level of success, start giving back. The paying forward of time, money, and resources is how the world goes 'round.

What is it about volunteering that creates such a strong bond?
Palmira: It is inspiring to see women helping other women and doing great work together. While we aren't saving lives like doctors, we use our talents to make an impact on the community.

Imelda: This is my town, and I am determined to give back in

What have you learned from your mentor or mentee?
Imelda: Palmira has helped me to demonstrate my passion in a more diplomatic, professional manner. She guides me when I don't know what path to go down.

Ariel: My anxiety tends to creep up easily. Imelda notices when I am stressed and talks me off the ledge. She has taught me to be a little more carefree.

Palmira: I have realized that I can learn from someone younger. Imelda offers a different perspective and knowledge in areas that I am not as well-versed in.

How has Methodist helped to facilitate your personal and professional growth?
Palmira: Methodist is a faith-based organization, and spirituality is what gets us through the day. Our servant leaders take their faith and role model status seriously. That reminds me of how lucky I am to work here.

Imelda: In my hectic days, spirituality reminds me of what is most important. We are here to serve our patients and God. That guides my professional agenda.

Ariel: The first time I sat in orientation, I felt like this was where I was meant to be. Even though I am not a very religious person, prayer is how I find my purpose and peace in every moment.

Palmira: A lot of the work at Methodist revolves around healing, but there are also times when we walk patients to God's door. I think it's important for patients, employees, and families to know a prayer has a place.

What does HCA's mission mean to you?

Imelda: The mission reminds me of why I got into HR in the first place, which is to stand up for others. We are a voice for Methodist employees. My personal goals and this organization's values completely align, which is a great feeling.

Ariel: Everyone wants to be treated with kindness and respect. I try to treat all of our employees as I would want to be treated, which is what our mission is about.

Palmira: We are devoted to serving humanity through offering the best possible healthcare. In unison, we march to accomplish that mission.

How do you hope that your work impacts patients?

Imelda: My goal is to make our employees' lives easy so they can give patients the best possible experience. Everyone in the HR family is easily accessible and willing to answer any questions so the medical staff can deliver exceptional service. All we want to do is support them so they can give to patients.

Ariel: I want to do any and everything that I can so our employees can channel all of their energy into the purpose behind their position. To help them reach their individual reason for being here is a really great feeling.

Palmira: I hope to give our employees the reminders, tools, and education they need to improve quality and safety for our patients. In addition, I want the community to know the exceptional work we are doing at Methodist and why they should receive their healthcare services here. Through communicating with both of those audiences, we can hopefully save more lives and help San Antonio to become an even healthier city.

Photo by Olivia Weetch

KATHRYN BEECHINOR, RGN, RM

{Nurse Midwife, *Portland Hospital*}

Kathryn Beechinor, a nurse midwife at Portland Hospital in London, United Kingdom, has a seemingly infinite capacity for empathy and an ability to coach others through tragedy. The frank, funny, and fearless midwife uses her own experience of bereavement to guide couples through the loss of a child. Beechinor, raised on a farm in West Cork, Republic of Ireland, always tried to heal anything in her path. After her father passed away, she found that people often dismissed her and her siblings' feelings. From then on, Beechinor vowed that she would always approach others who were grieving in a compassionate manner. While she uses bespoke methods to help each family through their mourning, kindness is always at the forefront. Beechinor walks to the dark places with her patients and holds their hands as they sort out their strife. The Excellence in Nursing Compassionate Care national finalist insists that her reward is knowing she's provided comfort to parents in times of sorrow.

How did you become interested in healthcare?
I grew up on a farm in West Cork, Ireland, in a typical rural setting. I would go to school in the morning and collect eggs with my granny from the hens in the afternoon. From an early stage, I loved babies and nursing anything that was ill. I even tried to resuscitate a dead rabbit on the road once. (Laughs) On February 13, 1989, I enrolled in Cork University Hospital's nursing program.

How did you wind up in London?
In the early '90s, Ireland had very few jobs for qualified nurses. After my mother suggested that I study to become a midwife, I applied and was waitlisted for my training. I had a year to kill, so I moved to London where I worked in a cardiac unit and did some work at a cosmetic surgery clinic. Afterwards, I returned to Dublin to do my midwifery training and then came back to London because of the buzz of the city.

How did you come to your current midwife position at Portland Hospital?
I began working at Portland Hospital as a midwife in 1997. The role of bereavement midwife requires someone with a particular emotional build. I fell into the role because I simply kept volunteering every time someone had a pregnancy loss.

Why are you not afraid to speak about death?
Death is similar to a dirty word in the way that people become very uncomfortable when you talk about it. When my own father died, I felt pushed to the side and not allowed to see him, even though that was all I wanted. I decided in that moment to always be honest with anyone who was grieving, ask him or her how they were feeling, and encourage them to get it out and express their needs.

What do you say to someone whose child has just died?
Firstly, I acknowledge what has happened and, while I cannot take the loss away, I show empathy for their loss. The parents should feel comfortable to grieve in their own way. Sometimes you have to show people how to grieve and other times let them be. Most importantly, you must understand that we are all human and open to frailties, which means we cannot always get it right. What is suitable for one couple could be completely inappropriate for the next. You just have to trust your judgment and use your experience to feel your way through.

Why do you think most people are not comfortable dealing with grief?
My grandmother died in our family's home. As a family, we nursed her for the last few weeks of her life, which is something people are sheltered from these days because so many people pass away in hospitals or hospices. Even in the medical world, dealing with the dead has become a specialty and skill. Many of the newer midwives have never delivered a stillborn baby. The majority of our training and responsibilities revolves around the arrival of new life. Death is the polar opposite of that positive outcome. No one ever wants to think about death, because it makes him or her uncomfortable. Being unable to take the pain away or fear of saying the wrong thing is unsettling. It's easier to avoid the grieving person or situation. Standing next to someone who is grieving makes us question our own mortality, which is not always something we are ready to do.

GRIEF IS LIKE A WOUND THAT NEVER HEALS, AND INSTEAD, YOU JUST GET USED TO IT.

How do you offer compassion and comfort to the parents?
When I go into the room, I introduce myself, ensure privacy by shutting the door, and acknowledge the parents' loss and make my condolences. Next, we discuss what the procedures are for the delivery process and go through all of the different funeral and cremation options. It helps to give parents some sense of structure to their day. I think the death of a child is like being hit by a truck. It makes people completely incapable of doing anything but sitting there in shock and grief. My job is to guide them through the initial stages of grief. I try to explain that their emotions will shift and they need to be patient and kind to one another.

Where does your great empathy come from?
Anyone in the healthcare world must recognize that the patient's pain is real. Emotional pain can be far worse than physical because only time can lessen it. Because I experienced death as a child and felt very alone, I am able to understand what my patients are going through. Understanding comes from experience. Over time, this is a skill we achieve.

How do you take care of yourself while looking after others?
I have great support in my colleagues and friends, who are all very supportive. We will have a chat and cup of tea during which they'll ask if I'm all right. However, my compensation is being there for the couples. I need little more than that.

Would you provide some guidance for those who might be grieving?
It is very important to have memories of the person that you've lost. That might be a photo, something they've written, or an item with their smell on it. You should have proof of their existence. Do not be afraid to express your loss through crying or speaking to the dead. There is something cathartic about sitting in a room and telling that person how much you miss them. I think everyone should have some form of professional guidance when grieving. Grief is like a wound that never heals, and instead, you just get used to it. There will be difficult days where it feels like the tide is hitting you frequently, fast, and hard. Others will feel brighter and better, but there will always be a part of you that feels the loss.

How do you think death changes a person?
No one is the same as they were before. Losing a child is particularly hard because they are part of you. We are also programmed to believe that a child should never die before their parents, which makes the experience feel like it's going against nature.

How has your job changed your perspective on life?
I have learned to be truly honest. When you deal with loss, there is no time to waste on falsity. Death took away my filter and has made me much more direct. I can go straight to the heart of a subject without fear versus tiptoeing around the edges. None of us have time to waste. Death cannot be avoided.

Can you tell me a bit about the memory boxes that you offer parents?
Some couples want a clean break initially but will oftentimes come back years later for their photographs or baby blanket. In the midst of great distress, it's very hard to make good decisions. People do what they need to survive, and that's okay. We keep all of the memories in case they should change their minds and want something tangible down the line to prove the child existed.

Can you explain the importance and significance of the cuddle cots?
A baby's body decomposes at a much faster rate than adults. The cuddle cot keeps them cool to preserve the body in case the parents would like it to be in the room with them. The parents might also want to bring in a brother or sister to say goodbye because the entire family was expecting a newborn.

What is your proudest accomplishment?
The best compliment is when a couple, whose baby has died, comes back two or three years later pregnant and asks me to look after them. I always worry that I bring back the bad times, so knowing that they want to see me feels good.

What does the HCA mission mean to you?
When I come to work, I want to do the absolute best that I can for the person in my care. HCA's mission is about giving the best quality service in each area of the hospital and treating each client as though they were your relatives.

Photo by Olivia Weetch

BUD & JEFF REED

{Past Maintenance Supervisor
& Maintenance Specialist, *HCA Healthcare*}

Father-and-son duo Bud and Jeff Reed can do anything maintenance-related—from farming to taking care of a facility. They are famous for fixing stuff side by side. As Maintenance Supervisors (Bud for 26 years, prior to his retirement, and Jeff for 37 years), the pair began working at HCA's Park Plaza headquarters when everyone knew everyone. Hailing from a family full of fixer-uppers, the Reeds, who finish one another's sentences, are proud to be tradesmen, something they consider a rarity these days. After Bud was introduced to HCA through a contracting company, he encouraged his son Jeff, then 14, to help him during school breaks. Jeff started in 1980, and Bud began his HCA career six months later, becoming a supervisor himself. When Bud retired, Jeff took over his position and carried on the family legacy. The self-proclaimed country boys, who used to drive into town together every morning, love this line of work that allows them to chitchat with their colleagues and catch a glimpse behind the scenes. Even now that Bud is retired, tinkering is simply how he operates. The work keeps the Reeds' minds sharp, social lives flourishing, and spirits up.

Can you tell me a bit about the early days?
Bud: Dr. Frist, Sr. and I were real good friends and fishing buddies. I would show people around the HCA grounds for him. He always said to me, "Bud, them boys up there have higher titles than you, but they ain't no better." That's the way he was. He was a down-to-earth type of person.

How did your upbringing shape your character in the workplace?
Bud: I grew up poor in Cheatham County, Tennessee. My dad worked, and I farmed. Back then we had to turn the land ourselves because we didn't have a tractor. I broke up 16 acres every year with a turning plow and then did everything else.

Jeff: I had it a little better. He worked all of the time and provided pretty much anything I wanted.

Bud: We were self-made. On the farm, you had to repair what broke. My daddy taught me a lot and I learned a lot from him. We grew our own corn and shucked it by hand. Then we would shell it and sell it for seed corn. Monday through Saturday I did that until I could leave home and get me another job.

Where did you go next?
Jeff: First, my dad drove a truck and then framed houses. Next, he worked for John W. McDougall contracting company that did all of the remodeling for HCA's Park Plaza facilities. After I graduated, I started helping them remodel stuff. I actually started there before my dad. (Laughs)

Bud: The guy who oversaw the maintenance department told Jeff that when he got out of school he had a job.

Jeff: I would do any and everything from plumbing to changing lights. There were three or four of us at the time on the east side of building one. That was all there was. I've watched every single one of those offices go up over the years. After six months, my dad came on in.

Was it strange having your dad as a boss?
Jeff: I never reported directly to my dad, since we were kin.

Bud: We worked alongside one another all day every day and never would say a word. Then on the weekends and at nights we would build houses together for our family members. He could read my mind and I could read his. When we drove in the truck every morning, that was really the only time we'd speak.

Jeff: Sometimes we'd just grunt. (Laughs) We're just real quiet.

Bud: If something exciting had happened, then we'd talk more.

Jeff: We knew everyone in the building at the time. Fortunately, the leadership and staff are still pretty friendly. We are the behind-the-curtain people who no one sees. Things break, we get them fixed and disappear. Middle of the night or day, it doesn't matter.

What is enjoyable about maintenance work?
Jeff: You never know what's going to come up, which makes our job interesting. We are always dealing with different problems and situations. And we know every nook and cranny of the building.

I ENJOYED THE HECK OUT OF MY CAREER. LOVED THE PEOPLE AND THEY LOVED ME. IT WAS A REAL GOOD RIDE.

Bud: The employees appreciated us and would bring Christmas presents and cakes every year. That felt real good.

Jeff: My guys perk up when they see that people notice our work and know we're there. However, most of the time the person whose office we're in is in a meeting. Today, we deal with people all day long, but there are a lot who we don't know.

What is difficult about the work?
Bud: Sometimes we'd go into work at seven and leave at two the next morning. If there was a move that had to be done, we didn't care if it took all night.

Jeff: When they would buy a building, empty, remodel it, and then ask us to put everything back in its place, we would be absolutely exhausted at the end.

What about the job has changed over the years?
Jeff: The work-order system used to consist of a pen and piece of paper. Now everything that we do is on the computer.

Bud: I am really old school, so switching over to technology was harder on me than on them.

What is one of your most enjoyable HCA memories?
Bud: The most enjoyable thing about our careers had nothing to do with work. We would play on a softball league across the street from Centennial Park. The maintenance team beat the A&B team—so bad they wouldn't play us no more.

Jeff: We put a whupping on them because we practiced every day after work. Dad was our coach and hit the ball like a bullet. One day he knocked someone out cold! (Both laugh)

What do you think makes for a successful maintenance team?
Bud: You lead by common sense and treating people how you want to be treated. If a rough situation came up, I would go in first. If I can do it, they can do it. Lead by example.

Jeff: Still today, my guys ask about Dad all of the time. They respect him. From him, I learned to ask my guys to do something rather than tell them.

Bud: If you think you're better than they are, you're in trouble. I'd never ask someone to do something that I wouldn't do myself.

Jeff: My dad and I got respect for one another. That's the way it is and all you need in life. Treat people like human beings, which is what we do.

What would you like others to know about maintenance work?
Bud: Making a lot of money and fixing things feels really good.

Jeff: Similar to when we used to build houses all of the time, you would stand back, look, and think, *I did that*. You feel proud of yourself—and deserve a beer.

Bud: Back in my day, if someone got married, we'd all get together and build them a house as their wedding present. I hope that the passion for making stuff comes back in fashion.

What do you like about work?
Jeff: If I completed my job, then I felt good.

Bud: You feel a sense of accomplishment by doing what had to be done. I never cared what it took, because people thanked and respected us. We never missed a day. I don't count the weather. Snow days don't factor in. (Laughs)

How do you feel about your career at HCA?
Jeff: Everything has its ups and downs, but for some reason, I've always enjoyed working at HCA.

Bud: I love HCA and was the talker, PR person, and ladies' man on campus. When I left, I had a huge party! It's a great organization.

Jeff: We're good to people, and people like us. I used to be real shy, but I'm coming out of it. This job has opened me up over time, which I'm grateful for.

Bud: Actually, I'll say it: I enjoyed the heck out of my career. Loved the people and they loved me. It was a real good ride.

Jeff: It's true. They still ask, "How is Bud?" every day.

How do you view your relationship with one another?
Bud: Jeff and I been like that (crosses fingers) all our lives. He isn't hard headed and listens to me.

Jeff: We have an unbreakable bond.

Bud: We're close as can be.

ANN NGUYEN, MSN, RN

{Clinical Nurse Manager, *Regional Medical Center of San Jose*}

Perceptive, passionate, and compassionate, Ann Nguyen, Clinical Nurse Manager of the Wound Care Center at Regional Medical Center of San Jose, shares the knowledge she has acquired in the United States with the nurses in her home country of Vietnam. She draws lines of communication between her home and adopted countries so they may learn from one another. Nguyen, born in South Vietnam, practiced as a physician before moving to the U.S. in 1989. As a non-English speaker, she chose to study nursing once stateside instead of continuing as a physician. Nguyen quickly grew fascinated with the American healthcare system, comparing and contrasting it with her Vietnamese experiences. In 2011, while pursuing her master's degree at San Francisco University, Nguyen was introduced to professor Gregory Crow, founder of the Vietnam Nurse Project. She was invited to tag along with his team overseas to teach nurses and providers about the basics of wound care. Afterward, those same clinicians were welcomed back to the U.S. to continue their learning experience. Since joining the organization, Nguyen has used travel and technology to translate American medicine to Vietnamese specialists. Recognized for raising the profile of Vietnamese nurses, Nguyen became the first nurse to address the Vietnam National Institute of Burns congress meeting. She believes human improvement is instrumental in healthcare.

Why did you decide to become a nurse?
Since English is my second language and communication is critical in healthcare, I didn't want to jump into medical school. Instead, I moved slowly and studied English while also taking community health classes to see how Western medicine worked. After taking on a part-time position in a nursing home, I became interested in bedside work and the value it brings to the medical industry.

What is it like to be a nurse?
I believe that nurses lift the team up to give the patient the best level of care. We stand in the middle as the uniting force between physician and patient. Our job is to transfer the diagnosis from the physician's perspective to the patient and their family. Nurses also pick up on small discomforts that the patient is going through. We see all of those nuances because we are at the bedside.

What do you uniquely bring to the nursing field?
I try to use my compassionate nature, which comes from my heart, to bring my patient back to their normal condition. I am just so passionate about working with my patients to heal their wounds. To do this, I always try to put myself in their shoes to feel what it is like to have a wound. Patients want attention, empathy, and information. My reward comes from standing at the finish line and seeing a wound heal. Knowing I made a difference energizes me.

How do you take care of yourself in order to care for others?
I take care of myself by leaving everything at the hospital. Three days a week I do yoga and hike in the morning. Also, studying for my doctorate helps me to forget about the stressful moments of my job. I focus on my study at night so in the morning I come back feeling clearheaded. Often in those hours I come to new realizations simply because I gave my mind a break. I am also a nursing teacher at a community college. I find teaching relaxing and restorative. I enjoy teaching other nurses how to balance school, work, and life all at the same time.

How did you find HCA and what has kept you here for six years?
I found HCA through the patient network. My goal was to become a wound care nurse, so when this job opened up I applied. As I've worked here over the last six years it's been really exciting to see the Wound Care Center grow. I really love the team here, which works together to give the best possible patient care. Since we have so much respect for one another's areas of expertise and assessment skills, we are able to heal the patient efficiently. We make it a point to listen to one another and acknowledge that there are always two sides to every situation.

Do you think a strong team has an impact on patient care?
Absolutely, and we make sure the patient knows they are a part of the team as well. We communicate with the patient constantly because

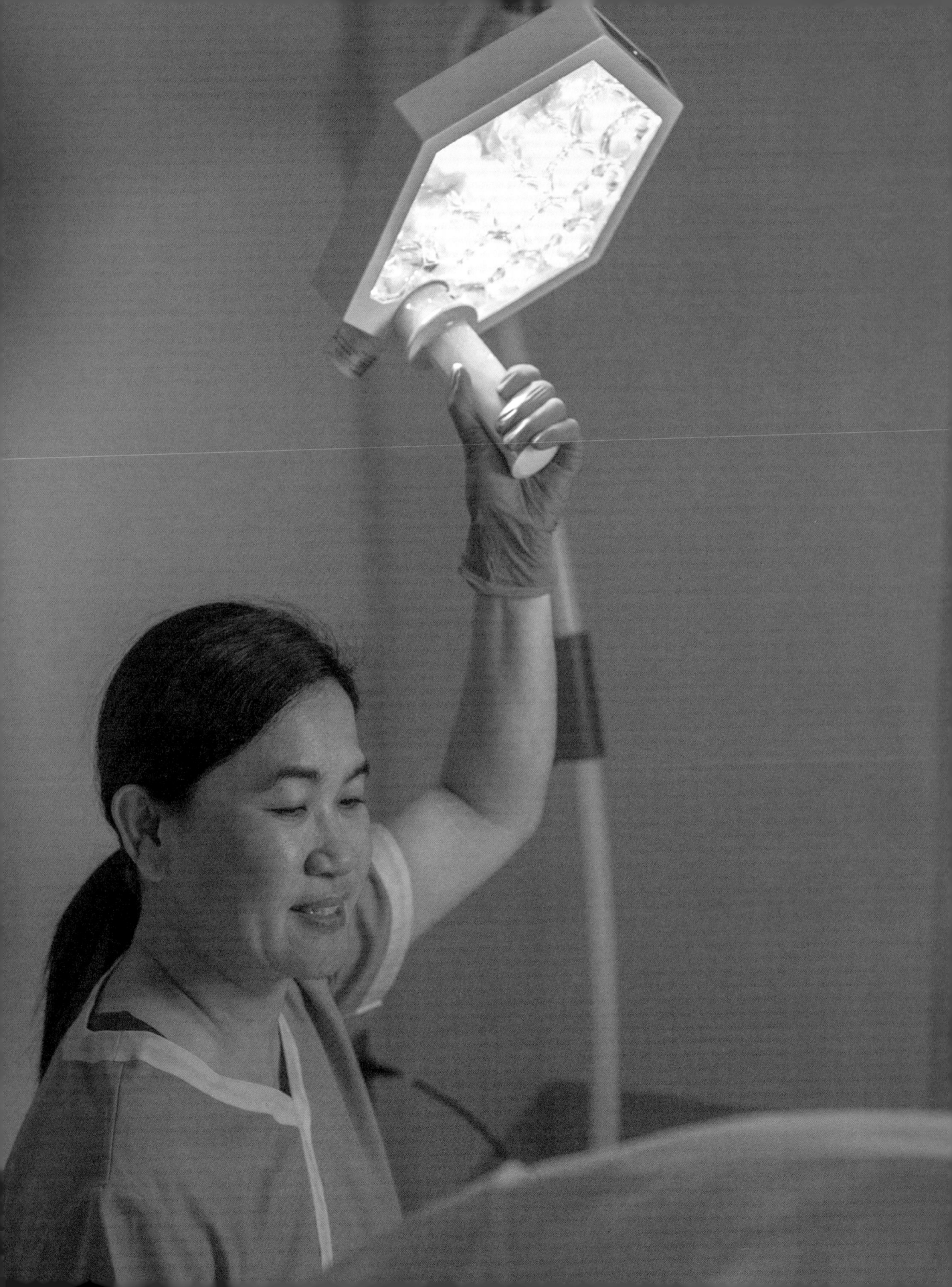

MY REWARD COMES FROM STANDING AT THE FINISH LINE AND SEEING A WOUND HEAL. KNOWING I MADE A DIFFERENCE ENERGIZES ME.

knowledge is power. We also use palatable language so they can understand every part of the diagnosis. I am always paying attention to make sure the patient understands what we say or asking myself, *Could I phrase this differently?* If a patient is in pain, then our communication style changes. Some people don't want to be touched or talked to so we have to find the best way and time to communicate.

Did you have any mentors who particularly inspired you?
My first mentor, Edith, called me up one day and said, "I feel like you have a teacher in you." That inspired me to begin my career as an educator in 2006. When I teach my students, I learn the information much better myself. I get back what I give to them. You don't always know the answers to a student's or patient's questions, so from there I have to do my homework so I can figure out the answer. I learn every day because new questions constantly arise. My second mentor, Dr. Gregory Crow, has helped me to transfer the theory of nursing into daily care. My boss, the director of our center, David Beckham, teaches me daily through his leadership style.

How do you view the role of a nurse?
I think nurses and physicians see things from different angles, which means we are allowed to question one another. The goal is to match the medical and nursing diagnosis, which means that all minds must come together to create a consensus. Nursing is a combination of your knowledge, self-belief, and the information that you acquire at the bedside. That is the key.

How did your wound-care work in Vietnam develop?
After joining the Vietnam Nurse Project, I began traveling there annually to teach workshops at the hospital and the nursing school. The more knowledge and skill the nurses acquired, the better they could handle themselves. Today, we host virtual classes in which our Vietnamese team presents their projects to an American team situated across several states. We give them feedback in regards to their problem based on American evidence-based medical expertise.

What are the benefits and challenges of sharing information?
The healthcare system in Vietnam is very different from the United States. Historically, the nurses tended to do whatever the doctors told them versus applying their own critical thinking. We encourage them to collaborate with the physicians and use their own knowledge to make clinical diagnoses. Slowly, we have created change.

Why do you think empowerment in Vietnam is so important?
The Vietnamese culture tends to follow what the generation before them did. Sometimes it can be hard for them to accept alternative solutions. Instead of telling them what to do, we show them what we are working on in the United States. Then they are much more willing to try a different way. Due to our work in Vietnam, the nurses and doctors are learning to collaborate, and the patient outcomes are improving.

How do you feel technology is an asset to the medical community?
Technology makes it easier for us to teach physicians and nurses without having to jump on an 18-hour flight. Technology brings physicians closer to other medical professionals all over the world. Every clinician wants to do a better job, and if we have the resources, why wouldn't we share them? It's been so rewarding to watch Vietnamese nurses value their intellect and insights more, which in turn, gives them strength. The education pathway is also improving with more nurses going back to school for higher degrees, which is inspiring.

What is it like to spend your life taking care of other people?
Taking care of people is the meaning of life. Helping my patients release pain and heal their wounds is what gives me energy. If I were reborn, I would become a nurse again.

How has HCA helped you with your philanthropic support?
HCA provided me with the practice, education, and opportunity to grow within the organization. They also allow me to use my vacation time to teach in Vietnam and the US when we invite the Vietnamese physicians to study at the Wound Care Center.

What does the HCA mission mean to you?
The HCA mission is about delivering excellent, consistent care.

Why is teaching so gratifying?
I believe we all learn every day, but it is more meaningful if we are able to share our lessons with the next generation. Nursing and teaching go hand in hand and are a part of one another. Both help me grow personally and professionally.

What is your proudest accomplishment?
After being the first nurse in Vietnam to speak at the Vietnam National Institute of Burns congress meeting, more nurses have been invited to join their conference. That makes me feel as though we are further integrating the Vietnamese medical system by bringing nurses and physicians together.

SAM HAZEN

{President and COO, *HCA Healthcare*}

HCA Healthcare President and COO Sam Hazen spreads the culture of HCA across departmental, professional, and corporate lines. In an industry that often operates in silos, Hazen lends cohesiveness by championing core values and best practices. Hazen hails from the hardworking, humble roots of an Appalachian coal mining region in Kentucky. It is there where he learned his customer service skills, working at his father's 5&10 stores, gas station, and Tastee Freez. After studying finance and business administration, he began his healthcare career in 1983. He served at Humana as a chief financial officer for a couple of hospitals before joining HCA. Over the years, Hazen's fear of falling behind has been his primary fuel. As he pushed himself forward, he eventually passed others by. Yet, in his 33-year tenure, while he is always itching for more, Hazen never had to look outside HCA. The expert goal-setter was able to create his legacy within while building a more viable and productive organization. His enthusiasm for HCA is energizing to others.

How did your upbringing influence your demeanor in the workplace?
I'm from a second-generation Lebanese family. My grandfather migrated to Eastern Kentucky in the early 1900s when all of the big steel companies were starting to mine coal. They would buy up all of the mineral rights in the mountains and start these coal communities. After he followed the herd of immigrants, he began bartering goods for food or shelter. That was the beginning of his 5&10 business, which was like a mini version of Walmart, which also started out as 5&10 stores. My family built stores adjacent to the coal camps. I worked in retail starting at age 12.

How did your part-time retail job shape your character?
My father wanted his customers walking out happy so they'd continue to walk back in. Retail taught me how to give great customer service, which is critical to running an organization like HCA, where, on any given day, we have 120,000 patients getting care at our facilities. We're in the people business at HCA, and those forced interactions growing up taught me how to navigate a wide variety of situations.

What sparked your interest in healthcare?
Here's the simple story: When I was a senior in college, I was offered a position at JCPenney, which I just could not do. I had to get out of retail. Fortunately, my dad sponsored me to attend one more semester at college so I could get a minor in accounting. In one of my classes, I had to create and follow a portfolio of stocks. One of them was Humana, and during my research I noticed that they had a Financial Management Training Program. I knew nothing about hospitals, but as my dad put it best, "Zero versus a salary of $18,500. You're a smart boy. I know you will make the right decision." He was right, and so I took that job. I have never looked back.

Over time has your passion grown for the industry?
Absolutely. I love the people in healthcare and their passion for what they do. I also love the competitiveness of the industry. In my role, I support a process which helps clinicians do their best work, and it is rewarding.

What is stimulating about the business side of healthcare?
While there are common threads in healthcare—a nurse, doctor, and sick person in a bed—the strategic nuances are what I find stimulating. Healthcare is a local business, and HCA operates in 43 distinct markets. That constant engagement with different markets and different situations makes my job very interesting.

What was appealing to you about HCA as a company?
The most appealing things to me about HCA were the opportunities to be around capable people and to grow personally and professionally. I think the opportunity to work for a strong, reputable company was very appealing also.

Why have you stayed so long at HCA?
There is great pleasure that comes from leveraging your talents and knowledge. At HCA, I have been able to do that, and I have been fortunate to grow and be around smart and good people in this company. I also have a significant family investment in HCA, so I look at it as owning my own business. Lastly, I love being able to have an impact on the lives of others. While I may not have the same interaction with our patients as a nurse, I know my work positively affects the organization.

How did you develop your own leadership style?
I've moved six times during my tenure at HCA because, when you work in the field, movement is how you get on a pathway to growth.

By observing others, I have learned how to make decisions, think about organizational processes, and how to react in certain situations. In developing my leadership style, I melded those experiences into what I learned from my dad, which was treat people right, work hard, and understand your business. HCA recognizes that we need great leaders throughout the company in order to be successful and push the company into its next phase.

What do you hope to do at HCA in your leadership role?
Build the business, solve problems, and help others capitalize on their strengths. I try to bring different components of HCA together to help our team function as smoothly as possible. My role is to make this massive organization run efficiently, harmoniously, and effectively. The goal is to help our team understand what we're doing and how we do it.

to different audiences. While I used to dislike speaking in front of groups, I've learned to embrace it as an opportunity to share our values and business plans and make sure that folks feel they are in the know. In terms of a speaking style, I try to be approachable, down-to-earth, and clear about the fact that I am committed to getting the HCA team the resources that they need.

Why is face-to-face communication so important to your role?
Face-to-face conversations are needed to ensure we get the necessary information to run the company. Communication in a big company is difficult, but it is necessary to ensure our teams understand our mission, our strategy, our approach, and get their questions answered. It creates a sense of familiarity and connection to something bigger amongst our employees and physicians who work in our 1,800 facilities. While I get tired of hearing myself talk, these conversations and visits are critical.

THE MOST APPEALING THINGS TO ME ABOUT HCA WERE THE OPPORTUNITIES TO BE AROUND CAPABLE PEOPLE AND TO GROW PERSONALLY AND PROFESSIONALLY.

How do you take in all of the factors to create a strategy?
I visit our hospitals and talk to a wide variety of people across our organization to get the necessary inputs to make decisions. I have routine meetings, interactions, and field visits so I can touch the organization and frequently find out what the staff needs. Getting in front of people to communicate the message may be exhausting at times, but it's also fundamentally needed to ensure our leadership is connected and can support the organization appropriately.

How would you describe HCA's business climate and approach?
First and foremost, we want to give our patients what they deserve, which is a safe environment and top-notch, compassionate care. Second, we partner with our physicians to give them a voice and provide them with state-of-the-art nursing, equipment, sub-specialty support, and any assistance in terms of their individual needs. The third fundamental is bringing the best business principles to HCA in terms of leveraging our unique scale to drive down costs, sharing the best practices from one facility to the next, and developing our employees so they can be the best providers of healthcare.

What is one of the most important skills in terms of your job?
Communication in a big company is very important. We have to be frequent and intentional with how we relate our mission and plans

What did your dad think about your success?
He passed in 2008. I believe he was immensely proud. My freshman year of college he got me a job at the coal mines because I wasn't sure if I wanted to finish school. Three days a week I went a mile deep into Black Mountain with my backpack, light, and steel-toed shoes. I worked alongside people who had been there their whole lives. After seven weeks, I quit, to which my dad responded, "Good decision, son." That was his way of saying, "Get the heck out of here." Generationally, where I grew up, health, education, and general welfare were a struggle. It was hard to escape for many people because they got stuck in a difficult generational cycle.

What does the mission of HCA mean to you?
It's simple: people taking care of people. We are celebrating our 50th anniversary. We have survived through different economic cycles, different strategies, and different managers. I think this survival is because of our unique culture. When you combine a great culture with strategy, execution and the right leadership, then the sky is the limit.

ALONZO SMITH

{Sergeant, Security Officer, *Wesley Medical Center*}

Security guards often give patients their first impression of a hospital, and Alonzo Smith's warm, compassionate, and welcoming presence provides a great impression of Wesley Medical Center in Wichita, Kansas. In his 29 years at the hospital, the security officer has worked his way up from Traffic Officer to his current role of Supervisor. From every opportunity Smith has had—at Wesley Medical Center, or in his previous careers in professional baseball, modeling, and chemical engineering—he has acquired invaluable wisdom about life. Each new set of responsibilities gave Smith more energy. During his night shifts, the security officer makes face-to-face connections with colleagues, patients, and families, and gains knowledge about what is happening in the community. He feels grateful to work at a facility where, similar to his hometown, all walks of life mix together.

Can you tell me a bit about your upbringing?
To be truthful, my life has been kind of strange. I was adopted at age two and raised around all Caucasians on a farm in Victoria, Texas. I was blessed for a young, black man because my godfather was the town mayor, which opened up a lot of doors for me early on. I was raised with a solid moral compass and around a lot of respectable folks. In my early 20s, I played professional baseball for the Philadelphia Phillies and also went to college for chemical engineering and business. Ironically, as a kid, I wasn't interested in sports; I was more of a mama's boy who liked to stay inside and lick the cake bowls.

What is the best piece of advice anyone taught you growing up?
There may be people who are willing to help, but you have to help yourself first.

How did you transition from playing professional baseball to becoming a security guard?
I played professionally for two years and then tore my rotator cuff. Baseball was something that we did for fun as children in the backyard. Once I got into the field it became more of a business and therefore less appealing. Afterward, I studied chemical engineering for a few years and then got into modeling and bodybuilding. None of those industries gave me the satisfaction that I have today. I landed in Wichita at age 29 because of a modeling agency contract. Initially, my position at Wesley was just for survival. Twenty-nine years later here I am!

What made you want to stay at Wesley Medical Center?
Law enforcement was never on my radar. In fact, the gentleman who hired me still jokes that he thought I would be one of the first people to leave. Yet, nearly 30 years later, I feel that my work here isn't over. Wesley is a pillar of the community, and every single person here uplifts one another. Since the early years, I have seen this hospital as an opportunity to make my city a better place.

How would you describe the Wesley environment to others?
Wesley, in the best way possible, reminds me of the community that I grew up in: here, all walks of life mix together. Working somewhere with such a diverse population widens your perspective. I have been able to learn so much simply by listening to the stories of our patients and my coworkers. By getting outside of your own bubble you can find out what is truly going on.

What is it like to be a security guard?
Back in the day, we sat at post and guarded a specific spot. Now we have more leeway in terms of what areas of the hospital we can become involved with—as granted by the sheriff's department. The complexity of my job has made me stronger as a person. While I feel that my job will be needed until eternity, the position itself is always changing because of society.

How would you hope that others perceive a security guard?
Usually security guards show up when something has gone wrong. My team shows empathy, gives others comfort, and takes away fear from a situation—rather than instilling it. We alleviate problems by not bringing our own into the situation.

How would you describe your Wesley Medical Center family?
Similar to the Southern culture, everyone at Wesley is friendly, easy-going, and genuine. People take pride in their work and are willing to pitch in wherever they are needed. Even if someone has a complaint, they will turn it into something positive. If your home is your castle, then Wesley embodies that exact mentality.

SINCE THE EARLY YEARS, I HAVE SEEN THIS HOSPITAL AS AN OPPORTUNITY TO MAKE MY CITY A BETTER PLACE.

Why does it feel so good to be a part of something?
A lot of my life, I felt like I was on the outside looking in. I was a bit of an oddball as a kid. This is the first place in my entire life that I have always felt included. The dedication of our staff is why I stay here. The vision at Wesley has never changed: to approach every person as if they were your own family members. Everyone here wants to respect others and do well for our hospital and city.

What is the number-one misconception about your job?
Some people may see us as the bad guys who throw people out. However, my team and I are really the ones who listen to people vent and hold their hands through the tough times. That face-to-face connection is why I love my job.

What is one of your favorite achievements at Wesley?
I speak Spanish, and before we hired an interpreter, I was able to translate for our Hispanic population. Closing the gap by giving those who don't speak English the chance to express themselves made me feel really good.

What advice do you have for others in your industry?
You get whatever you seek out of life. There is so much wisdom to be learned at this hospital, yet you also have to remain open to it. When I wake up and come to Wesley, I feel like I am walking into life. That intense exposure to humanity—and the knowledge I have acquired because of it—keeps me motivated every day.

Why are you so passionate about mentorship?
I want to give the kids that I mentor what my parents gave me: guidance. There are many roads in life, and I think that young kids need someone to help prepare them for the future. If I can somehow make their lives easier, then maybe they will be able to pass that on to someone else. Life is a give and take. Our role as human beings is to better ourselves and uplift others with the wisdom that we obtain. The icing on the cake is when people are thankful for your service.

When did your job take on a deeper purpose?
When I was promoted to Supervisor, I felt a tremendous amount of responsibility to uphold the Wesley image in the community and serve as a leader. I felt like a true part of the operation because my role wasn't just about me anymore. To also know that an organization had faith in me meant that I had to take my actions a lot more seriously. Other people were watching.

Why are you so committed to the Wesley community?
I love people in general, so my goal in any position that I've held at Wesley has been to make others' days better in one way or another. I have learned more about life here than anywhere else and want to return the favor by being a great company representative and making new hires feel like family. When something or someone is good to you, then it's only right to return the favor, don't you think?

What is one piece of advice you give to the kids that you mentor?
If you ever want to amount to something, surround yourself with the kinds of people that you want to be like. Your environment and the choices that you make are everything and can always be changed. If you start off in one lane, that's not where you have to finish. I also try to teach them that we all have problems, and the solution is structure and positive passions that take your mind off of them. Lastly, in life we are all in this together and need to look after one another.

What are you proudest of during your HCA tenure?
I am proud to still be here after almost 30 years. I could get a job anywhere but have stayed because of the wonderful people and ability to give back. There is no sense of hierarchy at Wesley. We all know that we can learn from one another. The vets show the young go-getters the way and vice versa. We're all driven by a collective mentality: to make this the best hospital in the world.

Do you have any last words about your 29 years at Wesley?
There are so many moments that I could tell you about, but the bottom line is my joy at Wesley comes from the fact that my job isn't about me. I truly feel like I am being used for good by a higher power at this hospital.

SANDRA OSMOND, BSN, RN

{CNO, *St. Mark's Hospital*}

Sandra Osmond believes everyone should want to work in medicine. Since the Salt Lake City native began her St. Mark's Hospital career as a candy striper in 1977, she has consistently dug deeper to develop her philosophies on the art of nursing. Thirty years of service later, the Chief Nursing Officer maintains a strong enthusiasm for her craft. St. Mark's Hospital, a 145-year-old community gem founded by the Episcopal Church, is treasured for its small-town intimacy. Osmond never dreamed of working anywhere else. She began her career as a medical surgery and delivery room nurse and has since explored a number of her industry's avenues, from hospice to women's health. While she finds great satisfaction in her current CNO role, she never anticipated being in an office job. Osmond is first and foremost a nurse, and her contentment will always come from contact with her patients and staff. As she tells new nurses, every patient is somebody's someone and needs to be treated with compassion and respect.

How were you first introduced to St. Mark's Hospital?
I grew up five miles from St. Mark's Hospital and have worked on this same corner most of my life. When my mom signed me up at age 14 to become a candy striper, the white socks, shoes, and striped pinafore did not exactly appeal. (Laughs) In the OB unit where I was assigned, the nurses taught me a great deal and allowed me to interact on a personal level with their patients. It was then that I began to consider nursing, because I wanted to help people.

When did you first realize the impact of a great nurse?
About four years after I became a candy striper, my mom had heart surgery at St. Mark's, where she did okay until day three. I was sitting in her room when a nurse came flying through the door and thumped her on the chest. When the precordial thump didn't work, I had to watch them shock her in order to bring her heart rate back. After two more full cardiac arrests, they figured out that she was having a bad reaction to a medication. As I walked out the same doors that I had entered five years earlier as a candy striper, I saw the sun coming up over the mountains and I knew I was going to become a nurse. I wanted to make a difference in the lives of families just as my mother's nurse had that night. Not only did I credit him with saving her life but also I was deeply touched by the concern he showed for our family and the emotional distress we were going through. I applied for nursing school within the next couple of weeks and chose one that did its clinical rotations at St. Mark's Hospital. I knew I had to be there.

What were your first nursing experiences like?
Although my goal was to become a labor and delivery nurse, one of my instructors recommended that I take a year to work in the med-surgical department before taking on a specialty. I am so happy that I followed her advice because during that time I refined my skill set and learned how to trust my eyes and gut. I left St. Mark's for just a few months to work alongside midwives at a birthing center. Then I came back to St. Mark's when a position opened up in labor and delivery. Being present at a birth is a beautiful experience. The nurse has a one-time shot to create a positive memory for that mother and family. I loved being part of bringing new life into the world and changing a family tree forever. Equally as important, a nurse can have a great impact helping a family work through the grief of a stillbirth. Those moments are indescribably painful, and while a patient may not remember your name, they will always remember how you made them feel and the support and compassion that was shown towards them.

What has been your most meaningful job in healthcare?
In 2002, I started what would become five years of Saturday night shifts at a hospice unit. I loved my role as Executive Director of Women's Services but also missed touching patients. Death is an amazing opportunity to make someone's final breath as comfortable and pain-free as possible. I have been fortunate to be present at close to a thousand births and a hundred deaths, as well as everything in between.

What is one piece of advice you have for other nurses?
When I talk to nurses at graduations or white coat ceremonies, I always tell them, "What a gift it is to be present at the widest spectrum of human life." There is no do-over in our industry. We can't give someone a gift certificate if we get his or her birth or death wrong. Yet, it's also critical to focus on everything in between. At St. Mark's, in a single day, people will be told that they have cancer, an incurable disease, or are on the fast track back to a healthy life. In

what other industry can you stand with people at the most critical junctures in their lives?

How can nurses care for themselves while also caring for others?
Our job is taxing because as nurses and all other care providers we take on everyone's emotions. While we are all busy, it is essential for us to not forget about ourselves. Do something kind for yourself every single day. When I meet with new nurses, I hand them a "blue day folder" into which they are instructed to save positive notes from patients and coworkers. Nurses sacrifice a lot of normalcy because healthcare is a 24/7 job. Those reminders are necessary on days where you are feeling low. They immediately snap you back to the joy that comes from changing someone's life.

How did you transition from nursing to management?
It was never my intention. However, after eight years in the delivery room, I felt slightly restless. From there, I worked part-time in our mammogram clinic, which was not for me, having come from a fast-paced, chaotic delivery room. When I was about to transition back into delivery room full-time, I was voted by our staff into a managerial position. That was the first time that I had been in a position of power since I was promoted from waitress to manager at the local restaurant. (Laughs) Aside from the fact that we are saving lives and waiters are serving meals, the industries have some similarities. In both environments, people want to know they are going to receive great service and that they are cared about.

Can you tell us about a time where you faced a challenge and overcame it?
The first big test that I had as a hospital manager was being instructed by my CEO that I had 60 days to get our mammogram center in the black. I quickly pulled the entire staff together, and we worked tirelessly to find ways to be more efficient, decrease expenses, and grow our volume. We successfully flipped that operation in 60 days. However, it was a stressful experience that made me realize that I had to go back to school in order to understand the business side of healthcare. After finishing my degree, I followed the advice of our CNO who said, "Keep busting your tail and finding situations in which to prove yourself. Reach as high as you can." Shortly after, I had an opportunity to open a reproductive care center, which was absolutely outside of my comfort zone. I had never managed a physician practice, let alone started a practice from scratch. Therefore, I learned a great deal about an industry I knew nothing about. When we built and opened the first Freestanding Women's Pavilion in the state, an executive director position of Women's Services opened up, and because of my outpatient, inpatient, and physician experience, I felt prepared to take on this new role. After twelve years in that role, I had an opportunity to move into the CNO position at St. Mark's in 2014. To have the opportunity to grow and develop into the CNO role in the same facility that I started at as a candy striper was pretty remarkable.

What do you most enjoy about your current role?
As CNO, I let my nurses know that assisting them in any capacity makes my day. I will always get my hands just as dirty because I'm not above any nursing duties. Plus, I want to be with the patients and nurses more than anything else. I never want anyone to scatter or to think that something is wrong when I appear on a shift. I simply want to be a resource. My greatest joy comes from finding out what concerns my team members have and problem-solving with them. I am grateful every single day for St. Mark's and my role as CNO. It is an honor to oversee the care of our patients and provide support to the staff of such a great facility.

TO HAVE THE OPPORTUNITY TO GROW AND DEVELOP INTO THE CNO ROLE IN THE SAME FACILITY THAT I STARTED AT AS A CANDY STRIPER WAS PRETTY REMARKABLE.

What is one fun fact about your facility that most people wouldn't know?
Interestingly enough, there are several nurses on my team who chose this field as a second career. These former real estate agents and wedding photographers are so joyful to be here making a difference every single day. As a one-time banker told me recently, "You can't get this kind of satisfaction giving out loans."

How would you describe the culture at St. Mark's?
St. Mark's is like a family. This place rallies around our peers like nobody's business and pulls together in times of crisis. Even though we have all of the services that a larger facility offers, St. Mark's is a community hospital. That is why we have so many employees with 30 and 40 years of service who, like myself, are deeply dedicated to this place. Just like the HCA mission statement says, "Above all else, we are committed to the care and improvement of human life." Every decision we make must put the patient and their families front and center. By making the patient and their family the focus, we can't go wrong.

ERIC WARD & RYANN SCHNEIDER

{President and CEO, *Parallon Business Performance Group* & Senior Counsel, *Parallon Business Performance Group*}

It's easy to become excited about volunteering when you see the tangible effects it has on the lives of others. Eric Ward, President and CEO of Parallon Business Performance Group, and Ryann Schneider, Parallon Business Performance Group's Senior Counsel, share a strong commitment to community service. In anticipation of moving to the new Parallon corporate offices, Ward was looking for ways to engage with and support the surrounding community. At the same time, Schneider saw many opportunities for her coworkers to conveniently connect with their neighbors through Buena Vista Enhanced Option Elementary School. BVEOES is located less than two miles from Parallon BPG's headquarters and serves a population of roughly 280 students—pre-K through fourth grade—most of whom face unique challenges due to poverty and homelessness. Working closely with local non-profit and business partners, Buena Vista is able to offer access to a clothing closet, food pantry, laundry services, and many other supportive activities for its students, their families, and the surrounding community. Following Ward and Schneider's lead, the Parallon Caring for the Community leadership team took time to understand how Parallon could meet Buena Vista's existing needs. Parallon is regularly engaged in one-on-one mentorship and tutoring at Buena Vista and has generously donated food, clothing, laundry detergent, toys, books, money, and more to support the needs of Buena Vista scholars and their families. Engagement with Buena Vista is interwoven into Parallon's culture and is just one example of the company's depth of commitment to community service.

How did you both find your way to HCA?
Ryann: I grew up in Minnesota in a family that was committed to community engagement and the belief that education is a key to opening avenues for success. My path to HCA, and ultimately Parallon, was somewhat winding. Initially, I was taken by the music industry and moved down to Tennessee to study recording industry production and technology. As part of that curriculum, I took a copyright class and unexpectedly fell in love with law. After studying at Vanderbilt University Law School and starting my career at Bass, Berry & Sims, I joined HCA in 2012 as part of the Technology Law Group. I supported Parallon in that role and really enjoyed the culture. When a position opened up, I was excited to move over here and become a permanent part of the Parallon team.

Eric: I grew up in McMinnville, Tennessee, and then attended college at Tennessee Tech University where I received my degree in accounting. I spent the first couple of years of my career in the restaurant industry, but I soon realized that I didn't feel like my work had a real purpose. A friend of mine mentioned that a position as an assistant controller was open at an HCA freestanding emergency room in Smyrna, Tennessee. I applied and was offered the job. After a short time in the position, I began to understand the impact that HCA has in the lives of our patients and that I was able to contribute to that through my work and make a real difference. I worked in several hospital/division controller positions and as CFO of TriStar Health System before I accepted my current position as President and CEO of Parallon Business Performance Group. Over the next 18 years, our team built out the Shared Services platform for HCA that became known as Parallon Business Performance Group.

How would you describe the company culture at HCA?
Eric: HCA has a patients-first philosophy and a culture of caring and respect for others. At Parallon, we see our role as the engine that takes on the administrative business functions for the hospitals so their management teams, physicians, and nurses can focus their energy on delivering high-quality patient care.

Do you remember the first time you felt an emotional connection to your work?
Ryann: It is hard to recall a specific first time because the client-patient impact is so ingrained in every single activity at HCA. However, the first time I was able to shadow at an HCA hospital and saw the technology that I negotiate contracts for in use, I felt a renewed connection to the impact my work has. I'm happy to work for a company that allows me to help patients and caregivers.

Eric: I became connected to my work while working at an HCA hospital. I really saw the impact that our company has in the lives of our patients and their families. The other key connection point for me is working with amazing people and being part of the HCA culture.

What do you think is unique about the HCA culture?
Ryann: HCA is very mission-driven, and every element of the culture reflects that. The HCA mission statement serves as an operational directive and a collective touchpoint for the organization

Eric: HCA has always promoted a culture of philanthropy to its employees. Dr. Frist established this culture of giving because he believed it was our responsibility to give back to the community and others who are not as fortunate as we are. HCA provides employees a platform to give money, time, and talent to the organizations for which they have a passion. Ryann's passion for Buena Vista quickly became a passion for many members of our team.

What are the benefits of doing your service work through HCA?
Ryann: Seeing the immense collective impact we can make with the support of a strong organization is a phenomenal benefit. You are never alone in the community service work you do here; HCA will match your commitment in whatever way you choose to engage.

Eric: As I mentioned earlier, HCA provides a platform for its employees to give money, time, and talent to organizations. This platform exposes our employees to other giving opportunities and

YOU ARE NEVER ALONE IN THE COMMUNITY SERVICE WORK YOU DO HERE; HCA WILL MATCH YOUR COMMITMENT IN WHATEVER WAY YOU CHOOSE TO ENGAGE.

when working through complex or challenging discussions. In an advisory role as legal counsel, I am grateful for the trust I share with my colleagues and faith I have in HCA's mission.

Eric: I have been with HCA since 1991, so the HCA culture is all I've ever known. As I progressed through my career, I was given the opportunity to interact with other companies and began to understand the uniqueness of HCA's culture. Through these experiences, I have developed a real appreciation for the people and culture in HCA. I believe one of the key aspects of HCA's culture is the expectation that everyone will be treated with respect at all times.

Ryann: Sharing that strong mission with good people also really drives success in our work. This work requires your brain to be operating on all cylinders, so working with a great group of people removes that extra layer of stress. We can focus on what's important, rather than the periphery, and achieve better results.

How does HCA promote philanthropy within the organization?
Ryann: Service is a part of Parallon's identity and culture, which is why it was easy to build such a strong partnership with Buena Vista Elementary School. As soon as Parallon employees learned about the needs out there, they jumped into action. Their response was swift and overwhelming.

allows them to share their passions with coworkers. Serving together also builds teamwork and strengthens our organization as a whole.

How do you think giving back improves your overall well-being?
Eric: The benefits we get from giving are much greater than the money, time, or talents that we give to organizations. We get to see how our actions impact other people's lives, which gives us a sense of fulfillment and contentment that only comes from giving. Volunteering makes us better people and enhances our sense of purpose.

Ryann: Parallon employees come back from their service engagements and comment on how revitalized and reenergized they feel. On the other hand, our neighbors know we are invested in solving the challenges facing our community. It's mutually beneficial on every level. Not only do our programs fulfill academic and social needs, but also they give our company a chance to directly impact someone's life in a lasting way. I don't think you can put a value on that.

Eric: Most of us at Parallon aren't super touchy-feely by nature, and our work is primarily administrative. (Laughs) We do get the opportunity to work with patients in patient access or customer service areas, which gives us the opportunity to make a personal impact.

Service work gives us the opportunity to use our other talents such as sensitivity and empathy to make an impact on someone's life.

What incentive would you give to someone to volunteer?
Eric: We have some employees who come from families or cultures where volunteering or service isn't the norm. We introduce them to giving through our Caring for the Community efforts and service opportunities that we participate in as a team. We hope that they will develop a passion for service as they watch their coworkers in action.

Ryann: All it takes to inspire someone to volunteer is educating them on the impact it has on others. Once projects get moving, the energy around these activities is contagious.

Eric: We're always looking for team-building activities. Volunteering together allows you to get out of the office and get to know your coworkers a little better. Team service opportunities also allow you to see the best in others.

What's your favorite thing about what you both do?
Eric: I really enjoy taking on big organizational problems and developing solutions for those problems. My current job has allowed me to do this over the past 18 years. The most enjoyable part of my job is the amazing people that I work alongside. They make my job worthwhile and fun.

Ryann: I love helping my coworkers work through a complicated issue. Being the one they trust and call in to assist in critical situations means a lot to me.

Eric: Also, healthcare is a very complex business that keeps me motivated with new and exciting challenges every day. Plus, we are providing a service that matters.

Ryann: At the end of the day, we're helping people. I can't think of any other industry I would rather be involved in.

What would you like others to know about HCA?
Ryann: HCA is a place people can be proud to work. This is an excellent company that seeks to have a connection and positive impact on patients and the community.

Eric: HCA is an amazing company that truly lives out its mission and values on a daily basis. The company believes in doing the right thing no matter the circumstance. HCA is a company full of wonderful, talented people with really strong characters and cores. I am honored to work at HCA.

DEVON MOORE, RN, CCRN

{Direct Care Nurse, *Metropolitan Methodist Hospital*}

"I always felt that way" is often the medical community's reaction to Devon Moore's musings. On her popular blog, the 21-year-old direct care staff nurse has a propensity for putting into words the joy and suffering of her job. Moore's astute observations articulate what it means to be a nurse at Methodist Healthcare in San Antonio, Texas. Born and raised in Albuquerque, New Mexico, Moore, as a child, watched her dad, a physical therapist, examine patients, and she played with her mom, an X-ray tech, in the darkroom. At age 17, she enrolled in nursing school where she pushed herself to step it up, study twice as hard, and overcome skepticism surrounding her youth. Nursing is a calling rather than a career choice for Moore, who feels blessed to be at the bedside. However, the wordsmith is equally drawn to describing her experiences and processing her emotions in a cathartic, creative way. Through her blog, Moore articulates what others want to say. Despite only three years of floor experience, the old soul has already become a poster child for her profession. She loves being intellectually stimulated while making an impact.

Where did the idea arise for your blog?
Last February, Methodist announced that they were hosting a conference, and our CNO asked if I would speak at it. I had written a Facebook post a few weeks earlier about the heartache that you feel as a nurse, which many people are blind to. Writing that post gave me closure on a very tough patient situation. When I finally spoke, I noticed halfway through that everyone was crying. My intention wasn't to sound profound but rather speak about the reality that we live in as nurses. Afterward, the executive team encouraged me to continue writing.

Is writing a form of self-care?
Absolutely. In school, they teach you the technical parts of the job, but you don't learn how to deal with the parts of you that are equipped to care for others. For 12 hours at a time, three or four days a week, my well-being comes second to my patients'. As a preceptor, I am passionate about teaching nurses how to be competent on the unit but also how to look after themselves. Critical care nursing can lend itself to more heartache than other units because we deal with such sick patients, and it can be quite sad.

You have a rare gift to say the things that others might not know how.
I constantly think, *How can I not tell people about this profession?* People ask me all of the time why I'm not a physician because, in their mind, it's so much more glamorous. I became a nurse because of who I am. I love the families who appreciate our ability to break down complex information in a palatable way. I treasure the days where a patient gets better despite the odds stacked against them. It's very easy to only live in the grief or in the mountaintop, miracle moments, but the reality is most of our patients get better. And as a bedside nurse, I'm a large part of that. Therefore, I focus on the run-of-the-mill cases in which we still change lives.

How has your job as a nurse changed you?
This job has shaped my personality for the better. After dealing with life and death, you learn to let go of a lot of stress. For example, you learn to be much calmer about how the dishes get put in the cabinet.

What is your relationship like with your fellow nurses?
The ICU is so fast-paced and crazy that on some shifts the only time I get to talk to my coworkers is when we are taking care of a non-responsive, sedated patient. Methodist's team of physicians and nurses is incredibly supportive when it comes to boosting one another's professional careers. It feels amazing to know that doctors realize we are capable of caring for their sickest patient. Equally as awesome is when another nurse says, "I read your new blog post and shared it with my parents so they would better understand what we do." They're not just a team of fellow nurses; they're family.

What about your personality makes you good at your job?
I've only ever wanted to work in critical care because I love the autonomy, intensity, and intellectual stimulation. I am a bit of a perfectionist and a control freak, which is necessary in our world. While no one is mentally prepared to deal with this job, I also grew up fast, which helps me to deal with the trauma.

IT'S AWESOME WHEN ANOTHER NURSE SAYS, "I READ YOUR NEW BLOG POST AND SHARED IT WITH MY PARENTS SO THEY WOULD BETTER UNDERSTAND WHAT WE DO."

What gets you through the toughest days?
My faith. Faith has always given me strength during times of trouble. My entire life I've also been blessed to have the right people placed in my path at the perfect time. I made the decision to become a nurse early and, ever since, have worked ridiculously hard, asked a million questions, and read and studied everything I could get my hands on. This is the best job in the world, and anyone who isn't doing it is missing out.

What was it like to pursue your profession in a nontraditional way?
Nursing school, while I love learning, was always a means to an end. I wanted to work versus studying in a confined, secure classroom. I craved the reality of my profession because you never know what a job is like until you do it. The day I was supposed to be at my senior prom, I was in a hospital learning how to save someone's life. What would have been my first summer off from college was spent starting my career in the SICU at Metropolitan Methodist Hospital. I wanted to be a part of something bigger than myself. That was most important to me.

What is it like to be a nurse and how do you feel about what you do?
I think a lot of people assume that nurses just clean up fecal matter and hand out pills. However, there is a lot more that goes on behind the scenes. Nursing stretches your patience and empathy—from calming down a patient who is yelling for ice cubes, to conversing with a newly widowed wife about her husband's death. We have to constantly prioritize who needs us most at that moment. When people are dying, petty concerns become a lot less important. What's most sobering is that you can't be everything to everyone. It's impossible. You have to know that you did the best you could and put the rest to bed. All that said, it's still absolutely the best job in the world.

How has this job impacted your personal life?
In my personal life I have very little patience for nonsense. After going home from a 13-hour shift when I've been trying to keep people alive all day, I can't be bugged about something stupid. Your priorities change, and I don't know if it's good or bad, it's just something that happens. You learn to really see what matters more and not get hung up on the rest. This job also can be very isolating if you let it be. While my mom understands a lot more than others because she worked in healthcare, it's even hard to describe my worst days to her. Sometimes I feel guilty saying, "I had a 37-year-old dad die today," because I don't want her to carry that burden. On the flip side, my best friend who works in women's health tells me daily about the babies that she delivers, which is a beautiful contrast to the death I so often see. It's a reminder I need a lot of the time. She lets me sit in my darkness while bringing in a bit of light. I think the answer is that I've learned to let myself be sad and happy all at the same time, acknowledging the real grief and joy that define this calling.

What would you like others to know about nursing?
My best friend's fiancé, a cop, has called me and asked, "Why won't she stop crying?" to which I responded, "Something sad probably happened. Don't try to fix it, because you can't. She'll be happy again." Nurses don't want a pity party for the rough shifts, but rather for others to understand the intensity of our experiences and the breadth of knowledge we possess. We do far more than most people understand, and it's hard work. Fortunately, 95 percent of the physicians I work with acknowledge this and are unbelievably appreciative. It means the world when they walk into a patient's room and say, "You have the best nurse today." That level of respect has a great impact on the care that we give, and I'm unbelievably grateful for it. If more people understood that, the world of bedside nursing would be a better place.

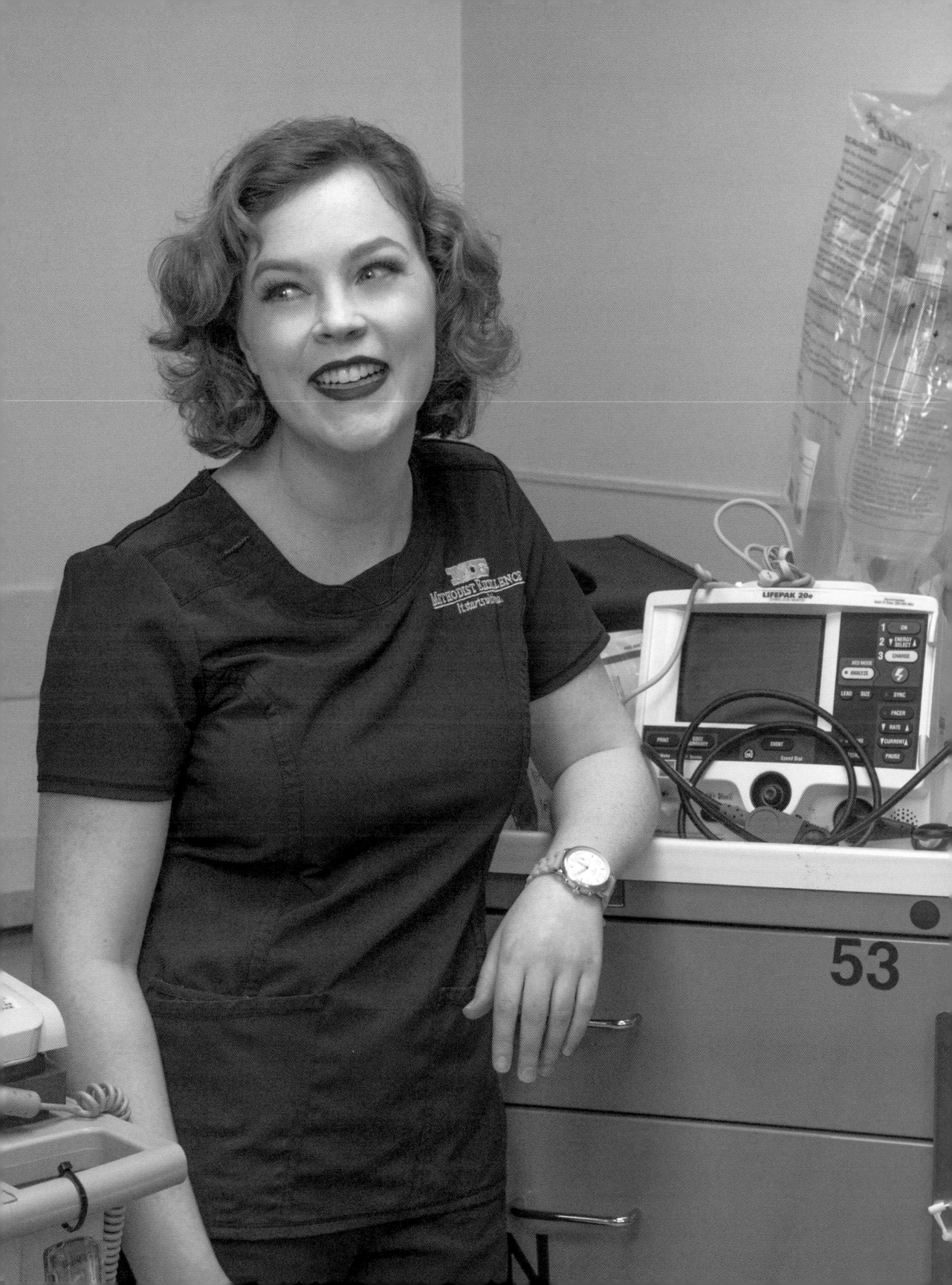

DR. JON PERLIN

{CMO and President Clinical Services Group, *HCA Healthcare*}

Jon Perlin, MD, came to medicine to serve and pursue a scientific path. However, the chance to make worldwide changes drew the big-picture thinker, Chief Medical Officer, and President of Clinical Services away from one-on-one patient care. For 11 years, the former Under Secretary for Health in the U.S. Department of Veterans Affairs has used his experience leading the nation's largest integrated health system to set the clinical agenda for HCA. Perlin recognizes that medicine, science, and human beings are imperfect. Therefore, he is motivated to use his passion for technology and big data to provide the most effective care. The healthcare industry lauds him as one of the most influential physician executives and health leaders in the country. Perlin attributes these accolades to the social responsibility and adventurous mentality that were instilled in him from an early age. At HCA or the Veterans Health Administration, Perlin confidently pushes the envelope to produce world-class care provided in the context of extraordinary compassion. His gratification comes from watching successful initiatives spread like wildfire and set new industry standards.

How did your upbringing influence your character in the workplace?
I am the first-born child of an academic physician and art historian, which means that I had a 70 percent chance of becoming a doctor. The real question was, what specialty? In college I was an English and philosophy major, and that background has been extraordinarily helpful throughout my career. Individual interaction with patients is based upon good communication, and I'm happy that it's now a critical part of medical school preparation. It is also pretty useful in healthcare leadership.

Did you always have an intrinsic love for medicine?
I wanted to help others through my work and do something meaningful. My father was a bit of a renegade in the academic sense. He worked in Baltimore in the '60s and '70s, which was a turbulent time with a lot of civil strife. He was the head of the psychiatric hospital at Johns Hopkins and created community mental health clinics. At the time, it was absolutely revolutionary to buck the hospital model so individuals didn't end up institutionalized or incarcerated. It was a profound experience to watch someone whose career was both scientifically interesting and also served vulnerable communities. My father grew up very poor and felt blessed to have the ability to study medicine and send his kids to great schools. Yet along with the privilege I experienced came a requirement to pay it forward.

Can you speak to that great sense of responsibility that you felt?
Watching my parents invest in others through education and social service and witnessing exceptional economic and educational disparities inculcated and amplified that sense of responsibility. Accepting things as they are would have been easier. Going against an established social norm is about seeing things differently and doing something that hasn't been done before.

Can you give me an example of how you did this in your own career?
When we built the first national electronic health record (EHR) in the VA, everyone accepted that paper records were adequate. It was obvious that the dependency on paper-based information had its risks. We felt a sense of urgency to create an EHR and use technology in a new way that would serve individual hospitals as well as an entire U.S. health system.

How do you educate a nation on something entirely new?
At first there was the small group of early adopters who were the converted. Eventually people took notice and a sense of pride was instilled once they saw that we were making progress in making information more easily accessible. Proof and a sense of appreciation move initiatives forward. One of the things that I'm most proud of in my tenure at the VA was the measured performance of our healthcare becoming better than the private sector. Today, at HCA all of our 30 million yearly patient encounters are measured electronically. That aggregation of data is used to learn, improve the system, and discover new treatments to improve care. Our goal is to be the new benchmark.

What was one of your most pivotal moments at the Veterans Administration?
We had the opportunity to display and demonstrate the EHR at the White House to Bill Gates. He was only moderately impressed and

asked a really important question: "Why aren't you learning?" He saw the future of "big data" and wondered how we could accelerate discovery, learning, and improvement through this massive amount of information. That outlook inspired me greatly in terms of the REDUCE MRSA study, which helped HCA set a new worldwide standard for cutting the risk of infections in intensive care units by almost half. It is now the recommended practice worldwide, proving Dr. Frist's adage: "If you change care in HCA, you change care everywhere."

What has it been like to witness healthcare change over time?
There are constants, like the love for patient care and the mission of serving the health of communities. One of the most profound changes, however, has been the advent of big data. The tracking of patient care now comes from a trail of information that, in aggregate, answers questions like, *What works best for a disease?* or *What will work best for a specific patient?* As we use computers to discover and track relationships that people may not see, we can improve care and save lives like we are currently doing to combat sepsis. Our ideal clinician would be watching their patients all day, every day, all of the time. A human can't do that, but a machine can. Together, they are the perfect team.

How much does the human connection play into the clinical agenda?
The human connection is the secret sauce of HCA. Despite the fact that we are a massive organization, we also retain many of the elements of a family-founded organization. We are community driven by a collective mission: the care and improvement of human life.

What brought you from direct patient care to healthcare leadership?
I can trace the change to a particular moment. After doing the PhD part of my MD/PhD program, I came back to clinical care. The very first patient assigned to me was a heart transplant patient. I went to his room and he wasn't there. He was out on the deck smoking a cigarette ten days after his transplant. I was disturbed by the resources that had been used, including the heart of another human. I went to the dean who informed me that since Virginia was a tobacco state and we were a state institution, taking on the tobacco lobby could be problematic. He offered that if a student were to take on this case he wouldn't get in the way. So I partnered with some dedicated faculty who knew how to effect change and we became tobacco free in one year. From there on, I wanted to intervene at a policy level to achieve outcomes that would help an entire population. Everything I love about the physician-patient relationship was amplified by caring for populations.

What goes into setting the clinical agenda for HCA?
My job is to bring together science, technology, and behavior change to improve the human condition. I am constantly asking myself, *How can we eliminate harm? How do we consistently apply our knowledge in the most effective way? How do we drive waste out of the system to make it more efficient?* We want to democratize technology, data, and systems so everyone can make decisions like the most seasoned individuals in the most sophisticated institutions.

> # GOING AGAINST AN ESTABLISHED SOCIAL NORM IS ABOUT SEEING THINGS DIFFERENTLY AND DOING SOMETHING THAT HASN'T BEEN DONE BEFORE.

What is unique about HCA's leadership culture?
We are disciplined about making effective decisions. The benefit of HCA is that we are able to test initiatives around the country. If you see something that works, then you perfect, replicate, and disseminate it. We also don't believe in size for the sake of size, but rather to methodically test ideas and bring them to scale. Our success comes from merging operational and clinical expertise.

What about your personality has made you successful?
First is a sense of purpose to make healthcare better. Secondly, I work well with others, value their input, and share power. Great things happen in interfaces, which require partnership and teamwork. Only then can you create a synergy that results in a greater success than you could have achieved on your own.

Was there a moment in your life where you knew that you could lead?
Around the time of 9/11, I went to the Secretary of Veterans Affairs' office and asked how I could contribute. In the month that followed, I spent my time in a secure, undisclosed location, helping to provide healthcare for the country. The privilege of serving in that circumstance was transformative. I learned to be present, roll up my sleeves, and do what it takes, which paved the way for future leadership opportunities. Life is preparation for the next opportunity, which you either create or answer when it comes knocking.

How do you stay grounded in your current role?
When we are so consumed by information overload, staying present is a challenge. I make a conscious choice to give individuals and situations my full attention and also step away to other interests. For fun, I enjoy photography, sailing, tennis, and guitar. I figured, *Where better to learn guitar than Nashville?* (Laughs)

LENORA EVERETT-GAYLE, RN

{Direct Care Nurse, *Ocala Regional Medical Center*}

Lenora Everett-Gayle, a direct care nurse at Ocala Regional Medical Center, gleans strength during times of struggle from her spirituality and support system. The native Jamaican, who has spent the last 20 years in the United States, describes her home country as one in which the entire society looks after one another. She likens the culture there to the one shared by her hospital's nursing staff, a group that selflessly gives to their patients and colleagues. Her mother, also a nurse, initially suggested the field as a career path, but Everett-Gayle originally shied away from the profession because of squeamishness. However, she couldn't deny her desire to be of service. She moved to Ocala, and through her studies there, as well as a mind-over-matter mentality, overcame her earlier reservations about the field of nursing. In 2015, after 14 years in the medical industry, Everett-Gayle's daughter Janae was diagnosed with a rare, life-threatening disease of the liver and bile duct. Despite being the main breadwinner of her family, Everett-Gayle took months off of work to ensure that Janae received a liver transplant. One day, knowing that Everett-Gayle's family was struggling to make ends meet, her manager suggested that she apply to the HCA Hope Fund, a public charity through which employees help employees. She accepted the assistance with appreciation, which allowed her to focus all her energy on her daughter's care. Although she's still faced with struggles, Everett-Gayle maintains an optimistic demeanor. She believes that she is a better nurse because of them.

How did you become a nurse?
I came to the United States at age 16 for better opportunities. My training was done in Florida where my mother lived, and I transitioned from a home health aide to a medical assistant and finally a nurse. I moved slowly because I wanted to make sure that I could handle it. I had to condition myself to get over the horrific things that we see every day and realize all that matters is helping patients shift from poor health to their new norm.

What qualities make for an unbeatable nursing team?
There is nothing more reassuring than teamwork. It makes you feel less alone to know that you can call your buddy down the hall to ensure that your patient gets everything that they need. We are all there to achieve together.

What were your first thoughts upon entering the healthcare industry?
I am responsible for people's lives. Even though that was slightly intimidating, I would coach myself and say, *You can do this*. I love helping people, so I stepped up to the challenge. It is an amazing feeling to help someone maintain his or her dignity by getting over a stumbling block. A nurse brings the patient back to their previous state or helps them to manage a new life.

How would you describe what you do every day?
A nurse's role is to make a patient feel safe while preserving their independence. We are constantly assessing patients, prioritizing and meeting their needs, and asking them what they want and need from us. We also are relentless about education in order to help the patient live a healthier lifestyle.

What makes someone a good nurse?
You have to be compassionate, altruistic, and have a high sense of integrity. We must do the right thing. Otherwise the patient suffers.

What do you like about a job that is in keeping with your beliefs?
I worship and serve God, so this job aligns with my faith. If I do the wrong thing, I won't feel right inside. That's what keeps me on track.

What is it like to work in a trauma unit?
The environment is fast-paced, so prioritization is key. We have to set emotion aside to know what comes first. Should I tend to this person who has to go to the bathroom or to the one who feels faintish? To know the answer, intuition, common sense, and critical thinking come into play. Talented nurses are honest, team players, fast learners, and critical thinkers.

How do you stay calm in chaotic situations?
I go to my spiritual place, which allows me to filter out the negativity and focus on the positive. Through prayer, I can be calm in the midst of the craziness. I cannot afford to get worked up or lose my cool, because that is how you make mistakes.

How do you deal with a difficult patient?
I try to imagine what kind of pain they are in or how frightened they must be. By constantly asking myself about their behavior, I am able to empathize.

my attention—Mommy had to maintain so we didn't lose it. A supportive husband was also a great help.

You're quite a woman for holding strong under all of that pressure.
I did what I had to do. One morning I blurted out at our huddle, "My daughter is getting a liver transplant, so you might not see me for a while." My coworkers could not believe I had kept quiet for so long. From there, my daughter and I went to Georgia for her surgery, and my husband watched our other two children.

How did the Hope Fund first cross your radar?
After I received the call for our liver transplant, my boss, Beth Richland, said, "You're going to need financial assistance!" That had been the last thing on my mind. My only prerogative was to get my child fixed. Beth got the ball rolling and filled out the first round of paperwork for the Hope Fund. I really admire and thank her for that because I'd never have thought of it. How many bosses do that?

THE HOPE FUND HELPS FELLOW HCA EMPLOYEES AT THEIR LOWEST POINT, WHICH IS A BEAUTIFUL THING.

What did it feel like to find out that your daughter was very ill?
December 31, three months after her birth, we found out she had biliary atresia, which is a rare disease of the liver and bile ducts and can only be fixed with a transplant. That was the beginning of our new year. From there, our plans were put into motion of finding her a transplant.

What goes through your head when you hear that kind of news?
It felt like a nightmare because, as a healthcare professional, I was well aware of all the complications. I was overwhelmed as a parent rather than a medical professional, because my child had a rare disorder that could take her life.

How did you console yourself?
I prayed all day long. My faith and family are a huge part of who I am. When I went into work, I would compartmentalize and leave my struggles outside. For a long time, I didn't tell anyone what was going on; I separate personal and professional.

What was it like to be under financial duress?
It was a difficult period, and to be truthful, I do not know how I managed. I would constantly repeat to myself, *We're going to get through this as a family.* I had to keep up a positive façade for my family, which was exhausting. However, if I let my upbeat demeanor crack, I would have crumbled. Sick baby, medical bills, and other children needing

When you share your experiences, people want to help.
Exactly. Had I continued to be discreet I would have been doing this on my own and tearing my hair out. (Laughs) Having a support system is a great thing. The Hope Fund helps fellow HCA employees at their lowest point, which is a beautiful thing. I could properly function once I knew I had financial support.

What did it feel like to have your fellow HCA colleagues help you?
If every organization could support its employees similarly, the world would be a different place. Not only did the Hope Fund help us to pay our mortgage and monthly bills but also the application process was simple and straightforward. A Hope Fund employee also calls to congratulate you on your recipient status, which I found to be very comforting. After months of falling, I finally felt like I had a safety net.

Was there any hesitation to accept financial assistance?
Never. My prayers had been answered. God had worked it out. There was no judgment about taking the financial aid, so why would I allow myself to suffer?

How is your daughter today?
After her transplant, we've had a few hiccups, but so far so good. The last few years our family has adjusted to a new norm. Some days I have my moments and think, *God, why me?* But I quickly bypass those thoughts because I can use my story to help someone else get through their troubles.

Will you tell your daughter what happened to her when she's older?
I want her to know that she is a miracle and incredibly strong. By understanding what she went through as a baby, she'll be able to overcome anything.

Do you have a support system that you rely upon?
My husband and our families are our support system. We also frequently talk to other parents who have gone through the same disease. Other parents whose children are healthy don't know what it is like to deal with a life-threatening illness. But if I call up one of my other "liver mommies," as we call them, they can say, "We had to deal with that situation!" From there I think, *We can work it out, because they did.* They understand everything that we are going through.

Has your daughter's disease changed your approach to nursing?
Yes, because I have been in the bed even if I wasn't the patient. Being on the other side has allowed me to be more empathetic and give better care. Even though I fought it tooth and nail, I know that is why I was chosen to be a nurse.

What does the HCA mission mean to you?
At Ocala, we are here to provide the community with outstanding, compassionate, and innovative care, and we make sure every patient knows they will be looked after.

BILL RUTHERFORD

{CFO, *HCA Healthcare*}

Bill Rutherford, Chief Financial Officer and Executive Vice President of HCA, isn't someone who sees his role merely as a budget manager. In his 30 years at HCA, his goal has been to grow professionally, contribute to the community, and achieve a 360-degree view of the healthcare industry. After graduating from the University of Tampa with a bachelor's degree in accounting and finance, Rutherford joined HCA as a staff auditor in 1986. Every promotion felt like a bit of a stretch to him, but Rutherford always stepped up to the challenge. At HCA, he has been able to exercise his entrepreneurial inclinations, build a professional path tied to social good, and achieve a level of success beyond his aspirations. While he calls himself a "simple accountant at heart," Rutherford takes the time to self-reflect and ensures that his career path mirrors his moral compass.

What has been most meaningful in terms of your HCA career?

There always have been characteristics I was in search of during my professional career: I wanted to believe in the organization in terms of its services and mission, make a meaningful contribution, enjoy the company of my coworkers, and have the opportunity to grow professionally. HCA has allowed me to experience all of that.

Can you tell us a bit about your upbringing?

While I was growing up, my family and I moved about every three years. I had lived in eight places by the time I was 16 years old, which is why I feel like I can drop in almost anywhere and make it home. My dad was the first person in his family to graduate from college. After a stint in the army, he joined one of the largest oil companies at the time, from which he retired with a 40-year tenure and the position of EVP of Operations. I've always found his story to be very inspiring. As a kid, I wanted to stretch myself. I was athletic and I spent time as a drummer in a rock 'n' roll band. I aimed to be a touring musician, but fortunately, my dad talked me into going to college instead. (Laughs) I took an accounting and business class in high school and immediately took a liking to it.

How did you go about pursuing your chosen profession?

Originally, I wanted to work for the FBI, so I double majored in criminal justice and accounting at the University of Tampa. My junior year I pivoted and went full-time into accounting. Straight after graduation, I started with HCA, which as you know, has a big presence on the West Coast of Florida. One hospital there had an assistant controller development program. They hired college graduates with accounting or finance degrees, trained them, and placed them. One of my professors referred me for the program, but the slots were already filled. Fortunately, I was quickly referred to HCA's regional office in Clearwater and hired on in internal audit in 1986.

What were your first jobs in the healthcare industry like?

Back then my job was 80 percent travel, and the average tenure was roughly two years. I lasted seven, traveling around the country, meeting lots of great people, and seeing tons of operations. When HCA spun out HealthTrust, I moved to Nashville with internal audit, this time at the corporate level. There, I was assigned to special projects and the operations side of the company, which allowed me to network with the regional leaders. In 1993, HCA did the Columbia merger, and there was an opening as a division CFO in Atlanta. The company promoted me from internal audit to division CFO of Georgia, one of the largest divisions at the time. They gave me that opportunity when I was 30 years old. There I was, running a billion-dollar division. That's the great thing about this company. You develop relationships that allow you to prove yourself, and that creates opportunity. Leadership looks at your character, positivity, business intelligence, and ability to communicate. That can count for more than just experience.

What happened next?

After being a division CFO for two years, I was given the opportunity to be the Eastern Group CFO in 1996 and help develop the northeast corridor, where historically we hadn't had a presence. Then in 1997, Dr. Frist, Jr. came back from retirement to restructure HCA, which is when the company went from five operating groups to two: the Eastern Group and the Western Group. I held the position of Eastern Group CFO for 10 years. Dr. Frist's paradigm shift spoke to the fact that HCA could get stronger by getting smaller. In 1999 and early 2000, we began to hit an operational excellence era at HCA.

What did your experience away from HCA teach you?

In 2005, I was 40 years old and had accomplished a lot at a young age. I decided to leave HCA to run my own training and development company, which was a great plan terribly executed. As I started to raise a lot of venture capital, a group introduced me to Psychiatric Solutions, one of the largest behavior health companies in town. I became COO of Psychiatric Solutions for about two years as the company was on a hyper growth path. At a point, I realized it wasn't where I wanted to be and came back to HCA in 2008. Bruce Moore asked me to come back as the CFO of the Outpatient Group, which he was running at the time. There was a lot of entrepreneurial growth happening in that group. I spent the next three years there until Richard Bracken, CEO at the time, asked if I would take over as the interim CEO of Physicians Services in 2011. They were growing rapidly and needed operational and financial focus. After that, I wasn't sure what I wanted to do until one day, Milton Johnson, who was CFO but about to become Chairman and CEO, called and said he had his eye on me to become the next CFO of HCA. Five years later, here we are.

That time away from HCA was priceless, simply because it gave me a renewed sense of appreciation for our culture. I joined HCA right out of school, so it was the only organization I knew in my professional career. Coming back with an even greater admiration made my return that much more rewarding.

How do you feel about what you do?
I can't think of anything more inspiring than to support caregivers and impact the healthcare industry. That is what gets me up every day. Also, to have that as a common bond amongst your coworkers is pretty cool. The first time I drew a connection between my job and the HCA mission was as an auditor. While doing clinical and financial audits, we immersed ourselves in the individual hospital environments, which taught me all about the industry and allowed me to make friends with the clinicians and nurses. The overarching goal of HCA is to deliver the best clinical quality in the most cost-effective manner with the best patient service. Every single function and role at HCA can be tied to that overall mission. I feel satisfied knowing that my time at the office is tied to improving healthcare as a whole, which in turn helps people across the country.

What are your proudest accomplishments in your HCA tenure?
One of the most rewarding things we have done as a company was to create Shared Services. I was the CFO of the Eastern Group at the time and helped to support that evolution. However, the consolidation posed some challenges because we now had to find new ways to hire, promote, and reward our CFOs. We began focusing on developing the CFOs so they could spend their time strategizing growth opportunities, deciding where to apply capital investment, and gain a deeper understanding of what was going on in the marketplace. During that time, I developed a great appreciation for training and development. Also, by evolving the role of CFO—they have become a critical component in our company's success.

What is something most people don't know about you?
The first mentor I had was our VP of Audit, Leon Drennan, who helped me create goals and a professional development plan. Together, we charted a course on how I would achieve them, from shadowing in a department to improving my communication skills. In my wallet, I carry around a tattered sheet of paper with my goals written on it from 1991. One of them was to become CFO of HCA.

HCA OFFERS AN AMPLE FORUM FOR PEOPLE TO EXPRESS THEIR THOUGHTS AND OPINIONS IN A SUPPORTIVE ENVIRONMENT.

What is some advice you might give to young professionals?
I always liked to have a mentor who was in the organization but in another department so they could give me solid, unbiased opinions. I tell the young people I mentor to establish the professional and personal goals they're in search of, commit them to writing, and make sure there is congruency between the two. I have a sense of peace when I know there is synergy between the two. If there isn't, you tend to have a lot of internal conflict and friction. I see too many people pivot from one role to another without being fully aware of what they're pursuing. When I stepped away from HCA, I woke up one day, literally and figuratively, and realized that I wasn't happy even though I had the biggest title and was making the most money I had ever made. That's what caused me to come back. Our mission, the culture, the people, the ability to achieve your goals are what I love about HCA.

How has HCA helped you to grow personally and professionally?
The organization also helps me to scratch my entrepreneurial itch. Each business has its own executive team, growth trajectory, and organizational management systems, which makes each feel like its own entity. HCA is so broad in terms of operations that you can work with any of our businesses as if they were your own. We also have a culture of listening to people's ideas and innovations. HCA offers an ample forum for people to express their thoughts and opinions in a supportive environment.

Do you have any last thoughts on your HCA tenure?
Over 30 years or so, I've worked in almost every area of the company, which gives me a unique perspective. To operate at the macro-strategic area and the micro level, too, is an important ability for an executive to have. I believe it's why I've been able to help fulfill our organization's objectives to the best of my ability.

It's incredible to be one member of a large team like HCA and take care of 30 million people a year. I can't think of a nobler cause than delivering healthcare to your community. (Long pause) No, I really can't.

KRISTIN BAKER, RN

{Direct Care Nurse, *Oak Hill Hospital*}

Saving lives isn't always pretty, but for Kristin Baker, an emergency room nurse, it keeps her perspective in check. Originally from Maryland, Baker and her husband landed in Spring Hill, Florida, after his retirement from the military. The Nurse of the Year honoree, admired for her steady compassion and composure, fell in love with Oak Hill Hospital's ambiance upon arrival. From its democratic nature to the collaboration between departments, the hospital's dynamic suited her sociable, take-charge personality. After working in nearly every available nursing position and a vast range of medical facilities, Baker finally found the friendship she craved at Oak Hill. It is an environment in which the resident prankster can crack jokes when appropriate or cry on her coworker's shoulders. In the ER, Baker, who thrives on adrenaline, gets her chaos fix. She's highly competent, yet humble enough to admit she doesn't know everything; in the ER there is no room for an ego. When it comes to patients, no task is below her pay grade.

What were your first impressions of Oak Hill Hospital?
It was a culture like I had never seen before. When you are 10 feet away from another person in the hallway, you smile. Five feet away you say "hi." I immediately felt like I was part of a family. I know who the CEO is because he makes himself available. I feel heard and know that my voice is taken seriously.

How do patients view the culture at Oak Hill?
Oak Hill has been here for over 30 years, yet in the last five, our intake has increased dramatically. Surrounding communities choose to go out of their way to come to our hospital rather than their local facility, because of the culture.

How does that kind of tightly knit community nourish you?
A family dynamic is critical to success in our industry. Recently, my husband and I renovated our backyard into one that resembles a resort, complete with a hot tub, kitchen, and grill. Weekly, we have Wine Wednesday, to which I invite all of my coworkers. Some of my teammates don't have a family to process their work life with, so they find our group to be very therapeutic. I also see patients around town who stop and thank me for taking care of them. That is the blessing of working in a small town and makes me know that I have left a mark on their lives.

What is the best compliment you have ever received in your nursing role?
Leisa, who was a travel nurse when I was a charge nurse, came in on a regular basis once or twice a year. In 2013, she asked if she could feature me as her subject in a school paper. The topic was a breakdown of the ideal characteristics of a nurse manager and hospital leader. I was really flattered by what she said I did right in the workplace, which was that I was fun to be around, made every nurse feel useful, and was able to work with others to achieve results. Lastly, she noted how much she admired the positive reinforcement that I gave my coworkers and said it was a breath of fresh, empowering air.

Which mentors in your workplace have impacted you?
Our hospital is in the process of construction to give us more room in the ER. Currently, we are running a second ER out of our lobby, which has been a huge learning curve. How we've made this new brand of nursing a success is because of the guidance of our director Kim Loucks. She is a former ER nurse who is unbelievably giving and kind. Kim comes into work when we're short staffed, listens to our needs, and encourages use to invent systems that will keep the patients safe—rather than always telling us what to do. The reason I am so positive is because I know she is behind the patients and staff at all times.

You create monthly lists for your fellow ER nurses, reminding them how to make light of the tougher moments. What are some of those key points?
For every list, I write three to five reasons that I love being an ER nurse. Next, I tack it to the bulletin board in our break room. Nurses tend to get overwhelmed because we take in so much action and emotion on a daily basis. Even in the bleakest moments, you must have a sense of humor so you don't get burned out. My daughter, who is 23 years old, is a certified nursing assistant at Oak Hill. I send my patients up to her unit to tease her. I'll tell them to do things like ring her call bell every five minutes so she's always running into their room. (Laughs) During Hurricane Irma, I hid fake snakes and spiders in my coworkers' sleeping bags when they weren't around. Security knows me well because I have plastic-wrapped my coworkers' cars in the parking lot. (Laughs)

What is most exciting about your job right now?

Oak Hill is growing really quickly, which means the other nurses and I are always tossing around design ideas. It's really fun to be involved in that process and have the administration staff tap us for insight. Recently, I made what I call the "ugly tent city," with recliners and curtains on wheels, in our lobby. We needed separation to know who had been treated and who was waiting for their treatment. One day, the higher ups were rounding and asked, "Who did this?" When the other nurses answered, "Kristin Baker!" they said, "Well I guess it was needed." What I saw as practical at the time turned out to be a great way to speed up the construction. (Laughs) My coworkers and I live to problem-solve. If something works, great. If it doesn't, we let it go. We're just a group of nurses trying to do our best for the patients. The best thing is that if we prove our ideas are safe and suitable then the administrative staff green-lights them.

How does everyone remain focused on the same goal?

While I tend to take the lead on a lot of situations, the entire team at Oak Hill hospital always works together to achieve patient satisfaction. We also have shared governance, which means that the nurses in every branch of the hospital have a voice. On these various committees, we talk about changes that are needed, put action plans on paper, and push them towards the division. You can be involved on every level and with every medical department at Oak Hill.

Can you tell me about a time where you put yourself in another's shoes?

I had a patient recently who had a heart attack. All of a sudden, his wife came in to the ER and asked me to find his tattered T-shirt that we had cut off him minutes earlier. While I didn't quite understand why it mattered so much to her, I rummaged through all of the linen bins until I found it. When I handed it to her, she thanked me and said, "I wanted something that still had my husband's smell on it in case he didn't survive." Something minute to me was monumental to her. That was a moment I truly understood empathy.

When you are in chaos, how do you make your patients feel important?

I use a bit of positive scripting to explain what is going to happen. Information is everything in a hospital environment. "While we're full in the ER right now, we will get your care started right here in the lobby. We'll have the doctors and CT scan team come to you. We'll work as quickly as we can, which means you might even get discharged from here." All the patient wants is to be informed and acknowledged. Ten minutes in the ER can feel like an eternity, so if a doctor or nurse pulls up a chair and has a chat with a patient, that makes a world of difference. Oftentimes there is much more going on underneath the surface of someone than just the physical symptoms. People in pain want to be recognized.

YOU CAN BE INVOLVED ON EVERY LEVEL AND WITH EVERY MEDICAL DEPARTMENT AT OAK HILL.

How do you facilitate communication between the various departments?

Donuts are a great incentive for conversation. (Laughs) I will routinely go to the different departments and floors and ask if they have any issues with the ER. Communication breakdown disrupts everything. Both sides truly trying to understand an issue builds a respectful rapport. If you explain the *why* to someone rather than demanding something, they will generally do what you ask.

How did it feel to win the Nurse of the Year award at Oak Hill?

Amazing. I get a lot of satisfaction out of connecting various departments. In turn, hopefully they know one another better than they did before. Keeping myself plugged in with all parts of the hospital builds my capacity for empathy.

How has being a nurse changed your perception on life?

My HCA family and I take advantage of every single moment because we realize today could be your last day. Things could always be worse and usually are for someone else. Pick yourself up and keep on moving. Every day when I go home I say, "I love you," to my kids and husband and give them a huge hug. My work keeps things in perspective, and I try to pass that frame of reference on to others.

What does the HCA mission mean to you?

I believe it comes down to seeing and appreciating our patients as individuals, no matter how busy we are. Caring for them in that manner is the goal I constantly strive for every single day. The second I stop trying to be a better ER nurse, then it's time to move on to something else.

DR. FERNANDO TRIANA

{Cardiologist, Chief Officer for Strategy and Innovation, *Cardiology Clinic of San Antonio*}

Fernando Triana, MD and Medical Director of the Cardiology Clinic of San Antonio, believes uncomfortable conversations can result in great change. Born in Bogotá, Colombia, Triana decided as a child that he would devote his days to serving humanity. He was born in a house without running water or electricity, but Triana transcended the socioeconomic divide by becoming the first physician in his family. Driven by survival and the desire to become renowned in his industry, he enrolled in medical school at age 15. At 21, he was performing surgery. Shortly after, as a non-English speaker, he moved to the United States to train in internal medicine at Tulane University in New Orleans, Louisiana. Today, in speaking engagements across the country, he champions a renaissance approach to physician work life, the benefits of continuous care, and treating each patient as a whole. Enhancing the lives of his patients during his time on earth, within an enterprise like HCA, feels like heaven to him.

Were you emotionally prepared to become a physician at age 15?

We become ready when we need to be. The plasticity of the human brain and our capabilities are limitless. My father had to work in the coal mines at age nine after his father lost his leather business and all of his money. When I moved to New Orleans and was sleeping on sofas, I would think, *This is hard but not as bad as what my dad experienced.* That gave me a lot of mileage.

Do you think you have to grow up faster in Colombia versus America?

Absolutely. Some have described the Colombian society as people drinking champagne and those without water living on the same block. At age 57, I still have that survivalist mentality instilled in my youth that dictates my every action. I am criticized occasionally for still trying to prove myself.

How did you become a master at your craft?

A sense of purpose has been essential to my path. The initial drive was to be the best physician possible. I greatly admired my grandmother's physician, who did everything he could to keep her alive until she passed away in our house. In contrast, my brother's physician misdiagnosed him as a pre-teen with epilepsy, which completely flipped his entire world upside down. That was the first time I realized the significance of words and the magnitude of my responsibility.

What does it feel like to witness the toughest moments of your patients' lives?

When you are vulnerable with someone else, your own vulnerability shows. Not everyone is cut out for that. You have to be willing to walk to a threshold where you lose the fear of being exposed. Very early on, I learned that it was okay to cry with my patients. What else do you do when a 20-year patient has heart failure? A lot of people go through trauma, and it is a privilege to empathize with them. Empathy is a huge part of the personal, holistic relationships that I create with my patients and enriches my own life greatly.

What is your current passion?

I want to give physicians a voice. We are at the single most important crisis in the history of American medicine, which is that physicians live in three universes: the art of medicine, the science of medicine, and the business of medicine. As a leader, it is my job to balance and integrate those worlds. Some people call me a visionary; however, I view myself as someone who simply took a step back and realized there is more than one angle to everything that we see. This polarization in a physician's work life is reflective of our lack of willingness to see the other side. Once we do that, we will have much more interesting conversations.

What are you contemplating most recently?

I write a lot about various issues, which then, similar to a fertile planting ground, start to expand. Recently I've been thinking about the level of satisfaction amongst physicians throughout the industry,

WHAT GIVES ME THE GREATEST JOY IS TALKING WITH MY PATIENTS ABOUT THEIR HAPPY MOMENTS AND DIGGING DEEP INTO THEIR SORROWS.

which I believe stems from face-to-face connection with our patients. I personally cannot wait to get out of bed in the morning; however, many physicians struggle because of the overload of information. The battle lies between entering data and trying to have a conversation with your patient. I've learned to juggle these two elements without sacrificing what gives me the greatest joy: talking with my patients about their happy moments and digging deep into their sorrows. That revitalizes my spirit and injects life into my journey. The more I understand the world I live in, the more I am able to adapt.

What is most satisfying about your job?
Contentment is derived from the enrichment of the patient experience. I look for the essence of every single patient by empathizing with all aspects of their experience.

Can you talk a bit about your philosophy in regards to continuous care?
In the business of medicine, I analyze the productivity of our physicians, locally and nationally, which led to assessing my own practice patterns. I noticed two dichotomized forces in terms of patient care: episodic care, which is where a patient sees their doctor, is treated, and goes home, versus continuous care, which involves assessing their condition and lifestyle choices over time. Continuous care, which I practice, allows you to collaborate with the patient and come up with a toolkit to help them lead a healthier life. That connectivity between patient and physician is critical to seeing what lies beneath the surface. Continuous care is critical to developing an optimal healthcare delivery system because our health, similar to emotions, is always in a state of transition.

What does the HCA mission mean to you?
HCA is devoted to delivering healthcare at the highest possible level. My responsibility here is huge and humbling beyond belief because of the opportunity to enhance human life throughout the world. Hippocrates wrote an oath 2,500 years ago, which says, "I devote my life to serving my fellow human beings." I will always put the lives of my patients before my own personal means, which is in absolute synchrony with HCA.

TINA BILLBERRY, RN

{Transfer Center Coordinator, *Rapides Regional Medical Center*}

Tina Billberry used her insight and relationships to facilitate top-notch cancer treatment for her father and aunt. Being able to handpick her family's caretakers at Rapides Regional Medical Center was the greatest privilege of her medical career. Introduced to HCA as a high school student by her neighbor, who was a nurse, the transfer center coordinator began working for the organization in 1996, and she still thrives on the versatile nature of the industry. After beginning her career in psychiatric nursing, Billberry moved into case management and home health, and next to a role as oncology nurse navigator. In that role, she walked patients through the various stages of their healing process, which are impossible to emotionally prepare for. When it came to her own family's arrangements, she found comfort in choosing the caretakers. Yet, while Billberry didn't have to walk into that situation blindly, she assures anyone who does that Rapides provides compassionate, cutting-edge treatment.

How did you first become interested in healthcare?
My sister was born with a congenital heart disorder. When we were in high school, she had an infected cyst on her chest. After the surgeon drained her cyst, they couldn't close the wound due to her condition, and it had to be packed three times a day. My neighbor at the time was a nurse and showed me how to do wound care in order to help my sister. Ironically, many years later that same nurse was diagnosed with breast cancer, and I was able to take care of her at Rapides. That brought everything full circle and was an incredible honor. It gave me the chance to give back some of what she had given years before.

Why are you proud to work at Rapides Regional Medical Center?
I am a lifelong Louisiana native. My first nursing job was at an HCA facility in New Iberia. After a family member passed away, I was able to transfer to Rapides so I could move back home to Alexandria. Rapides Regional Medical Center is a large referral center where patients come from surrounding areas to receive cutting-edge care. I take a lot of pride in the fact that I work at such a well-respected facility, which serves so many of the surrounding communities because of our specialties.

What was your role like as oncology nurse navigator?
As I was working on my bachelor's degree in 2015, I needed to scale back because 12-hour shifts were not working for my family. The navigator role opened up, and while I had never worked in oncology, it applied my mental-health and case-management backgrounds. A cancer diagnosis takes the wind out of you. Until you catch your breath, many don't know how to handle it. Patients appreciate having someone to hold their hand and make sense of all the foreign information.

Cancer care is multidisciplinary, and the diagnostic process involves many specialties. The navigator helps to explain and guide the patient through their care because, often, their head is spinning. The navigator organizes the steps of cancer care while the patient sorts out their feelings.

How do most people react to a cancer diagnosis?
Some cancer patients are very emotional. Others aren't. Some want to hear every bit of information. A lot want to know very little. So many different factors come into play when you are dealing with a life-changing diagnosis. I had to figure out what each patient needed and go there with them. A lot of patients want peace and time with their thoughts versus being doted on by their family. They crave normalcy because their life has changed so dramatically. Some days I would shut my door and let the patient cry, scream, or do whatever they needed to do to get their emotions out. It's devastating to realize you have no control.

How has innovation played into your HCA career?
When I stepped into my navigator role, we wanted to market the position so people knew that it existed, so we thought of the patient

pillow project. The patient pillows, which we initially looked to purchase but could not find anywhere, became a way to connect with our community and alleviate discomfort. The goal became to give away a locally made product that would protect a patient's wounds from rubbing against their car seatbelts. After finding a pattern for the pillow online, we posted it on our website. High schools, churches, and sewing groups came forward and began producing them. Everyone wanted to take part in our mission. We had so many at one point that they were stuffed into every closet in Cancer Center. (Laughs) We have homemade pillows to give away to patients for years because of the support of HCA, Rapides, and the residents of Alexandria.

What is it like to have your father and aunt be treated at Rapides?

When it came to coordinating treatment for my father and aunt, I had confidence in our staff because I knew everyone from my navigator role. I had watched their work with my own eyes and knew everyone would take expert care of my family.

schedule had been pre-arranged so I could be of assistance along with my other family members. You can never give as much as you want to. It's normal to feel that you could or should have done more. Even in a chronic or terminal illness, you know that the end is coming, but it's still a surprise when it does.

How has that experience changed your perspective?

While I always had the knowledge and compassion, personal experience altered the way I approach my work. I am more aware of what my patients and their families experience. I understand how frightening cancer can be and why it's imperative to get people treatment as fast as possible. Lastly, I know how great of an impact our staff has on people's lives.

What does the HCA mission mean to you?

HCA's values are practiced widely across the organization, which I can honestly say from having worked in several facilities. All life is valued and everyone has the intention of contributing equally to the wellbeing of the patient. It is a culture that builds you up and cherishes each person's unique compilation of knowledge.

CARE AND COMPASSION FOR THE PATIENT, STAFF, AND COMMUNITY ARE DEEPLY WOVEN THROUGHOUT OUR CULTURE.

Last year was intense. My aunt was diagnosed in February and my dad in April. They passed away within ten days of one another in the exact same room in August. While my entire family did everything they could, unfortunately, both of their stories ended with death. Caring for the dying takes more courage and compassion than caring for the living, honestly. It isn't for the faint of heart, but both my aunt and my dad received the best possible care until their last breath at Rapides.

What was most challenging about that time in your life?

Knowing the answers to your family's questions takes some of the anxiety away. However, trying to maintain a positive attitude despite knowing their prognoses were grim was a challenge. Fortunately, I was only working two shifts a week, so I could take my dad and aunt to doctor's appointments and also make sure they had some fun. You don't always know what's going to happen, but I do believe my

How would you describe the HCA company culture?

At my first HCA hospital in New Iberia, the staff took me in and taught me everything they knew. The team understood that I would then, in turn, be able to teach others the information that I had acquired. That value system has a beautiful cyclical effect and is why growth is limitless at HCA. After I first arrived at Rapides, I worked with a wonderful group of nurses who were pivotal in my personal and professional growth. Much of what they taught me set the stage for my current job. They instilled in me the belief that everyone benefits from one another's expertise. I am proud to be a part of an organization that contributes on such a significant scale to so many communities. The HCA values are what make every one of its facilities feel like home. Everyone knows and wants to help each other. Care and compassion for the patient, staff, and community are deeply woven throughout our culture.

DR. LARA M. LANE

{OBGYN, *Women's Care of Colorado*}

Lara M. Lane, MD, a Women's Care of Colorado partner and practicing obstetrician, develops some of the strongest bonds of female solidarity in the delivery room. She is flattered that her patients follow wherever she goes. After thousands of deliveries and 18 years of doctoring, Lane still lacks words to describe what it's like to witness such an intimate moment in a woman's life. The South Dakota native, who admired her physician and college professor father, always felt a calling to pursue a career in medicine. Once she earned her master's degree in nutritional science, Lane realized that writing diet plans didn't fully satisfy her desire to care for others. She changed course and enrolled in medical school. Lane discovered her passion for obstetrics during the first semester of her third year. The magnitude of responsibility that came along with bringing life into the world matched her take-charge personality. At Women's Care of Colorado, Lane practices a bedside manner built around kindness. It is an ideology that involves taking her time with patients and listening to their concerns. In a fast-paced, impersonal world, Lane finds that moving slower with her patients just makes sense.

How did your upbringing influence your character in the workplace?
My grandfather was a surgeon and my father a gastrointestinal doctor. On my office shelves I have my grandfather's medical bag and his bottle collection from the 1930s. I didn't want to go into medicine at first and was discouraged by my physician father because he was never home. Every Thanksgiving dad was gone because someone had choked on a turkey bone. (Laughs) He also tried to convince me to pursue another path, which is why I got my master's degree in nutrition at first. Yet there was always a deep-seated multi-generational calling to practice medicine. That passion kept pulling at me until I enrolled at Sanford School of Medicine at the University of South Dakota, where my dad was a professor. He actually taught my pharmacology, medical, and GI classes, which was very rewarding.

What about medicine appealed to you?
I love caring for others and developing bonds with my patients. The social drive in me made other career choices seem almost boring. I knew I could never sit in a cubicle. I like taking care of the entire patient, from the beginning of their pregnancy until delivery and beyond. I like hearing about how their children are, knowing I played a small part in helping start their family. (Laughs) I guess that's why I like being the leader of this center and my patients' care plans.

What kind of personality makes someone good at your job?
First, you have to love people, all kinds of people. It is your love for people and families that makes it right. Then your love has to be wrapped by a thick skin and a decisive and influential intellect. It is critical to sense your patients but also be able to develop a decisive course of care at even the most stressful moments. And when this patient whom you love pushes back on your course of care, you need to have the ability to calmly explain to the patient why it is in their best interest to pursue your recommendation.

What is difficult about your job?
There is never a guarantee of the perfect outcome, no matter how good the plan is. When outcomes occur that are not perfect, it is hard to not take that personally, especially with the way I practice medicine. I care so deeply for my patients that when an outcome isn't absolutely perfect, I find it very hard to not feel responsible. Science helps us increase probabilities of perfect outcomes, but in the end, I believe a higher power also plays a role. Accepting that you can't control everything in the miracle of birth is both incredibly difficult and a miracle all in one.

When did you know you wanted to work with women and babies?
Going into medical school, I was clueless about what I wanted to study beyond my core requirements. In my third year, I was able to experience OB for the first time and thought, *I absolutely love this.* The first time I delivered a baby as a medical student, the patient, the father, and I all broke down in tears. (Laughs) It was such an intimate moment that I will never forget it as long as I live. Taking care of women from beginning to end during a life-changing experience is amazing.

What are your relationships like with the mothers-to-be?
You get to know them on a very deep level because they talk to you about everything. Those friendships are what keep me working after 18 years. I have delivered thousands of babies, and it's a different experience every time. I get to be a part of one of their most private and miraculous moments in their life, which is very rewarding.

What are some popular questions that patients ask?
The internet has changed medicine forever. Access to information (both right and wrong) typically arms patients with a laundry list of questions. Often these questions create a basic paranoia that I wish patients didn't have, but they certainly make for a more well-informed patient. A few questions that are probably asked by almost every patient: Can I dye my hair? Can I paint my nails? Are you sure that medicine you are prescribing is safe?

Have you ever lost a baby?
Yes. It's gut-wrenching. But if you practice long enough, it will happen. It's the worst experience imaginable. When it happened, I wanted to quit afterwards. But instead, you keep going. It's very hard not to take things that happen at work personally.

How do you develop a connection with your patients?
I spend time with them. I learn their story. I want to know what their fears are and what their dreams are. We see patients from 8 to almost 40 weeks, and then see patients through delivery. Developing strong relationships with my patients comes naturally. This is a huge event in their life. After delivery, you see these patients for years after. You become very close with them.

TAKING CARE OF WOMEN FROM BEGINNING TO END DURING A LIFE-CHANGING EXPERIENCE IS AMAZING.

What do you wish for your patients to know?
Pregnancy is the easy part. The hardest is raising kids and doing a good job at it. (Laughs) While patients are pregnant, I try to reassure people they should enjoy their pregnancy. It goes by very fast. Kids are a lifetime responsibility, but the "kid" part is very, very short. I have two teenage daughters whom I love with all my heart. Love and hug your kids every chance you get.

What was it like the first time you delivered multiples?
I'm an identical twin—yes, I was born first (Laughs)—so multiples always have a special place in my heart. In residency, I delivered twins for the first time, and I thought, *This is what my mom went through!* Delivery of multiples always brings me joy, as it reminds me of my mom, and in some small way, reminds me of my twin sister, with whom I am very close.

What is it like to save a life?
It is both terrifying and rewarding all at the same time. Hemorrhage is not uncommon in the delivery and postpartum setting. My job is to make sure everyone is calm, to talk with patient, and to talk with husband—all the while leading numerous people (including nurses, anesthesia, ancillary staff) and moving quickly if necessary to the operative room so that the patient is safe. People are very grateful afterwards. I still have a note from one patient that says, "Thank you for saving my life." That meant a lot. And, yes, we are close friends.

What do you love about your job?
I could talk to women all day long. I suppose I just like to talk and I love people. I love to be real with women and say it how it is. I feel grateful that patients pour their hearts out to me. Maybe I missed my calling in psychiatry. (Laughs)

How did having children change your career?
Even though I love my patients, I had to prioritize my family. I cut down to part-time when my daughter Alli was in kindergarten and Courtney was three-and-a-half. Because my patients care for me, they accommodated my schedule. Many might think this choice likely "set me back" professionally. I believe this choice actually propelled me forward. It helps me identify with the choices mothers need to make not only during pregnancy but also throughout life. It's not easy being a mom, and only a mom knows what it feels like to be a mom (laughs).

What was the number-one thing you learned from your father?
The first time I took a test in biochemistry it came back with a C on it. I panicked and was so distraught. My dad was very comforting. "Buck up, girl, and get yourself graduated," is what he said. He was kind, well-respected, and had an amazing bedside manner, which he viewed as the most important quality in a physician. Patients still call my sister and me to say how much they miss him. While I didn't go into medicine for my father, he did help me to believe in myself.

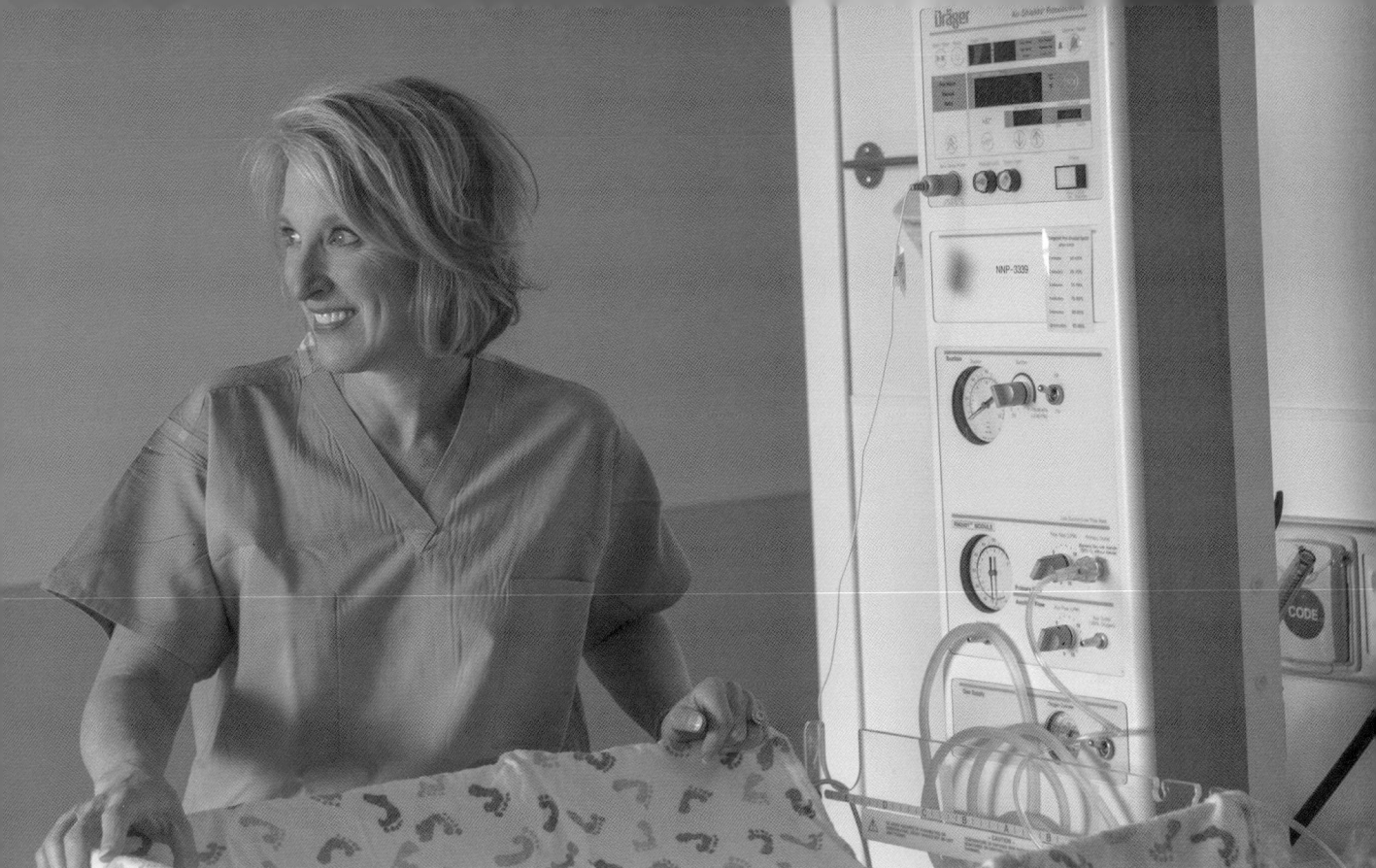

How would you describe the culture at Women's Care of Colorado?
Women's Care was the first employed OB practice at Sky Ridge Medical Center, which Dr. Juliet E. Leman and I helped to build. Kind, warm, and intimate is how I would describe the atmosphere. We are small, and patients are greeted by their first name like old friends. Time is taken with each patient. Care is not only in our name; it is likely the one word that describes how we feel about our patients: we care.

How is that kind of atmosphere created?
After beginning with a core group of compassionate physicians, Dr. Leman and I have been really picky about who we hire. We want a team that truly cares about women. OB patients are anxious and must be listened to and taken seriously. Medicine isn't hard. People just want to be heard.

Why is seeing and hearing your patients so critical to care?
In today's world, hardly anyone wants to have a genuine face-to-face conversation. Everything is so fast-paced and not in a good way. Medicine is old-fashioned in a sense because interpersonal skills are absolutely essential. Many times, my patients just want someone to listen, which I am more than happy to do.

What does a great bedside manner mean to you?
A physician must spend a sufficient amount of time with their patients. Never give the impression that you are rushed. A patient told me recently that her doctor didn't have the courtesy to take off her coat and purse during their visit. That's ridiculous. It is critical to ask, "Do you have any questions?" and let the patient ask whatever they like. I also make it a point to ask my patients about their spouse and kids. Remembering those details is why they come back. Even if you have 30 patients on your schedule each day, every patient has a story and every patient is special.

How do you care for yourself when caring for others?
That's the hard part. I try to exercise, eat right, and get enough sleep—all of which are almost impossible to do. You put yourself second and family third or fourth. I've never figured it out. Doctors can't have it all and should be aware of what they're getting into. Fortunately, my family is very understanding. When my daughter graduated from high school and was asked to give a speech, she said, "Mom, you're my rock, the strongest person I know, and I've looked up to you for so many years. Thank you." After grinding it out for so many years, I needed that validation.

What makes those sacrifices worth it?
I get a lot of self-worth from my patients. They are everything to me. I receive so much love from my patients, which makes me realize that I am living out my purpose. The power of female solidarity is incredible. I also love being witness to all stages of life.

FREDDIE WOODS

{Manager of Network Engineering, *HCA Healthcare*}

As Manager of Network Engineering, Freddie Woods fine-tunes his legacy and finds great pride in taking care of his team. Since becoming interested in technology as a teenager at the suggestion of his grandmother, everything in his life fell into place. He never wanted to do anything else. Woods credits HCA, a company he has always been connected to in some form or fashion, for allowing him to live up to his potential. He got his first taste of the medical world working in the kitchens at General Hospital and Park View Medical Center. His first job in IT, after earning his his associate's degree in Computer Science from Nashville State Technical Institute, was working for the state of Tennessee as a computer operator and programmer. Next, he was hired in the network department of HCA's newly founded IT division. In his 31 years at HCA, Woods has tried to use technology to bring nurses and doctors back to the bedside. He believes in the power of face-to-face connection and that quality time between patient and physician is critical to healing. The manager is proud to work for a company that provides the best healthcare to patients. If he had to relive his career, he would do it all the same.

Can you tell me a bit about your background?
Nashville is home for me. My father was a truck driver and my mother a nursing technician. I started working at HCA on her birthday, March 10, 1986. I've been blessed and have no complaints. When I came out of high school, I couldn't make my mind up about what I wanted to do. I started working in the kitchen at General Hospital with my grandmother and stayed there over three years. We walked to work together every morning. She instilled a great work ethic in me from a young age. One day, my grandmother, who pretty much raised me, said, "Son, I think you need to go back to school and get into that computer stuff." It was something that her intuition told her would be good for me. I trusted her more than anyone else, so I went after it. That's how I fell in love with computers.

What's the best advice you've ever been given?
I had some medical issues early on in life, like a dislocated hip, which meant that I had to have surgery and wear built-up shoes. However, my medical issues never stopped me from achieving. As my grandmother would always say, "You only limit yourself." I found computers and technology to be fascinating from the get-go and just stayed focused on IT. I never felt like I was limited and don't allow people to put that on me. I try to be an example of the fact that good morals and self-belief will allow you to do anything. Nothing can deter you but yourself. All of my brothers are taller than me, but I'm the one they look up to because of how I carry myself.

What goes through your mind while you go to work every day?
I am constantly thinking about what kind of legacy I'm going to leave when I retire from HCA. How I walk, what I do—my beliefs are all related to that. I've been blessed with a great team of people who appreciate the fact that I check up on them every morning. People know when you're phony, and people know when you're real.

What were your first years on the job like?
HCA used to outsource all of our IT until we built our own data center. When I came for my interview, the gentleman who facilitated it became my very best friend, Mr. Ronnie Johnson, who was hired from AT&T to put HCA's network together. He said to me, "Young man, how about you try working in networking to learn something different?" And I said, "Yes, sir, that'd be fine with me." Underneath his watch, I learned about wiring, fiber optics, and cable schematics. I was fascinated by everything because it was all changing the world! My team and I would work seven, eight, nine days in a row building the network and shipping it out to the hospitals. We just loved it.

What is one of your favorite HCA memories?
One day I was up in the data center installing terminals throughout the building. Dr. Frist, Sr. happened to come in and said, "Good morning, sir. Welcome aboard. I am glad to have you here, and I hope you're glad to be here." He then proceeded to ask about my job and encouraged me to let him know if I needed anything to do it better. We took a picture together, which I keep in my drawer today. You could tell that he was serious, cared, and wanted to know about your thoughts and feelings. I will never forget how he made me feel like I was a part of this company. That's how my whole HCA career has been. There are always ups and downs, but overall, I can't complain about nothing here. Life has been good, and HCA has been good to me.

LIFE HAS BEEN GOOD, AND HCA HAS BEEN GOOD TO ME.

What is your biggest motivator?
I am driven to create a legacy. Integrity means everything to me, which means that when people see Freddie, he is the same person all the time. I stick up for my team no matter what, and always have their back. They mean everything to me and are the reason for my success. When I walk out this door, I want to make sure I can go home, lie down, and be at peace. Whatever the consequences are, I have to do the right thing. You feel it here. (Taps heart) It's taken me awhile to achieve peace, but once I did, nothing bothered me. Life is about challenges and anything, bad or good, all comes down to how you deal with it. There is no reason to get down if you live everyday like it's your last.

What makes a healthy, happy team?
My team is one of my primary support systems, and we even talk outside of work. They're all good, seasoned professionals who've been here 10 years or longer. We respect each other. I know their spouses and children. It's my goal to find new ways in which I can support them every single day. Most importantly, they know that family comes first. Whatever I have to do to show that support to them I will. They know I mean what I say.

What makes you happiest?
Helping someone take his or her career in a certain direction is the best feeling. I want their children to witness them going after their dreams. As I tell my daughter, "Nothing is impossible." We all have to take care of ourselves, keep teaching what we know, and learning what we don't. The second you stand still you get left behind.

Have you conquered any obstacles recently?
One of the big projects we worked on this past year was an authentication migration project. We only had five months to install and implement a new product across the organization. Everything was done from scratch, and while stressful, it all came together because of my staff. I am proud to say that when we switched the entire network infrastructure over the impact to our facilities was very minimal, which was a miracle.

How do you keep your cool when faced with high-stress situations?
Working under pressure inspires innovation. For 28 years, I worked in the network operations center, where you are constantly fielding calls about data circuits that have gone down. We were troubleshooting hardware problems to facilities in multiple states. That was a pressure cooker, and you had to know what you were doing. I ate, slept, and breathed it because I thrived in that environment. You know them calls are coming, but if you know your stuff, then you recognize what to do.

What do you find particularly fascinating about the healthcare industry?
How technology has changed, especially in healthcare, is extraordinary. Everything in the industry—from how you pay your bills to your hospital stay—has grown dramatically. HCA has made it possible for hospitals in the most rural communities to have up-to-date technology, which otherwise they wouldn't have the capital for. It's just wonderful.

What changes are currently happening in healthcare technology?
Currently, our industry is trying to get back to the bedside, which is where you want your best experiences. Technology has, historically, pulled nurses away from their patients because of how much administration work they have to do. We are trying to put a lot of their admin work onto mobile devices, which moves the nurse back to the patient. Instead of logging on to fifteen or twenty different applications, we're aiming to put a front end on everything to simplify and make it more efficient.

What challenges are you currently facing in healthcare technology?
Technology is both good and bad. It's hard to reach people these days because they would rather text than talk on the phone. That means a lot of them are lost when they engage in real-life conversations. I love technology, but it has its flaws.

What advice do you have for other IT people looking to connect on a deeper level with their job?
IT people should all live at a hospital for a week to see what the environment is really like. When you walk through a nurse's daily routine, you see how critical your job is. Not being able to access a particular application can be highly problematic. I always think, *What if my mother was in that situation?* My job is to provide whatever the nurses or doctors need when they need it. I think you have to take your job personally in order to be effective. That's what makes you care.

How would you describe your own management style?
My mentor has always been Ronnie Johnson, who hired me. Matter of fact we're having lunch today at one. One day there was a power outage, and my team and I were doing everything that we could to get the systems working again. There was a man who kept coming into our workspace and demanding why everything was down. Ronnie saw that he was prohibiting us from getting our job done and told him to back off. If that man had any more problems, he would come directly to Ronnie instead. That interaction has influenced my own style of management and is why I watch out for my people.

Last words?
I will leave you with this: If you want to be blessed, you got to keep your hands open. Otherwise, you can't receive a blessing. And that means you can't bless anyone else.

NOEL WILLIAMS

{SVP and CIO (retired), *HCA Healthcare*}

In Noel Williams's mind, technology is a critical part of caregiving. Whether she found HCA, or it found her, the former CIO and Senior Vice President of IT&S is grateful to have used her gifts to improve the lives of patients. As an undergraduate at Vanderbilt University, where she studied computer science, Williams had the good fortune of befriending the stepson of HCA founder Jack Massey. His confidence in the success of HCA, at the time a startup, was contagious and piqued her interest. Post-graduation, she pursued the traditional technology route for several years and finally decided to apply for a systems analyst position at HCA in 1979. Williams may attribute her entrée into healthcare to good luck; however, once she entered the industry, her go-getter mentality propelled her forward. Williams became a pioneer in the world of IT&S, systematically introducing multiyear initiatives such as the electronic health record system and upgrading the core clinical system. Still, her most memorable milestone is building a culture around collaboration, a concept that is still alive and well today at HCA. As she knows, genuine care for one's team results in collective success. The Noel Williams Award of Excellence says it all: it is an accolade reserved for high-achieving IT&S employees with a high moral compass who set the bar for others.

How did your upbringing influence your demeanor in the workplace?

I grew up in Nashville in a lower-middle class family. My mother was a secretary and a stay-at-home mom. My dad was self-employed as an engineer and manufacturer's rep. My brother and I both have his mathematical and analytical mind. However, my father's self-employment was erratic, so our family struggled to rely upon him for a consistent paycheck. Yet my father always told me, "You can do anything you want to do and be anyone you want to be." I learned that was true, which is why I can handle just about anything. I've always been driven to take care of myself.

What were your first impressions of HCA upon arrival at the company?

My first job was in information systems, which was a small department at the time, but very exciting because we were doing things in healthcare that hadn't been done before. The company and department were growing, which created opportunities. My coworkers were hardworking, smart, and enjoyable to be around. One of them, Tom Cato, who became a significant mentor in my life, would often call me into his office to discuss areas of the company that had nothing to do with my job. His reasoning was, "You'll want to understand how it all works because one day you'll be sitting in my seat." He pushed me outside of my realm of responsibility to teach me about the broader aspects of the business. That was probably a key inflection point in my career.

Did you feel comfortable making mistakes as you learned?

I'm not sure anyone is really comfortable making mistakes; however, it's human nature, and hopefully I always learned from them. When I headed up IT&S, I encouraged my team to move around to different parts of the department to broaden their knowledge. "Be open about your errors and then let's move on," I'd say.

You've compared technology in terms of importance to the clinical instrument.

Absolutely, and that is increasingly true since the early 2000s. Prior to that, technology in healthcare was mostly used in terms of finances, medical records, and scheduling systems. For a while, I struggled with how we in IT were connecting to patient care until we began working on patient safety initiatives. That allowed us to come out of the back office to the bedside. The stakes were higher; however, I loved being directly connected to the mission. There is nothing better than using your gifts to better lives.

Did HCA help you gain confidence in your abilities?

It's been a blessing to be surrounded by great people who are committed to the HCA mission, which I view as doing the right thing. In my tenure, I had the support of mentors and colleagues who worked side by side in order to achieve our goals.

How does camaraderie fuel success?
The patient-first culture at HCA is palpable because it starts at the top and flows throughout. IT&S is "mission motivated," which means leaving your ego at the door, focusing on the team, and treating others the way you'd want to be treated. It's not about the *I* but rather the *we* component of being a mission-driven organization. Collaboration increases employee engagement. Who doesn't want to work on projects that are interesting, alongside equally committed employees? Positive energy gives you a greater ability to get things done. HCA's focus on people pays off because it fuels trusting relationships, which are critical to constructive conversations. Great ideas arise when a team sits around a table and says what they think without fear that they'll be judged. If conflict does arise, then you can generally work through it to reach a consensus and resolution.

> ## IT IS A TEAM SPORT. WE ALL RELY ON ONE ANOTHER AND ARE DEVOTED TO THE MISSION.

What does it feel like to have the Noel Williams Award named after you?
We started the IT&S Award of Excellence to recognize one corporate and one field person who exhibited the values of IT&S. When I retired, they named the award after me because of my focus on culture and employee engagement in my last years at HCA. Having an award named after me is incredibly humbling and kind of embarrassing. (Laughs) However, it's definitely an honor, and I love the times I am able to go back to present it to the recipient.

What do you consider excellence within the IT department?
Integrity. Accountability. Keeping the team at the forefront more than your personal success. IT is a team sport. We all rely on one another and are devoted to the mission.

What was it like to rise through the ranks of IT?
It was a challenge because technology and HCA were a man's world at the time. Fortunately, I had mentors who saw qualities in me that they felt they could nurture, which made all of the difference. Sometimes it was hard to have my voice heard, so I tried to come to the table well-prepared every time. I also freely gave myself pep talks before big meetings. In time, I think I became respected, and fortunately the landscape shifted. Still, it wasn't easy. Speaking my mind has been a lifelong journey.

What initiatives were the most memorable?
There are many, but the initiative I'm most proud of leading is the implementation of the new IT support model. Back in the day, every hospital and some divisions had their own IT staffs which functioned at varying levels. We rolled out a new staffing and support initiative to 170 hospitals, which required an investment but was seen as an investment in HCA's future. In essence, it consolidated and streamlined HCA's scattered IT capabilities by building skilled staffs in each division to support the technology of the future. That allowed us to prioritize and have multiple initiatives going on across the company and country simultaneously. We were finally able to truly take advantage of HCA's very savvy IT department and capabilities.

What was hardest and most rewarding about your role?
Almost every strategy at HCA has an IT component. We were constantly challenged to support the company's strategies, which is very fulfilling. It also meant the IT pipeline was always full. The hardest thing was the negotiation that occurred in order to try and meet everyone's needs. Fortunately, we established a process and the Strategic Program Committee, which became our forum for prioritizing initiatives. This group is presented various ideas, discusses them, and makes the ultimate decisions.

How did you constantly adapt in a rapidly changing industry?
First, we had many talented people who remained knowledgeable and current on the latest technologies and industry trends. But also, HCA never does technology for technology's sake. During my tenure, we looked for and chose proven technologies to incorporate into our company strategies. We also ensured that we had the right people and processes in place. Let me say though, many of our best technology ideas bubble up from the field. Those who do hands-on work constantly hand us visionary concepts.

What was most inspiring about your HCA tenure?
The roll-out of our patient safety initiatives, which used technology to directly improve clinical care and save lives. Hearing doctors and nurses say how a specific technology met a clinical need was fulfilling. An example of this would be our electronic medication administration. We used simple barcode-reading technology to ensure we gave the right patient the right dose of the right medication at the right time. As we rolled it out, nurses often said, "This caught a mistake which could have killed a patient!"

What does HCA's mission mean to you?
The HCA mission and culture are about putting patients first, improving lives, helping others, and treating each other with respect. That mission and our culture is what motivated me to stay here for 33 years. I hope that I helped create a culture in which our employees can thrive and our caregivers can save lives by means of technology.

HEATHER J. ROHAN

{President, *TriStar Division*}

Healthcare flipped the switch for Heather Rohan. Upon first exposure to the industry, the TriStar Division President knew it was her calling. In high school, Rohan watched her father, post-heart attack, receive exceptional care at their local hospital. Following her high school graduation, Rohan was admitted into a Florida-based nursing program where her fellow residents woke a deep empathy in her. Ever since, Rohan, formerly a shy individual, has become a force in her industry. She seeks out personal connections with her colleagues and strives to instill self-confidence in others. After spending a decade in critical care, the nurse listened to her inner voice, which told her she was ready to make a difference in the healthcare industry in a different way. Answering a blind ad, she applied for an Associate Chief Nursing Officer position at Northwest Medical Center, part of HCA. She has since earned one promotion after another, including becoming CEO of TriStar Centennial Medical Center, until 2017 when she became the first nurse in the TriStar Division to take on the role of Division President. Witty, wise, and transparent, Rohan has a relentless passion to support patients and staff.

How did you pursue your career in nursing?
Seeing my father, whom I considered my hero, suffer from a heart attack when I was in high school was my turning point. I watched the nurses tend to him with such compassion, which compelled me to follow in that path. One day I was sent a catalog from Barry University in Miami, Florida. My mother suggested we check it out, and off we went. The college was small, and I immediately felt at home. The second I arrived, I sealed myself up in my room and studied nonstop. I knew that this would be important for me to be successful.

What else did you learn in nursing school?
Nursing school helped me to develop the compassionate side of my personality. My parents were very stoic and reserved. In South Florida, I saw emotions and feelings expressed freely. I learned to be comfortable with my emotions. That was huge.

Do you think that compassion can be cultivated at any point in your life?
Yes, and nurturing that ability has enriched my own life. Being in environments that fostered a sense of openness was instrumental in terms of my own success. I can be tough when necessary, but I care deeply about people and the relationships I have with them. The founders of HCA are a great example for us in terms of being kind, caring human beings. The desire of Drs. Frist to make a caring connection with everyone has always stuck with me. I also greatly admire their visionary perspective in terms of looking forward and shaping the future of healthcare.

What did your time as a critical care nurse teach you?
In college, I took my LPN boards early because I was anxious to get to the bedside to help others through a crisis. That was truly gratifying to me. I also loved the teamwork that comes along with being a nurse and how we all take care of one another. My ICU team was like a Camelot, where no one sat down until everyone could take a break.

How did nursing shape your personality?
Nursing has shaped me into a detail-oriented person who is very observant. I meditate every morning and hike several times a week. I strive to experience moments to their fullest extent. I encourage my staff to exercise, take vacations, and find time for fun outside of the workplace. The nature of our job is inherently serious; therefore, it is important to have ways to find balance.

When did you decide that you wanted to be a leader?
The day that I finished a critical care class, I was asked to be the Assistant Head Nurse of the ICU. Deciding to give it a shot, I became conscious of the fact that I enjoyed coaching others and suggesting different ways to improve care. Through interfacing with many different departments, my lenses started to broaden. I found that I wanted to influence outcomes on an even greater level and sought positions with increasing responsibility along that path. At one point, I made the decision to be a director in an area I had not worked in previously, the emergency room, which ultimately taught me a great deal about leadership.

How did you move forward despite your trepidation?
In my heart and mind, I had set a goal of what I wanted to achieve on my path. I was willing to be uncomfortable and courageous in order to learn new things. This director role in the ER was exactly the right thing for me at the right time.

OUR COMPANY IS FILLED WITH BRILLIANT MINDS. WHEN I NEED ADVICE, I CAN ALWAYS LEAN ON SOMEONE NEXT TO ME WHO WILL OFFER SUPPORT AND GUIDANCE.

How did you know what you wanted for your career?
I have always enjoyed having a great deal of responsibility. Taking a sense of ownership is important in terms of leadership. While there is a healthy checklist I go through before making big decisions, I am always willing to take ownership of my actions. Once you know and believe in yourself, saying "I'm sorry" or "I made a mistake" doesn't lessen your value.

Did you have a moment where you thought, *I am a leader*?
There have been moments that tested all of my skills as a leader. Leading through a difficult situation successfully can, at times, demonstrate that best. For example, there was a point early in my career when I was the CEO of a hospital that had to close. This tested my fortitude and ability to lead the team, physicians, and community through a challenging and, at times, difficult transition. Ultimately, most everyone in the facility was able to find a new position. The physicians were also on staff at nearby facilities, and the patients were cared for. I learned many lessons during this time in working productively with team members who were under a great deal of stress, appreciating where they were coming from and achieving the objectives before us. This understanding has served me well through time.

Have you ever questioned yourself?
Absolutely, and I certainly did early on in my career. Yet, with more experience and knowledge, one's confidence level increases. I went through an acclimatization process when I moved from Florida to Nashville. The conscious decision to adapt my style of communication to the new environment enhanced my ability to engage while still allowing me to be straightforward.

What is the biggest lesson you've learned in your HCA career?
Some of my greatest lessons have come from thinking through difficult and challenging situations. I experienced a number of these in my career, such as the example I shared above, that have made me a stronger leader.

What did it feel like to become the first nurse in your TriStar leadership position?
It's humbling, exciting, rewarding, invigorating, and energizing. I don't think about my role in the terms of leading 15,000 people but rather the individuals that I connect with every day. Having the ability to work alongside such amazing people is what makes my job great. I am huge on appreciation, whether it is a personalized thank-you card or telling someone who is toiling away that I am grateful for their work. You can never recognize or thank people enough.

What advice would you give to other aspiring female leaders?
Focus on what fires you up. Identify what you love to do, set a path, and ask for what you want. Don't wait for it to happen. Even if you don't get it the first time, you will the next. Find mentors and ask them for guidance and constructive criticism. Be courageous enough to take on new opportunities. Lastly, get involved in your community.

What would you say has been critical to your own success?
I've had amazing mentors, coaches, and guides who were forthright with me about my strengths and opportunities. I admired them and was able to listen and adapt. We are never done learning, which makes life exciting. Our company is filled with brilliant minds. When I need advice, I can always lean on someone next to me who will offer support and guidance.

How do you feel about what you do?
I am so blessed to be where I am and do what I do. This doesn't feel like work. My job is to support the hospitals and their leaders to make sure they can give the best possible care to our patients. People don't have to choose our hospitals, and when they do, we respect and honor that by giving them our absolute best.

What is your proudest achievement?
Personally, it is raising my two sons who have grown into amazing young men. On the professional side, it is the relationships I have made over time.

What does the HCA mission mean to you?
The HCA mission is about caring with your heart and connecting with the patient. At HCA, we are passionate about making the patients', employees', and communities' lives better. The result is an ever-widening circle that starts with the care and improvement of human life within the walls of our hospitals.

LOUIS JOSEPH

{Group VP of Physician Services Group, *HCA Healthcare*}

Louis Joseph's greatest pleasure comes from pairing patients with first-rate physicians. The Group Vice President of Physician Services, who recruits and employs top-notch doctors to work at HCA, pins his faith on the fact that we live in an amazing age in terms of technology, pharmaceuticals, and treatments. Joseph, born and raised in a four-stoplight town in Georgia, worked at his family's clothing store as a young man. In college, he became an EMT/paramedic; however, his true ambition was always to run hospitals. He earned his MBA in hospital administration and completed his residency in Greenville, South Carolina. Charter Medical in Macon, Georgia, hired Joseph, then 25, to run one of its hospitals. About eight years into his career, when he first began hearing about HCA, known as "the University of Healthcare," Joseph accepted a job offer at PhyCor, a medical management company. In 1999, he was hired in Physician Services where he's stayed ever since. Joseph's pride comes from reading positive patient satisfaction surveys and knowing that he helped form the connection between patient and outstanding physician. However, his badge of honor is mission work, which is where his best memories have been made.

What do you do all day long, and what do you enjoy about what you do?

People call me regularly to ask who is the best physician because they know that this is my domain area of expertise. Everyone wants the best doctor. Doctors pull the wagon and are the reason that people choose a certain hospital. Patients trust their physician because they know the intimate details of their life. A friend called me one day because he had been in a bad accident. He needed a plastic surgeon who could put 60 stitches in his face and not leave a scar. After the procedure, he looked perfect. That's the difference a good doctor makes.

Have you ever been an HCA patient?

Funny enough, just a few months ago I woke up at 4 a.m. with acute appendicitis. I went to HCA Centennial Medical Center as an "undercover patient." Just a few hours later, my wife met me in post-op, and I walked out the door. Who does your work matters. You only want the best physicians to fix up your sister or your mother, and that's who works at HCA.

Why do you get such a kick out of being a resource?

It's meaningful to handle life-and-death decisions and help people survive whatever issue they are going through. My satisfaction comes from getting a patient to the right place. Whether it is a rotator cuff or hip replacement, there's nothing better than hearing someone say, "Thank you so much for that referral."

There are a lot of ways to help people. Why is healthcare your art form?

I am drawn to it. I didn't want to be a physician, because I'm not great at chemistry and math. As an administrator, I love being able to empathize with the physician mindset and give very gifted, smart scientists the opportunity to flourish. Doctors postpone satisfaction by staying in school until their early 30s. They make that conscious sacrifice because they genuinely love taking care of patients. Our physician turnover is very low because we give them the resources to get their job done. While HCA has always been the best operator of hospitals from a business standpoint, we are now more focused than ever on offering the best doctors, nurses, and patient experience.

How does HCA provide its people with the right context to succeed?

Most physicians come out of school with $250,000 in student loans. They don't want to hire an office manager, invest in medical records, or negotiate with insurance companies. They want to be busy, have a good call schedule, and deliver great patient care. HCA's culture is to do whatever it takes in order to take care of the patient like family. If we take care of the patient, the business will take care of itself.

How does HCA give physicians what they need financially all the time?

HCA has made very wise decisions about where to strategically invest. Our hospitals tend to be in urban areas where people are

having babies, surgery, or annual check-ups. We set up in areas where people need and want us. Everyone at HCA knows their job and performs at a fast pace. This is the "major league," and you're expected to play and thrive in that kind of environment.

What about your personality makes you a great fit for HCA?

I get bored really easily, have a short attention span, and dislike predictability. It's a little bit like drinking out of a fire hose. (Laughs) Things come at you left and right, and it's your responsibility to figure out what's important. Delegate, delete, or deal with it immediately is my philosophy. I would rather practice fire prevention than put out fires all day long. We are taught here to anticipate and deal with issues proactively. You have to get juiced by working hard. And HCA is the best place to do that.

can substitute for visiting a third-world country and helping out. On my mission trips, people are so visibly touched that you cared enough to come. They wear their finest clothes and share with you their cultural traditions. I always come back more blessed than the person I bought stuff for. Life isn't about you. It isn't about me. It's about people who are hurting and need help. We could very well be there ourselves.

Does HCA cultivate this mentality or attract those who already have it?

Both. I don't think truer words have ever been spoken than "Good people beget good people." Everything starts with one good person, and in my department, those are the doctors. A few years ago, I attended a dinner with Dr. Tommy Frist, Jr. when we had recruited some great orthopedists to join Centennial, and I saw

THERE IS NOTHING YOU CAN DO IN THE SERVICE OF A PATIENT THAT WILL GET YOU IN TROUBLE WITH ME.

How do you keep your cool under pressure?

I am a Christian, so I believe that everything happens for a reason. Prayer keeps me focused on the fact that every day is a gift from God. I am serving His purpose. If someone calls me and says, "I think I have cancer. Please help me," I consider that a divine assignment. There is nothing you can do in the service of a patient that will get you in trouble with me. If someone comes in and has left their insurance card at home, we see them anyway. If they need to work out a payment plan, we do it. We are very patient-centered, and we always want to treat people correctly. Now, that doesn't mean things are perfect all the time, but I always know we are directionally correct.

Why are you so passionate about mission work?

On my 11 mission trips, I've met people who don't have electricity or water. Here in America, we have 50 kinds of toothpaste in our grocery stores. Sometimes we lose sight of how phenomenally blessed we are, which is why I encourage people to experience how the rest of the world is. No video, documentary, or podcast

firsthand his passionate vision to build hospitals with great physicians. They heard it straight from our founder that we want HCA to be the best place for physicians to work. You can be a cog in a machine or you can come to HCA and have your voice heard. That attracts great people and keeps them here.

What does the HCA mission mean to you?

Every patient is unique and deserves to be treated like family. If you concentrate on the individual experience, people will line up around the block. That's how we expand into new markets, acquire new hospitals, and elevate our existing ones. No one really wants to be a patient in the hospital. So the question is, *How can we make what could be a dangerous, deadly, and life-altering experience as good as possible?* We get great people to work here who know what they're doing and love taking care of people.

BABY RUTH BOSWELL

{Volunteer, *Del Sol Medical Center*}

You get back what you give. Baby Ruth Boswell, a social butterfly who loves little more than striking up conversations with strangers, has been a volunteer at Del Sol Medical Center for more than twenty years. The cheerful soul chips in where she is needed, greeting visitors and serving as Vice President on the hospital's auxiliary board of directors. As the youngest of 21 children, Boswell became familiar in her youth with the comfort that comes from being looked after. During times of financial stress, she never failed to find solace in her family, spirituality, and sense of gratitude. Boswell raised six children and traveled the world with her second husband, whom she also worked alongside. Once she became a widow, she devoted her days to volunteering. Showering others with affection is what keeps her sprightly. From cofounding the Silhouette Club, an organization dedicated to the betterment of young black women, to chatting with children in the church pew, Boswell believes that a smile is as meaningful as a check. When the tears come down, her hugs are the first ones to go out. Love is her oxygen.

Is your real name Baby Ruth Boswell?
It is! I am originally from Shreveport, Louisiana, and have lived in El Paso, Texas, since I was 14 years old. I am 86 years old. In 1996, I started working for Del Sol Medical Center. This hospital has helped me as much as I've helped it. I consider my coworkers to be a part of my family. This job keeps me from sitting around and being lazy. To have a friend you have to be a friend. Del Sol is good to me.

What have your 86 years on this earth been like?
Every day of my life people tell me that they like my name. (Laughs) I am a mother, grandmother, great-grandmother, and great-great grandmother. Growing up, I got away with everything because I'm the baby. My second husband, the most wonderful man I ever met, was a retired army veteran and worked for a contract company. Together we traveled the world, which has always been my thing. Not having a big education, I learned a lot being out in the world.

What do you like most about volunteering?
My husband actually died in this hospital. Afterwards, I thought, *Why not help the staff who helped me through his illness?* This job is a joy and is what keeps me going. I get to see different sides of people and how they react to their loved ones being sick. In my heart, I feel for them. With my eyes, I see that my problems are never as bad as theirs, which makes me feel grateful for what I've got.

What about your personality makes you perfect for volunteering?
To be a greeter, you have to be personable and like running your mouth. (Laughs) I love being in conversation with people and especially children. However, I try not to dip in too much because I prefer to listen. That's how you learn. When two people try to talk at once, you can't hear anything.

What is a trademark of your volunteering style?
I try to carry myself in a way that will inspire other folks to treat people with compassion. The more love I put out there, the more I receive. I greet everyone with a smile and give as much love as I can. I have enough to go around.

What is so powerful about love in your eyes?
To give someone a hug or ask if there is some way that you can make their life better is the most meaningful thing you can do for them. It's important to stay in tune with the emotions of those around you. Empathy is free.

What was it like to win the Frist Humanitarian Award at the national level?
Wonderful. Aside from the beautiful ball that I was able to attend, HCA gave me money to donate to my favorite charity, the McCall Neighborhood Center. For the first time in my life I was able to give a sizeable contribution. I never felt so good. I have much

gratitude to HCA for affording me the opportunity to give others money with which they could do more good.

How does volunteering enrich your life?
I am a 34-year cancer survivor, which is why I believe that God is not ready for me. During my time on this earth I want to help others because that's what makes me feel most alive. It's an honor to take care of people and allow them to take care of me in return. What I have acquired in this life, I want to give back.

What would you like others to know about volunteering?
You don't need to be in the limelight to feel like you're doing important work. Every little bit helps. Piece by piece we make a whole. To bring a minute of joy to someone's life is the best thing that we can give. I get sad sometimes, but I never quit smiling. While I've lost two of my children and my beloved husband, my life has still been wonderful overall. Not every day is perfect, but what in life is?

Recently, I stumbled upon one from a few years back which had a $25 gift card inside of it. See how every gift always comes back?

How would you describe the environment at Del Sol?
The energy of Del Sol's team, from its volunteers to the executives, is why patients are so happy. The entire staff, which is a close-knit, comfortable team, is always trying to make Del Sol a better place. Still, not everyone gets along all of the time, because that is just reality. In any situation, there will always be people who you aren't fond of; however, by looking at the bigger picture, you can focus on the good. I try to encourage the younger folks in my life to watch out for one another. Like a family, you should want the absolute best for those in your life.

In today's world, why do you think compassion and empathy are so critical?
I understand that people are busy, but we need more compassion in this world. Even a simple hello or grin is effective. It means the

IN MY HEART, I FEEL FOR THE PATIENTS. WITH MY EYES, I SEE THAT MY PROBLEMS ARE NEVER AS BAD AS THEIRS, WHICH MAKES ME FEEL GRATEFUL FOR WHAT I'VE GOT.

How do you comfort people in a hospital setting?
Depending on who the person is, I will give a hug, cry with them, or offer a bit of the Lord's guidance. By getting a read on the person, I see what I might have for them. While my English isn't great, it doesn't bother me. I speak from my heart and offer wisdom and knowledge because that's what God gave me.

What volunteering commitment outside of Del Sol is most meaningful?
Fifty years ago, myself and ten other ladies got together to organize the Silhouette Civic and Social Club, which gives money throughout the year to different charities. Since I wasn't able to attend college, the partial scholarships are most important to me. Again, every little bit counts, in my opinion. Similar to my children, I want to give my fellow community members what I didn't have.

What is it like to spend your life giving to others?
I can't imagine my life looking any other way. I receive a lot of greeting and thank-you cards every year, which I typically put aside.

world to give someone your time. That is why the volunteers are critical to this hospital. We engage with the patients in a different way than the nurses can, sometimes simply because of their schedule. The medical staff is appreciative of our attention to detail.

What does the HCA mission mean to you?
The volunteers care. The hospital cares. We care. Love is healing, which we have a lot of at Del Sol. I have seen this from the volunteer perspective as well as someone whose family and friends have stayed here. That beautiful environment is why I stay. Everyone at Del Sol comes together for the sake of the patient rather than his or her own individual desires. And that is what life is about.

Would you like to leave us with any last words of wisdom?
How you carry yourself every day is most important. It isn't necessary to brag about your achievements when people see your actions. While I didn't grow up with silver slippers, I have always been loved, have eaten well, and had a place to stay. What you put out there comes back. The people in my life are proof of that.

EDWARD T. JONES

{President and CEO, *HealthTrust*}

Patients don't take rain checks. When a physician or nurse reaches for a product it has to be in the right place at the right time. Edward T. Jones, HealthTrust's president and CEO, wants his team to know that whether they work in a warehouse or are processing a transaction, their position is instrumental in saving lives. Jones, who began working for HCA as a senior in high school, has a deep and complex understanding of HCA. HealthTrust, a group purchasing organization and healthcare improvement company, ensures that each facility is properly stocked with medical devices and other critical equipment. From heart valves to computers to additional labor, Jones's team gathers the requirements, finds the goods, and transports them from manufacturer to facility. From his first day with HCA as a part-time employee in one of the hospital's food services departments, Jones has drawn a connection between his own contribution and the bigger picture. Today he finds great spiritual and professional satisfaction in understanding the overall objective of supply-chain management, how it relates to the industry as a whole, and why reliability in his area is so critical to patient care. A conversation with a nurse early in his career brought home this importance. "In other businesses, if you ask for a product and it's not in stock, you get a rain check. In our line of work, if you don't get us the supplies we need, if they're not there when we reach for them, people can die." Her comment hit home, and ever since, Jones has done everything in his power to awaken that same sense of purpose in others.

What was your first job at HCA?
I started at an HCA hospital part-time as a food service worker when I was in high school. I was 17 and I knew that if you had a job you were able to leave school right after lunchtime. (Laughs) That was an incentive as well as the desire to relieve some of my mom's financial stress. Then my mom had surgery at the hospital where I worked during the first year I was there. As I delivered her a dinner tray, my role became unbelievably real and rewarding. I knew in that moment that what I did really mattered.

What were your first impressions of the medical industry?
What struck me right off the bat was that everyone, no matter their position in the hospital, was committed to serving others. In 1985, at age 19, after washing dishes, serving food, and ringing the cash register for a couple years, I got my first job in supply chain. It's wild to think that was the job that set me on my path to becoming CEO of HealthTrust. My team stocked supplies for surgery, which I found fascinating. The first time I saw a surgeon use a tool I had supplied, it bridged the gap between my role and caregiving. It still never gets old seeing the products that we source in action.

How did you transition from studying pre-med to finance in college?
At Virginia Commonwealth University, I started in pre-med, which just wasn't a great fit. One day, a physician, Bill Holland, said to me, "Son, you need to get out of medicine. DRGs are coming. Finance is where your future is." I took his advice and switched over to finance. A year before I graduated, HCA alerted me to an operations manager position that was opening up. They wanted me to apply, but I was hesitant because I wanted to keep my grades solid. At their encouragement, I took the job because I knew it would put me ahead of my peer group upon graduation. My next job was an assistant director role at Chippenham Hospital. There, I worked under one of my most meaningful mentors, Bill Self, who was a father figure to me. He would always tell me whether I was ready to advance to another position. That was frustrating at first because I wanted to keep moving up, but I trusted him enough to take his words to heart, and I believed him when he said I wasn't ready. He knew I needed a solid foundation as I climbed the ladder. Because of his influence, I focused on doing my absolute best on the task at hand rather than just looking toward the future at the next job.

What else did he teach you?
He demonstrated the importance of staying connected to the bigger picture. If I wanted to work in supply chain then, as he explained, I needed to understand how a hospital functioned as a whole. How my personal responsibility fit into the overall context of HCA became my driving force. Thanks to him, I felt plugged in to the bigger objective of the organization. I am indebted to Bill for teaching me how to make tough decisions, to be a good steward of company resources, and to honor others' opinions even if they differ from my own.

In your own words, how would you explain what HealthTrust does?

Supplies have a huge impact on the financial structure of a company like HCA. Therefore, what we buy is critical to our ability to deliver the best possible patient care. HealthTrust's role is to take our purchasing power, which is our leverage, size, and scale, and negotiate the best possible price without sacrificing quality. To do this, we rely upon data and the opinions of the doctors and nurses who use our products. In the sourcing department, we negotiate contracts with suppliers to buy products that fulfill clinical needs at reasonable costs. We also run a distribution network, which manages inventory, places orders, brings the products into the hospitals, puts supplies away, and pays all the bills. HealthTrust is also responsible for HCA's pharmacies, which in itself is a huge operation. Lastly, we operate a labor management business, which aggregates and deploys additional people wherever they are needed.

How do you feel about what you do?

My job ties together patients, physicians, nurses, and HCA's partners, which I view as a privilege. I honestly love what I do so much that I would work for free if I could afford it. What fascinates me about my particular role is thinking about how products come alive in a caregiver's hands. Working with physicians and nurses to gain consensus and therefore reduce variation is what brings me the most contentment.

What is your personal leadership style?

At the end of the day, HCA is a servant-oriented business, which is why I consider it a privilege and honor to serve my team. As a leader at HCA, you have to be comfortable putting your personal ego aside and treating everyone as an equal. In my role, I try to set that tone and reinforce those expectations by living and breathing them every day. We all feel a sense of protectiveness for the HCA family, which starts at the top and cascades throughout the organization.

How would you describe the HCA culture as a whole?

We are all trying to save lives in our own way, which is a bigger calling, objective, and mission than anything I could have imagined for myself. The more you give, the more you get at HCA. That is the source of this highly philanthropic organization's success and also its key to unlocking individual potential. If there is any ego, it is around the satisfaction that comes from serving others.

Why is being a servant leader so important to you?

Our company is built around patients and their caregivers. If physicians and nurses are serving patients on the front lines, then HCA's leaders should cater to their employees in the exact same way. That ethos applies to every layer of the company and crystallizes our purpose: saving and improving human lives.

I FOCUSED ON DOING MY ABSOLUTE BEST ON THE TASK AT HAND RATHER THAN JUST LOOKING TOWARD THE FUTURE AT THE NEXT JOB.

When and how did you first make this connection?

Early on in my career, I tried to convince a physician to switch out his products. He kindly invited me to his operating room the following day and walked me through every single detail of his process. His goal was to make me understand how much had to be considered when changing out a product. That experience taught me to ask more questions and think deeply about the "why" in every decision. It also made my job that much more fascinating because, in order to create change, I had to know the medical professionals personally as well as his or her needs.

How has HCA helped your personal and professional growth?

Building a highly successful team and connecting them to HCA's mission is the crux of my personal satisfaction. I am eternally inspired by HCA's calling. Everyone wants to be a part of something big, and there is nothing more important than saving lives, in my opinion. Our people also inspire me daily for their relentless passion to deliver the very best in a selfless way. HCA isn't about personal gain but rather taking a sense of pride in the organization as a whole.

What currently is weighing on your mind as a leader?

Today I lead around 10,000 people, which is humbling because of where I started in this company. Every day, I am constantly thinking about how I can help the next generation. This literally keeps me awake at night. I've had incredible mentors in my own HCA career whose institutional knowledge I hope to capture and pass on. After witnessing them firsthand, I am highly sensitized to the vision, values, and culture that got HCA to the 50-year mark. Since this organization has given me a dream life, I want to help others achieve that as well. We have a huge responsibility to our patients and each hospital as the epicenter of its community.

What does the HCA mission mean to you?

HCA embraces people on their path of personal development and does everything that it can to help them grow. The more you invest, the more opportunities are available here; however, one can find contentment at whichever level they choose. To work at an organization where, no matter what department you are in, you know that your role is meaningful, is pretty special. I would never want to work anyplace else.

DIANE MCNEALY

{EVS Director, *Parkland Medical Center*}

At HCA facilities, we are healing people in healthier environments. By sharing that information and empowering her staff to spread the message, Diane McNealy, who is Director of Housekeeping, the Hazardous Waste Coordinator, and the Sustainability Champion, has made a huge difference in her New Hampshire hospital. McNealy, whose efforts with her facility's team have been honored by the Environmental Protection Agency and Practice Greenhealth, is deeply passionate about recycling, reducing, and reusing. She has also shared her voice through HCA Sustainability educational materials for fellow facility sustainability coordinators. Twenty years ago, she was hired at Parkland Medical Center as a housekeeper, the backbone of every hospital. Through that role, McNealy became aware of the negative impact hospitals could have on the environment. She looked for opportunities to implement new greening methods and reduce waste. With her leadership's help, they tested concepts at Parkland and made changes like removing water bottles from meetings, reducing food waste, and donating medical instruments. These purposeful steps have impacted Parkland, its community, and the planet.

Can you tell me a bit about your background?
I'm born and bred in Boston and have lived in New Hampshire for 25 years. My mother was a single parent and widow at age 21. She had six kids and was strict, driven, and instilled in us a strong set of morals. She worked in manufacturing, and while we were poor and lived in the projects, it was a great childhood. We didn't have a care in the world, and our family was very tight.

How did you become interested in the environment?
Every weekend we went to the beach because it was free. Boston Harbor used to be one of the most polluted water sources—so much that you couldn't swim in it. Not being able to swim in the water bothered me, which is when my interest in the environment first sparked. I thought, *Is this how it is everywhere?* However, over the years laws were passed, and finally the water cleared up so much that you could see fish in it! Today we live in New Hampshire, which is one of the cleanest states in America. Who wouldn't want to live here?

How did you land at Parkland Medical Center?
I didn't go to college. I am more of a business than a school person, but all kinds of things fascinate me. I worked at Massachusetts General Hospital from age 16 to 21 as a transporter and took patients to and fro, which I absolutely loved. You'd see people arrive in not such a good condition and then leave a little better. I liked being able to talk to a lot of people and make a difference in their lives. Next, I went to the postal service where I worked in the human resources department. In 1997, I came to work at Parkland Medical Center as a housekeeper. This was supposed to be a temporary job; however, I thought I could make a difference here so I stayed. Within three months I became the supervisor of the housecleaning department. As a team, we started to do things better, differently, and make changes slowly but surely.

How does one implement and educate others about green practices?
Back in those days, hospitals didn't appreciate fully the ways they could minimize their environmental impact. I started to look into organizations like the New Hampshire Department of Environmental Services and other healthcare environmental groups. We would get together as a group, meet with experts, and talk about different issues. In 2000, I started to work throughout HCA to help the company on initiatives that we could implement as an organization.

As the resident sustainability champion, my role is to educate and guide in regards to recycling, reducing, and reusing. In new-hire orientation, we cover hazardous waste and sustainability, so everyone knows the expectations when they walk through that door.

What inspired you to help other HCA facilities be more environmentally conscious?
The operating room technicians are some of our biggest champions because they also produce the most waste.

My team is active and willing to share. I think others at HCA think the same way. What we did to eliminate blue wrap, work with recycling, and composting, or be recognized by the EPA for food waste diversion, makes a difference. My hope was that by sharing information about our hospital I could make a difference across the organization.

AS THE RESIDENT SUSTAINABILITY CHAMPION, MY ROLE IS TO EDUCATE AND GUIDE IN REGARDS TO RECYCLING, REDUCING, AND REUSING.

What advice do you have for others to create greener hospital environments?
Everything starts with small steps. From there, you just keep growing and growing. My work also is tied to my moral compass.

HCA has given me a huge opportunity to make a difference. This is my hospital, and I have a big impact on what happens here. If you tell me something can't be done, I'm going to try until I can't win. We have to do all of the right things and not just some of them. Whether it's floods, fires, or diseases, I bring information to people's attention and let them run with it. Sometimes you can be asleep until an issue shows up on your doorstep.

I love challenges, and fortunately clinical people are very competitive as well. If a nurse recycles ten glove boxes one week, then another will recycle twenty the next. You give your staff incentives and empower them.

What drives you on a daily basis?
My passion for greening practices keeps growing and growing because I am always trying to learn more about it. My goal is to leave this planet a better place for my grandchildren, whether it's by reducing food waste or removing foam cups. We've probably saved a million water bottles here simply by offering pitchers in meetings instead.

What's the best advice you've ever been given?
My mother always taught me, "If you're going to do something, be the best at it." By doing that, one success will lead to another and another. We've gone from recycling to supplying less harsh chemicals and using less energy. It's just awesome.

What is your proudest accomplishment?
A lot of HCA hospitals have won greening awards because of the methods we've developed here. The goal is to get everyone to learn from one another, have a stake in the cause, and have a sense of pride about making their hospital environment safer.

I am so proud that a little hospital, director, and staff made a big difference. If my mother were looking down, she would be so proud. I've been through a lot in my life but consider myself very lucky. I'm most proud of the Making Medicine Mercury Free Award that was given to Parkland because of how excited the employees were to give up their thermometers. That memory sticks in my mind—it really does.

How would you describe your personal leadership style?
I'm always out and about because you have to know your team. Then they will be willing to work even harder for you. We have to be spot on every single day. I am a very competitive and passionate person, which is why I love HCA. They gave me the gift of doing what I enjoy every single day.

What does the HCA mission mean to you?
This company is compassionate and dedicated to making a difference to the patients whom we serve. Our mission is to give them the best healthcare that we can. HCA supports every single department so that we can do our best possible work.

Are there any last words of wisdom you would like to leave us with?
All you have to do is one good thing a day. If one person commits to recycling a water bottle every single day and then a million people do it, then guess what? We'll have recycled a million water bottles and reduced our carbon footprint. To see Boston Harbor polluted as a small child and then swim in it as a young adult was transformative. Everything we do at our hospital today will have a positive future impact.

DR. STANLEY WANG

{Cardiologist & Sleep Specialist, *Austin Heart*}

Stanley Wang, MD, JD, MPH, never forgot the words of one professor: "A doctor treats people respectfully, relieves suffering, and delays death—in that order." The Austin Heart cardiologist and sleep specialist collaborates with his patients by listening, asking the right questions, and assessing each as an individual. In his practice, healing is a delicate dance of technical skill, knowledge, and compassion. The son of Taiwanese immigrants, Wang grew up in Jacksonville, Texas, where his father was the local physician. As a kid, Wang worked summers in his father's office, filing charts and insurance claims. During this shadowing period, he learned the power a doctor has to shape lives. Today, the fourth-generation physician feels honored to treat an organ that dictates life or death. He strives to motivate his patients to take the best preventive measures and make lifestyle changes so they can extend their time on earth. Wang fell in love with evidence-based medicine during his internship and residency at Duke University Medical Center, and since then it's become his calling.

What is one of your earliest medical memories?
When I was a kid, my father and I would go shopping at Walmart. Patient after patient would want to converse with him so much to the point that we couldn't get to the check-out line. If they couldn't afford medical care, my father would accept bushels of apples instead. One even gave us a pig, which destroyed my mother's flowerbeds. (Laughs) He showed me how a good doctor impacts people's lives.

What about cardiology interested you?
My initial plan was to be a general practitioner until I became obsessed with evidence-based medicine. In the mid-'80s, outcomes-based trials began to guide how doctors made decisions. While you had to pay attention and study a lot more, there was also a greater confidence in the ability to help a patient. From the get-go, I embraced scientific empiricism. Cardiology also appealed to me because it includes many conditions for which there are both preventive and therapeutic treatment options. That offers a nice window of opportunity during which you can steer your patient in a positive direction.

What is something most people wouldn't know about cardiology?
Up to 80 percent of heart attacks are preventable, and this may be even more true for recurrent events. Yet I am occasionally surprised at how a lot of people are well behaved for a few months before going back to their bad habits. Whenever I can, I try to use information constructively to motivate my patients to stay healthy, even if it involves giving them bad news. I also emphasize hope, which I believe is a huge factor in terms of change.

How do you motivate someone to care more about his or her health?
Perspective is key. I try to help patients connect actions to consequences, and when possible, I involve their loved ones. If the patient's family members and friends act a certain way, then those behaviors become culturally acceptable to the patient, and vice versa. I often reinforce healthy dietary and exercise advice by pointing out to patients that their loved ones are likely to support and model such behavior and become healthier themselves.

How do you get your patients to trust you?
In today's age of computers and algorithms, it's easy to make decisions, but that is not the most important thing that the doctor does for the patient. It is just as important to educate the patient on their disease processes and treatments. This helps them understand the rationales for our tests and therapies and is crucial for gaining the patient's trust and boosting their compliance. Ultimately, this results in better patient outcomes.

What was it like the first time you transitioned from school into a clinic?
While I am a fairly social guy now, it was shocking the first time I had to lead a conversation with a patient. In school, we are taught what

typical symptoms and complaints to expect in each disease state, but in reality, patients do not always describe things in textbook fashion. Fortunately, I attended law school for two years, which taught me to absorb information fast, be quick on my feet, and communicate in a constructive manner. All of those skills are helpful in the medical world. Still, you can be told all day long that a disease has ten symptoms but realize, in the real world, it has three. The same goes for treatments, which often elicit different reactions and can produce unexpected results. It is difficult going from structured knowledge to fluidly applying information. Nature is weird, and people are unique, especially when it comes to their biology. Physicians must be fluid, react appropriately, and adapt to surprising results accordingly.

before he died, he said, "Thank you, doctor, for your compassion." I didn't help him live any longer, but I did try to improve his quality of life. His gratitude was beyond moving.

What is some advice you would give to other physicians?
I believe most physicians empathize with their patients to some degree, but I cannot overstate how important it is to continue to keep the patients' point of view in mind. Medical conditions and treatments can feel very frightening to patients, especially when their life is at stake. This is magnified by the use of medical terminology, which can be incomprehensible to some patients. Imagine the fear and vulnerability that comes along with putting your trust into the hands of a surgeon. It is crucial to establish confidence and competence early on with your patient by explaining information in a comprehensible manner. The rest of the job comes down to addressing their concerns in a kind manner and keeping their perspectives and personal contexts at the forefront.

WHEN SOMEONE IS IN NEED, SNAPPING TO ATTENTION, EVEN ON VACATION, JUST FEELS RIGHT.

Was it exciting or nerve-racking to draw your own conclusions?
At first it was scary to make new diagnoses and treatment plans because you risk being wrong, especially when dealing with life-or-death situations. Fortunately, I thrive when I have to react to shifting grounds. Perhaps going to law school and experiencing the Socratic teaching method helped me with this. Also, as a cardiologist, having been trained in internal medicine deepens my ability to calculate my own conclusions. Critical thinking keeps me interested in medicine and makes me passionate about keeping up with the latest clinical trials and medical discoveries. Great doctors learn until they retire.

How much time does studying take up?
I eat, live, and breathe medicine. The more we learn about the human body the less we realize we know. That seemingly endless exploration is so intriguing. Plus, I am passionate about science that impacts people's lives.

Can you recount any particularly meaningful patient experiences?
I had a patient with Huntington's disease, which is a condition that causes bizarre movements that can be very off-putting. He had lost a lot of his friends, and most of his physicians had thrown in the towel. However, together we worked on simple things like alternative strategies for holding a cup of coffee. The last time I saw him, right

What was it like to save a patient's life on an airplane?
On a flight to Barcelona, the flight attendants began yelling, "Code red!" which means passenger down. A woman had gone into cardiac arrest in the bathroom. Fortunately, we started CPR and got her pulse back, and she regained consciousness. After the patient received medical care in Barcelona, I ran into her on my cruise ship. Her entire family showered me with hugs and gratitude. It was incredible. When you have the skills to save lives, there is no such thing as being completely on vacation. When someone is in need, snapping to attention, even on vacation, just feels right.

Is medicine a calling?
Yes, it takes a lot of dedication to be a doctor, especially in today's fast-paced world with ever-increasing pressures to achieve quality care efficiently. However, it is a privilege to be entrusted with people's lives. Being a doctor feels so natural to me. Since I am a fourth-generation physician, I wonder if it's in my genes. I love what I do, and I can't wait to come to work every day.

How did sleep medicine become your second specialty?
When my youngest daughter was born, she had all sorts of behavioral problems. My wife and I were ready to take her to a psychiatrist because she was so disruptive. One year, we went on a cruise and all slept together in a tiny cabin. I was able to observe her sleep and noticed that she would stop breathing for 15 to 20 seconds at a time. Shortly after, we had her do a sleep study; it showed that she had severe sleep apnea. The surgeons removed her tonsils, which is curative for sleep apnea in children, and this completely changed her personality. She blossomed into a very sweet, caring, and high-performing girl. If we hadn't found this problem, she might have been on unnecessary pharmaceuticals and had fewer options for succeeding both socially and for her career. When I got into cardiology, I became fascinated by how sleep is intrinsically related to heart health more than any other organ, so I incorporated sleep medicine into my cardiology practice. I eventually became the director of Austin Heart's Sleep Medicine program.

Are you passionate about integrative health?
While pharmaceuticals have a time and place, I believe in assessing and treating the underlying problem for contributory behavioral issues. I try to help patients see that certain things they do could be interfering with their health. When patients say they eat healthily, I frequently ask what they had for dinner last night, and the answer is often something unhealthy—followed by an excuse. Hopefully, they recognize that they do sometimes rationalize their unhealthy choices without realizing it. I also emphasize that transforming your diet and increasing exercise has significant collateral benefits. Also, kids adopt the lifestyle their parents demonstrate, which is why it's so important to be mindful of your behavior. People with strong, positive support systems have an easier time changing.

What is your proudest achievement in your tenure at Austin Heart?
The patients are my proudest achievement. Their Christmas cards, thank-you notes, and nice survey comments mean the most to me. I feel so thankful that I am able to use my skills to change someone's life at a great practice that resides within HCA, which has been the best hospital organization I could imagine partnering with. Spearheading the cardiology and sleep program at Austin Heart, which HCA has fostered and encouraged, has allowed us to create a unique and important diagnostic center where we have been able to implement novel treatments that transform lives. HCA has been remarkably supportive of cutting-edge medical practices and innovation. I am very grateful to work with such a fantastic group of doctors at Austin Heart, and to be able to collaborate with HCA, an organization that has been very true to its mission statement and values.

LIZ HARMS, RN, CMSRN

{Direct Care Nurse, *Rose Medical Center*}

Liz Harms was diagnosed with colon cancer at age 34, right after the birth of her second child. The longtime Rose Medical Center staff nurse realized shortly after receiving her diagnosis that she needed to find "her people." She craved community support in the Denver area and sought out a group whose members were also going through cancer treatment to empathize with the trials and tribulations that come along with the disease. Cancer came down hard on Harms—a wife, mother, and dedicated worker bee. Not talking about the trauma could be just as toxic as the illness itself. Now, in addition to pursuing her doctorate degree, Harms volunteers for Stupid Cancer, an organization where she first sought support, and shares her own tales of remission. Below, she reflects on what it was like to come close to death and why it was so reassuring to find a community with whom she could share her feelings. Through her advocacy work, Harms has found a purpose for her pain.

How did you become interested in nursing?

My mother was a nurse, and my dad worked in healthcare administration. I wasn't initially interested in their industry, because it was too science-oriented. My first degree was in American history because I love storytelling and learning about where we all come from. Finally—after a period of time where I worked odd jobs and wondered, *What do I really want to do?*—I began taking nursing classes. It turned out to be the best decision that I ever made. However, I'm happy that I waited until I was mature enough to understand what it means to be a nurse.

What were your first impressions of nursing?

When I was in nursing school, I did rotations on the floor I work on now at Rose. I knew that I wanted to work on this floor because of the amazing sense of teamwork. If patients have a problem, we fix them up better than they were before.

In nursing, no day is ever the same, and there is always something new to learn. I enjoy the autonomy and the fact that I get to use my brain while helping others. My parents taught me to care for those in your community and do what you could for them. I love being able to make one of the darkest chapters of someone's life better. It's hard to find that kind of satisfaction elsewhere.

How has your own bout with cancer changed your perspective?

After my own illness, I have more insight into the patient's perspective. Cancer is a marathon and has its ups and downs. Being a patient myself, I understand the various physical and emotional stages of the disease.

What goes through your mind when you are first diagnosed with cancer?

Immediately after the doctors discovered my stage IIC colorectal cancer, I went into survival mode. While I was focused on the well-being of my two-year-old, newborn, and husband, I was also in a blissful state of denial. There was no family history, so the diagnosis was really shocking. The *Why me?* feeling still creeps up every now and then. Especially, when I've had fellow cancer survivor friends who have passed away. Then I really find myself asking, *Why them?*

The process of treatment is so much easier than the aftermath because you are actively working to kill the cancer. I still experience anxiety similar to PTSD symptoms because of my horrible treatment memories. For a long time I was simply concerned with moving forward for my children and spouse. To this day, we are still hashing out feelings which weren't talked about enough at the time.

How do you feel when you are going through cancer?

While going through treatment, I felt really angry all of the time. That's when I started to think, *I couldn't be the only cancer survivor in the metro Denver area.* My sister-in-law gave me a list of websites one day, and one of them was for the organization Stupid Cancer. I read a few of their blog posts, which articulated exactly what I was thinking and feeling. It was awesome to know that someone else was just like me.

One year after my diagnosis, my husband and I decided to attend the annual Stupid Cancer national conference. Being in a community of 500 other survivors who spoke my language was incredible. From there, I decided that I wanted to bring Stupid Cancer to

AFTER MY OWN ILLNESS, I HAVE MORE INSIGHT INTO THE PATIENT'S PERSPECTIVE.

Denver, which was sorely lacking a young adult support system at the time. We now have monthly meet-ups in which we bowl, bar hop, and have ice cream socials. Four years ago, Stupid Cancer decided to move their conference to Denver because the organization had such a strong network. My husband and I love it because the community feels like a second family.

Do most people have a hard time talking about cancer?
I think people who haven't been through cancer are afraid to talk about it. This is why the Stupid Cancer conferences were so liberating. There, we could talk about taboo topics and hear solutions others had tried.

What is one of your proudest accomplishments?
After being photographed for The Colon Club's annual magazine, I was invited by some of the other survivors to participate in some policy work through Fight CRC, which lobbies for colon cancer treatment. Through Call on Congress, we lobbied to our senators and House of Representatives, which was when I realized the power of putting a face in front of decision-makers. Presenting my story to Congress in attempts to sway them to pass a bill was an amazing experience. Everything circles back to the connection that I felt to that Stupid Cancer blog post. *There is a group of* me *out there*, is what I thought. I like the idea of belonging to a group.

What is it like readjusting to life post-cancer treatment?
Post-treatment, you struggle with everything from reconnecting with your spouse to returning to your career. When I finally came back to Rose, I had a few freak-out moments because of the neuropathy in my fingers and feet from chemotherapy. The first time I tried to take a patient's pulse, I couldn't feel it. That was scary, and I began to question, *What if I can no longer nurse?* Chemo brain also limits your cognitive abilities because it's difficult to formulate coherent sentences. Ultimately, I was driven to go back to school to prove that I could do it. Life can be exhausting, and there are definitely a lot of sacrifices to be made while in school. However, I knew that if I didn't pursue my doctorate now, I never would.

What is your advice to fellow cancer survivors?
If I had to give any two cents to a fellow survivor, it would be: *take care of your mental health and choose some sort of physical outlet.* That's how I became involved with First Descents based in Denver, which provides weeklong outdoor adventure trips for young adult cancer survivors. With that group, I was able to go surfing in Santa Barbara for one week and have one of the best times of my life. After that trip, I became involved with fundraising and created a Rose Medical Center team called Rose's Running Rumpers, through the Undy Run/Walk, which is a 5K race that occurs every June.

Ever since my diagnosis, I believe everyone needs to be in therapy. I think the stigma around seeking out a counselor for the sake of your mental health is crazy. Even my husband will tell the spouses of cancer survivors to focus more on self-care. He should have gone and hit more golf balls during my treatment.

How has cancer changed your overall perspective on life?
Today, I don't have a whole lot of patience for toxic energy. I've had to cut off some negative relationships because the drama doesn't help me. I don't have time for he-said-she-said conversations. Cancer made me realize that a lot of what we worry about in life really doesn't matter.

Has cancer changed the way that you approach your patients?
After going through cancer treatment, I like to think that I am better at communicating with patients. People just want to know what is happening in terms of their treatment. They might not know the right questions to ask, so I feel compelled to keep them in the know. Information is everything. As a nurse, I try to coach my patients so they can recover quickly, without complications, and go home. I use a lot of interpersonal skills to walk them through their illness.

How has this experience made you a better person?
I certainly have more patience with my patients because I can empathize with what they are experiencing. I really hesitate to tell someone when his or her prognosis is bad. As a glass-half-empty kind of person, I know the power of "faking it until you make it." I've had to reel in my pessimist nature because half of the cancer battle is about your mental state. I try to get off that highway in terms of negative self-talk before I start to spiral into a tailspin.

What do you love most about the HCA community?
One of the reasons that I love working at Rose Medical Center is because of its small-town feel. There is something comforting about connecting with others in your community. Rose is the flesh and body of HCA's mission statement, as our collective goal is to deliver the most positive healthcare experience. We want to make our patients feel that they aren't isolated in their experience. From my own experience, I know that a support system is life-giving.

BRUCE MOORE

{President of Operations & Service Lines Group, *HCA Healthcare*}

To keep himself on track, Bruce Moore asks himself, *How would I like to be treated as a patient?* The President of Service Line and Operations Integration, who recently received his 35-year HCA pin, relies on constant feedback from field experts and physician leaders to find the best practices in healthcare. He and his team assess what works and what doesn't to make the caretaking process as seamless and stress-free as possible. Moore was introduced to healthcare in his hometown of Laurel, Mississippi, where his mother was a nurse and father an accountant who specialized in healthcare. At age 44, his father had a heart attack that forced him to quit working. Seeing how life could change in an instant, Moore began making his own way in the world. After joining HCA as a staff auditor in 1982, he advanced to Vice President of Compensation and Benefits before taking charge of service lines, like cardiology, ambulatory surgery centers, behavioral health, and oncology. Moore, who strategically scales initiatives and technologies across the organization, believes that multiple perspectives produce the best ideas.

How were you first introduced to HCA?
I had accepted a job with an oil company straight out of college, which was the industry to be in at the time. I had worked on oil rigs as a summer job throughout college. However, the economy plummeted in the early '80s, and they retracted the offer. Shortly after that, I was on a spring break trip in the Bahamas where I met Dr. Frist's wife, Trisha, by happenstance. When she found out that I didn't have a job, she gave me the number for her husband's secretary, Judy Foster, sister to long-time administrative assistant Mary Greer. After interviewing with HCA, the HR person never called me back. Being a little naïve but persistent, I called back and left a voice message for Judy Foster. Low and behold, Dr. Frist, Jr. returned my call and asked, "Can you be here Friday for another interview with Bill Mitchell of Internal Audit who can make decisions?" The rest is history.

That's incredible that the founder proposed your first job at the organization.
I know, but I was a small-town boy from Mississippi who didn't know any different at the time! (Laughs) In my town, the owners of companies always called you back. Dr. Frist's actions exemplify the fact that he always took the time to do the right thing, an ideology that is intrinsic throughout this company. In the HCA community, most of us come from blue-collar, hard-working backgrounds.

Do you think HCA naturally attracts kind people?
I think most people get into healthcare because they are kind and compassionate. I do know most HCA employees want the best for the company and are willing to put in the work to achieve it. We also all really enjoy one another's company. While we have a lot of responsibility, we also know how to have a little fun. Many of my closest friends work at HCA.

Please explain what you do every day.
That's not as easy as it sounds! (Laughs) I take care of operations integration and service lines. As I tell my kids, I am a professional "meeter." We're charged with finding the best practices, inside and outside of HCA, for service lines like cardiology, oncology, and pediatrics. We also have support functions like Strategic Resource Group, Physician and Provider Relations, case management, and bundled payments. We try to innovate and find operating effectiveness. To do that, we hire great subject-matter experts and leaders who help us push those ideas across our 40-plus different markets. Our mission is to find the best way to do things so those who are running our operations and taking care of patients every day don't have to do as much research. HCA is massive and in so many markets, which is why we try and identify best practices from operations in Alaska to South Florida.

What about comprehensive service lines puts the patient first?
They fuel innovation and the desire to collect the best possible pathways in order to give patient-centric care. Whether it's patient care or making information more readily available, we work on a continuum to build out a healthcare delivery system.

Can you speak a bit to the collaborative relationship with physicians?
Our best outcomes come when hospitals and physicians work collaboratively to accomplish a great outcome for the patient. The amount of transparency and volume in clinical, operations, and financial data is unparalleled at HCA, and very helpful in guiding physicians on how they can improve clinical outcomes. Healthcare is complicated from a regulatory standpoint, yet it's always about caring for people.

What's your secret to creating a successful team?
I like to hire passionate, mission-driven people who will work hard and collaboratively to get the job done. The mission and team will fail if it becomes all about one person.

What if you don't hire the right person for the role?
You try and find the right role for them to be successful.

What advice would you give to those who want to move up the ranks at HCA?
One time in my early days, I did a presentation in front of Dr. Frist. He asked me what I saw as my job tresponsibilities. After fumbling around and giving him a very pat answer, he continued, "The people who really make a difference understand how all of the pieces of this organization fit together." They see beyond their job description and responsibilities and make connections that allow the business and team to thrive. I believe those who excel at HCA, and in life itself, ask, *How can I create a win-win for everyone?*

they were presented with a hard decision. Life is a constant interview. You have to remain aware of how you present yourself.

What has kept you at HCA for 35 years?
The people and the fact that I am always challenged, which is because HCA is constantly changing and trying to improve. Having the opportunity to advance and be influential creates an entrepreneurial spirit, which is inspiring. As big as the company is, it doesn't feel bureaucratic because we all know one another. HCA allows me to think outside the box, which is why I've made time and emotional investments.

What is the secret to your success as a leader?
Trying to create a vision and passion for improvement. Not surrounding myself with a bunch of "yes" people. Integrity is critical as is living out what you say. You need to be around those who will challenge the status quo and do things the right way.

GREAT LEADERS USUALLY LET PEOPLE AROUND THEM TAKE THE GLORY. THEY STEP UP WHEN THE TIMES ARE DIFFICULT.

Where does your collaborative mentality come from?
Growing up, every time I thought I was good at something, one of my parents would remind me how much better someone else was. (Laughs) I also worked under a lot of leaders who always considered how a decision impacted everyone on the team. I think playing sports also adds a team element to situations in your life. Great leaders usually let people around them take the glory. They step up when the times are difficult.

Was there anything else you picked up from other leaders?
Doctors Frist, Jr. and Sr. were always big on doing things the right way both at work and in the community. It's why they emphasized the importance of giving back. Jack Bovender was famous for saying, "It's not so much about what you do when others are watching but rather what happens when no one is around." He had to trust his team when

What does the HCA mission mean to you?
We'll touch over 30 million patients in a year, which is a huge responsibility. HCA always tries to do the right thing and at a higher level than many other companies. Being able to provide patient care isn't an entitlement; it is a responsibility. We constantly work to earn that privilege by giving our absolute best care to patients and their families in the communities we serve.

How do you hope that your work has impacted patients?
The healthcare system is difficult to navigate, and being a patient is one of the most difficult situations one can experience in life. The legacy I want to leave is to hire and develop leaders who are mission-driven and protect our culture. I also want to continue to improve on a more integrated, patient-centric model that takes into account each person's unique needs.

ELIZABETH BAUMGARTEN

{Director Service Line Solutions, *Sarah Cannon*}

Many people have been affected by cancer, however Liz Baumgarten, Senior Director of Service Line Solutions at Sarah Cannon, says the experience with her dad's diagnosis helped to form her into the professional she is today. She can empathize with the frustration of feeling in the dark; therefore she's motivated to make information more readily available to patients and their families. Baumgarten, an Ohio native, was first exposed to medical informatics while working at the Ohio State Medical Center. She had volunteered in hospitals since age 14 and originally pursued the physician route, but she changed direction when her dad became ill. After watching him go through radiation therapy treatment, which damaged his kidneys and resulted in his need for dialysis, Baumgarten grew determined to use technology to support clinicians so they can make better decisions for their patients. Since joining HCA as a senior clinical analyst in 2007, she has used the deeply complex layers of industry-data science to direct the design and development of EMR solutions.

How did you first hear about HCA Healthcare?
Right out of college, I worked for a startup software company based in Scotland. My role was implementation and training of the software and to educate my UK colleagues on U.S. healthcare. After living in Scottsdale, Arizona, for a few years and working for that same company, my husband and I decided that it was time to move closer to home. A recruiter alerted me to an open position at HCA, which is when I reached out to an OSU alumna and former HCA employee to get insight about the opportunity. She absolutely raved about the organization. Soon after, I interviewed for a senior clinical analyst position and was hired by the folks who would later become my greatest supporters.

How did your upbringing influence your personality in the workplace?
I am the granddaughter of immigrants on both sides. My mom's family is 100 percent Italian, and they have a very strong work ethic. My father was a Depression-era kid, and his parents were Jewish immigrants from Austria and Romania. Both families came to this country with nothing and made something for themselves. It was expected that you work hard and make life better for the next generation. My mom, while only four feet seven, owned her own steel company—a predominantly male industry. She is tough and taught me to stand up for what I believed in and take care of those you love. My dad taught me that any job worth doing is worth doing well.

Why have you devoted so many hours to medical technology?
It was by chance that I was exposed to this field by working at The Ohio State Medical Center while attending college. I had an amazing boss and mentor who introduced me to the CIO of the hospital, which led to multiple internships in health IT. It was my choice to choose HCA/Sarah Cannon as my career path, and it's been an incredible place to work and grow. I am continually inspired by health IT, where we get to see patients' lives being improved by clinicians who are empowered by technology solutions. While there is always room for improvement, it is remarkable to see how technology is responsible for creating, implementing, and supporting care. I am grateful to work for a company that is making such a positive impact on the communities it serves.

What was the first project you worked on at HCA?
When I was hired in 2007 as a senior clinical business analyst, I worked on defining the requirements for the legal electronic medical record. That project then evolved into implementing an electronic document management solution and supporting the consolidation of health information management into the shared services model. The intention was to find the most efficient, secure way to store information for patients and physicians with the least amount of resources. We freed up valuable real estate in the hospitals, created more easily accessible records for clinicians, and supported health information management workflows. During this time, I also met some of my closest colleagues to date.

Can you tell me a bit about the HCA community?
The people who work here and the patients we care for make up the culture of HCA. We have some of the smartest, most talented people at our company. If you make a mistake, they will help you fix it. They will drop everything to help you solve an issue. We all have one another's backs.

Why did you want to work for Sarah Cannon?
I am a strong believer that everything happens for a reason. I met Dee Anna Smith (CEO of Sarah Cannon) when she spoke at a women's leadership event in 2013. Naturally, I was very impressed and inspired. Next, several of my former HPF IT&S colleagues found their way to Sarah Cannon. After working in Clinical Services Group for several years as Director of Meaningful Use, I was ready to return to IT&S. The more I learned about Sarah Cannon, all signals told me that I needed to be there. Above all, I wanted to be around leaders who shared the same mission I did.

What is most rewarding about working at Sarah Cannon?
It is a privilege and honor to work on projects that directly impact people who live with cancer. One of the projects that I am working on today is the consolidation and standardization of radiation oncology information systems and implementing infrastructure to support failover/redundancy. In addition to creating an integrated platform with improved support and disaster recovery, the project also enables real-time performance reporting to reduce variation and adopt the best practices from an operational and clinical quality perspective. My father's kidneys were damaged due to an inappropriate exposure to radiation during his cancer treatment. It's so rewarding to work on a project that impacts the improvement of quality of care for patients like him.

How does your personal connection to cancer drive you?
Everyone has been touched or personally impacted by cancer in some way. My story isn't all that unique. However, I feel so fortunate to work in an environment where we enable and support technology platforms that help clinicians make the best possible patient care decisions. By supporting Sarah Cannon initiatives, I am able to see firsthand how we are transforming care and personalizing treatment through clinical excellence and cutting-edge research.

How much do communication skills play into your current role?
At HCA, we use an assessment tool to evaluate personality and communication styles by categorizing them as colors. It's interesting that my color has changed over time as I've moved from technical and analyst positions into leadership roles. The leaders I admire maintain the same personalities at the office as they do at home. I like to have fun and let my team know how much I care about them. Knowing what matters most to them is important to me.

How do you resolve conflicts amongst your team?
I find most conflicts stem from too much emotion and a lack of communication. Self-awareness and kindness give you the ability to understand another's perspective. While you can't fix their formative years, you can inspire someone to be their best self. One of the most important things I've learned from one of my mentors is not to take things personally and try to leave the emotion out of a challenging discussion. Those principles have worked in my career, whether it's giving or receiving constructive criticism.

> **IT IS A PRIVILEGE AND HONOR TO WORK ON PROJECTS THAT DIRECTLY IMPACT PEOPLE WHO LIVE WITH CANCER.**

What does the HCA mission mean to you?
I love the Dr. Frist, Sr. saying, "Good people beget good people." We're all here to continue his legacy. Every day I am inspired to come up with innovative solutions to make clinical care better, safer, and of a higher quality. Everything we do comes back to the patient, which for me obviously started with my father. As a byproduct, I hope to inspire my colleagues to make good choices in their professional and personal lives. If you're doing well in work, then you're doing well in life. What more could you want?

What is most rewarding about your job?
Being able to work with a great team who has the same fundamental values. I love mentoring others because of the guidance that I was given, which I most certainly needed, along the way.

VIC CAMPBELL

{SVP Investor Relations and Government Affairs, *HCA Healthcare*}

Vic Campbell, Senior Vice President of Investor and Government Relations, views everyone at HCA as a teammate. Despite his tremendous impact on HCA over his 46-year tenure, Campbell still jokes that he is the CEO's bag carrier, having worked for every HCA CEO since the company's founding. While clearly a company leader, Campbell doesn't view himself in that light. He is more interested in being a resource to others within HCA as well as those on the outside. Campbell learned his family-first values growing up in Anderson, Indiana. In this small Midwestern town and on the family's nearby farm where his father was raised, Campbell and his three brothers learned the importance of hard work. The lifelong athlete held his first leadership positions as quarterback and point guard. These roles taught him the critical nature of being a team player. As he puts it, "Even if one has the quarterback skills, if the line doesn't block for them, the game's outcome is unlikely to be a victory." Campbell joined HCA in 1972 after his first job out of college in the Treasurer's Department of E.I. du Pont de Nemours in Wilmington, Delaware, where he learned to give presentations and prepare filings with the Securities and Exchange Commission. Under the tutelage of founder Jack Massey, he would go on to establish HCA's Investor Relations function and become recognized as an industry leader. Still, Campbell relates his success to social skills, being straight with others, and staying at the level of a generalist. You don't have to know the answer to every question but rather where to get it, he says. Personable and charismatic, he leans upon the same rule whether engaging with investors or members of Congress: the deeper your connection with others, the more faith they have in you.

How were you first introduced to HCA?
After working in Delaware and realizing that I wasn't crazy about the East and didn't want to return to the Midwest, I began looking for opportunities in the South and West. I was told about an opening in Nashville with HCA. While I knew nothing about HCA or the hospital management industry, and wasn't too keen on Nashville, I decided to come down for an interview. When the taxi driver pulled up in front of a small hospital overlooking Centennial Park, I vividly remember saying "I'm looking for the corporate headquarters of Hospital Corporation of America." He turned back to me and said, "There it is!" pointing to a little white house in the parking lot of the hospital. I nearly stayed in the cab, but thank goodness I didn't. My interview, at the original house, was in bedrooms, the den, and even the kitchen. They needed someone who could oversee preparation of an SEC financial filing just like the one I had helped to prepare at DuPont. Never in a million years did I think, with my long hair and northern accent, they would see me as a fit for HCA. The HR guy even told me a couple years later that he threw my folder in the trashcan after I left. But the top two financial guys, John Neff and Sam Brooks, decided they would hire me, and once I completed the specific filing they needed, I could clean up my act—or else they would fire me. (Laughs)

What were those early days like?
While everyone was really busy, the office had a warm, family-like ambiance. There was a real sense of teamwork in the corporate office. Dr. Frist, Jr., or Tommy as he preferred to be called, was flying around the country buying hospitals and selecting properties on which to build new hospitals at the time. Dr. Frist, Sr. was revered as one of the best physicians in the South and a true humanitarian. And Jack Massey used his business and financial skills to raise the capital necessary to keep up with Tommy Jr.'s acquisition spree. There was a ton of energy at HCA!

How do you view HCA today?
I live and breathe this company. It's my second home, and many of my close associates are like family. Honestly, I can't imagine what I would do if I didn't come here in the morning. People tease me because I should be retired at my age, but I love the company and the people. As I tell my kids and young folks, "Find something that you love, and it will never feel like work."

When did you first meet one of the founders?
Early on, I got a call at home one Saturday instructing me to show up at the HCA private plane the following morning. I would be flying to New York City with Jack Massey, who was going there to

catch a flight to London. I had never been on a private plane in my life or met Mr. Massey, who was sort of a mystery. I was already pretty nervous, to say the least, and especially when he suggested that I sit next to him on the plane. After finding out that my title at the company was SEC Specialist, he proceeded to ask me SEC-related questions (all of which he knew the answers to but pretended not to) for what seemed like hours. When we arrived at one question to which I didn't know the answer, I responded, "I don't know but I'll find out!" I researched the answer and left a hand-written memo on his desk. When he returned from his travels, he called to thank me for following up. That flight and memo were key to him thinking of me when he returned as CEO of HCA a short while later. He asked that I assist him with some of his daily routine by reading his mail and taking notes during his meetings and calls. In that position, which I would equate to earning an MBA, I tried to soak up his wisdom. It was a blessing to see one of this country's greatest business minds in action.

I LIVE AND BREATHE THIS COMPANY. IT'S MY SECOND HOME, AND MANY OF MY CLOSE ASSOCIATES ARE LIKE FAMILY.

How did you get investment analysts to follow HCA in the early years?

Early on, Mr. Massey, Dr. Frist, Jr., and our CFO Sam Brooks were HCA's faces with Wall Street analysts and investors, but they were also running the company full-time. I ended up being the lucky one they picked to prepare information for our investors. Since investor-owned hospital management was so new, with only a few public companies in the industry, it was difficult for investment banking firms to justify paying an analyst to cover us. One of the biggest breakthroughs was convincing *Institutional Investor* magazine to add hospital management as a separate sector in their annual recognition. After pitching, or rather badgering, them for three years, the magazine added a hospital management sector, and the Wall Street analysts followed shortly after. Also, HCA leadership made a concerted effort to meet with investors and analysts in Nashville and take them to see our growing hospital network firsthand. Mr. Massey, Dr. Frist, Jr., Sam Brooks, and I traveled extensively across the country, to Canada, and several European countries to meet one-on-one with investors. At one point in time, HCA was the second-most widely owned U.S. stock among European investors. Our Investor Relations program, led today by my 30-year associate and teammate Mark Kimbrough, is still recognized as one of the nation's top programs.

How much does face-to-face connection play into your work?

I believe one-on-one, face-to-face conversations are critical to the success of both our investor and government relations efforts. In good and bad times, HCA's directness and honesty is key to why we have good relationships with investors and government officials.

When did you first figure out that you were ready to be a leader?

I was fortunate to have some incredible mentors at HCA, each of who taught me something different about leadership. Jack Massey, Dr. Frist, Sr., Tommy Frist, Jr., Don MacNaughton, Dave Williamson, George Mercy, Sam Brooks, Clayton McWhorter, and Jack Bovender are just a few of the men who have influenced me throughout my career. Identifying and learning from mentors has been a key to my success at HCA. Another key to success has been to surround myself with really good and smart people, like Mark Kimbrough in investor relations, Parker Sherrill and Warren Tardy in government relations, and Jana Davis in communications and crisis management. I'm not sure if I have been their mentor or if they have been mine, so I prefer to call them teammates.

How did you learn the business of government relations?

Clayton McWhorter, who worked as HCA's Chief Operating Officer for many years, called me in one day in the early 80s and asked me to get involved in government relations. I was hesitant, but he insisted that I learn that side of the business and develop political relationships similar to the ones I had with the analyst community. I really love it now. I was very fortunate to find a mentor in Washington, D.C., to teach me the ropes. Mike Bromberg, who headed our industry association, the Federation of American Hospitals, and I became close business partners and dear personal friends. To this very day, I find myself often asking, *What would Mike do?*

Did you ever have to do anything in your career that frightened you?

I recall being a little anxious on one of my early investor trips with Dr. Frist, Jr. when, right before we went on the podium, he suggested that we reverse our presentations. Without warning, he had me give his 15-minute overview of the company's operations and strategy, while he gave my 5-minute financial review. Afterwards, I was always prepared for unexpected mentoring practices when I traveled with him.

What is your favorite thing about HCA?

The people. The Frist family and the many incredible people they have brought to this company are what have kept me here for more than 45 years. Dr. Frist, Sr. was often quoted saying: "Good people beget good people." Not only was this his saying, but also HCA leadership today still lives by this motto. I have really been blessed to be a small part of the HCA team.

NATASHIA FLOYD

{Utilization Coordinator, *TriStar Division*}

Transparency is Natashia Floyd's gift. The HCA manager, known as a confidant amongst her team, believes that authentic conversation is the key to resolving issues in the workplace. Like many of her coworkers, Floyd rose through the ranks at HCA. She started as a medical records clerk before earning a promotion to office coordinator and then landing her current role as utilization coordinator. In that role, she helps navigate patients through their healthcare plans. She approaches every single person in her office with the same appreciation; whether they are sweeping the floor or doing data entry, the company, as a whole, could not survive without them. Floyd recently earned her bachelor's degree in healthcare administration after attending school in the evenings. Her 14-year tenure at HCA has taught this emerging leader that good things come to those who are willing to put in the hours. Her story proves that HCA's loyalty is a vital part of the company's legacy as well as what attracts employees who stay a lifetime.

How did your upbringing influence your character in the workplace?
After I was born in Murfreesboro, Tennessee, we moved right down the road to Smyrna. I didn't go that far. (Laughs) I grew up in a single-parent home where my mom, sister, and grandmother and I did everything together. We went to church every time the doors were open. Most of the people in my neighborhood opted out of college and went straight into a career in order to make ends meet.

What did you do after high school?
I initially wanted to be a teacher and change the world one child at a time. However, after graduation I went to work at a grocery store and then moved down the sidewalk to a few other retailers. I worked as a customer service manager, where I gained a great deal of patience and the ability to put myself in another person's shoes. If someone is chewing your head off, flip the role and pretend to be them. Once you sincerely empathize, then you can deal with the situation rather than flying off the handle.

Can you give me an example of this?
There was one instance where someone came in with a past-due balance, which was in the process of being sent to collections. They wrung me out hard. Still, I sat there and was attentive to their needs. After they got it all out, I counted to ten in between, and we were able to come to a common ground. Patience. (Laughs)

When did you become interested in a career at HCA?
I ran into a lady one day while shopping at the local discount store who said, "You should come work with me at HCA. It feels like family." Later on that week, my husband, a barber, came home and said, "One of my clients told me about a job opening at HCA which you would be great for." It turns out it was the exact same job, which was enough to make me go for it 14 years ago! It was a sign.

What do you like about the healthcare industry?
It's good to get to know people and how their health impacts their plans for the future. A lot of our patients were babies when I first met them, and now they're going off to college. That's an amazing transition to watch. Then there are others who, for whatever reason, had cancer take over their life and take away their dreams. It feels good to become a part of patients' families and allow them to be a part of ours.

What made you want to take on your current role?
My aunt is illiterate and went to the doctor's office one day. She signed in for her appointment, three hours went by, and she still sat there. Finally they were about to close and she went up to tell them she hadn't been seen yet. Their response was, "Didn't you see the sign that said if you've been waiting longer than 30 minutes tell us?" That drove me to be in a position where I could prevent that from ever happening again. Always check in on your patients.

What is one thing that surprised you about your current role?
Every conversation I have is on a case-by-case basis. I fluctuate between psychologist, psychiatrist, and counselor in my role. (Laughs) Fortunately, I love putting out fires. Also, the fact that people confide in me is an honor. I like to be trusted and show others that same trust.

HCA ENCOURAGES EMPLOYEES TO BE THEMSELVES BECAUSE THEY KNOW, HISTORICALLY, THAT'S WHERE GREAT IDEAS COME FROM.

Agreed. Did you have any mentors who helped you along the way?
Absolutely. Dr. Hixson, who I worked for, was a wonderful man. When he first came to Smyrna, he was the only person I ever saw exercising outdoors. Now, you constantly see people running and walking in our neighborhood. Because of his advice, their weight problems dropped. He walked the walk and talked the talk. I took that same concept and applied it to my work environment. If I ask someone to do something, I will do it first. Once people see that you're willing to get in the trenches they will go to battle for you.

What is it like to be in online school while working full-time?
Balancing school, family, and work takes dedication. However, I knew if I didn't sign up I would always regret it. I say to my girls, "From 8 p.m. on, my schoolwork and I have a date. That's our time." As far as studying healthcare administration, I needed to know what it was like to work in that field first. It's important to see what people do every day to know if you can handle it or not. I am practical and proud that I waited to go to college until I knew what I really wanted to study.

What did being in the workforce prior to becoming a student teach you?
It helped me develop a sense of loyalty, which is why I am so devoted to HCA. I also learned that you have to prove yourself in order to be promoted. You can't be a CEO straight out of college.

What do you love about working at HCA?
HCA invests in people who they believe will make great leaders. They are not afraid to give those who are lagging behind follow-up education to get where they need to be. We won't throw them off the ship because they don't run at the same speed as someone else. Rather, you show someone the skills they need in order to be a success. Maybe they lost them somewhere along the way.

What is one example of how HCA has shown you loyalty?
By providing financial assistance for college and putting me through different management and leadership classes. HCA encourages employees to be themselves because they know, historically, that's where great ideas come from. Confining gets you nowhere. The secret to innovation is freedom of the spirit.

What are some of your career highlights?
Being given the opportunity by both HCA and my peers to manage the office where I started. Also attending the first Emerging Leadership Academy, which was an honor and taught me what it means to be a part of this organization. While I gained a stronger sense of accountability for my actions, I also realized during that course that my team should know I'm human. It's why I wear funky shoes and try to show others who I am in my own way.

What does the HCA mission mean to you?
Above all else, we are committed to the care and improvement of human life. Whether it's donating to the homeless, giving a patient cab money, or an employee a college career, we are all about community.

How do you hope your work has impacted patients?
I hope they know someone is watching their progress and truly cares about their health. I've called to tell someone that their cholesterol was really high and laid out the consequences bluntly for them. They usually come back during their follow-up to tell me that they are thankful they took my advice. Everything at HCA is done for one reason: we want patients to live a happy, healthy life.

JACK O. BOVENDER JR.

{Chairman and CEO (retired), *HCA Healthcare*}

Jack Bovender is quick to praise others yet reluctant to seek accolades for himself. The humble, retired former Chairman and CEO accomplished a great deal in his 31 years at HCA. Thrice named Best CEO in America for Healthcare Facilities by *Institutional Investor Magazine,* Bovender attributes his success to the upward mobility HCA offers. While growing up in a closely-knit community outside of Winston-Salem, North Carolina, he witnessed a strong work ethic and camaraderie that would later influence his own leadership style. After majoring in psychology at Duke University, Bovender earned a master's degree in hospital administration at Duke, a move inspired by his mother, who was a nurse. He began his career as a U.S. Navy lieutenant before joining HCA in 1975 as an associate hospital administrator in Pensacola, Florida. Bovender relocated to Nashville in 1987 after having served as CEO of the HCA-owned Medical Center Hospital in Largo, Florida, and West Florida Regional Medical Center in Pensacola. He has lived in Nashville ever since. Twice retired from HCA, Bovender spent his final term as Chairman and CEO leading the evacuation of Tulane Medical Center during Hurricane Katrina. He also negotiated the single largest purchase of a nonprofit system with the acquisition of the 16-hospital system Health Midwest in Kansas City and undertook the HCA-leveraged buyout in 2006, which was at that time the largest in U.S. history. Instead of a command and control structure, Bovender encouraged autonomy in his team to do what it took to give patients the best possible care. His trust brought out the best in others.

What was your upbringing like?
My father, born and raised in Winston-Salem, was in the Marine Corps during the Second World War, and my mother, who was born to a family of tobacco farmers in the little town of King, North Carolina, was a night-nursing supervisor. The area I grew up in was very rural. There were 62 students in my graduating class, if that tells you anything. (Laughs) We still get together every year because there's a sense of long-lasting friendships and a strong attachment to one another.

What did you want to be when you were a young man?
I contemplated medicine. However, when I arrived at Duke, I realized I wasn't very good in the lab. Because of my mother's career, I became interested in pursuing the MHA degree. At the time, however, I didn't appreciate fully how strong leadership in our hospitals could and would drive significant improvements in the provision of acute care. As an example, at HCA we started patient safety initiatives that were picked up, duplicated, and became standards in hospitals throughout the country. In an organization of this size, you can have a significant impact on healthcare on a national level.

Did you see the potential for upward mobility at HCA from the get-go?
Yes, but that wasn't my focus. After school, I went into the Medical Service Corps of the Navy, where I was a lieutenant for three years. I am proud to have served and to understand our military culture. When I left there in 1972, my wife, Barbara, who was a public health and school nurse, and I moved back to North Carolina. In 1975, I experienced the first of many serendipitous moments in my life. A physician with whom I had worked in the navy called me one day and said, "HCA is building a new hospital in Pensacola, Florida, in tandem with a group practice". In short, I was hired by the CEO as associate administrator.

What happened next?
HCA sent me to Largo where a 240-bed hospital, which had been started by another company, was under construction. With

HCA's resources we finished the hospital, hired staff, and developed a patient-centered culture de novo. After that, I went back to Pensacola, where I grew the hospital from 300 to 517 beds. In 1985, we moved to Atlanta, where I became Division President for the Georgia/South Carolina region. Finally, thanks to my most important mentor, Dr. Frist, Jr., I was transferred to Nashville as Eastern Group President. I could never have envisioned all of these opportunities. I simply grew up with HCA.

What about your temperament allowed you to climb the ranks?

The most important attribute of a leader is a sense of humility and the recognition that this is a team sport. We only succeed if we all succeed together. Someone gave me a plaque early in my career that said, "The goal of the usual leader is to make people think more of the leader. The goal of the exceptional leader is to make people think more of themselves." I took that to heart.

Why do you have such faith in others?

I'm not a suspicious person by nature. My basic belief is that people want to do the right thing—especially if they know you believe in them and have their back.

How would you define the company culture at HCA?

The mission statement is very personal to me because I actually wrote the first draft. (Laughs) "Above all else" is the most important phrase because it sets the precedent that the values you're about to read are held sacred at HCA.

It's your own version of the *Declaration of Independence!*

You're very kind, but it's not that good! (Laughs) Fortunately, the people who are attracted to healthcare have an intrinsic, service-oriented value system. You don't have to convince them they ought to act appropriately, because that nature is already present in them. The bottom line of the mission statement is that we put patients, their families, and our colleagues above our own personal interests and desires.

I COULD NEVER HAVE ENVISIONED ALL OF THESE OPPORTUNITIES. I SIMPLY GREW UP WITH HCA.

When you're running a massive organization, how do you stay connected?

When I was a hospital CEO, I spent most of my time on the floor talking with the doctors and nurses. When I entered healthcare, my mother advised me, "If you listen to your nurses and do what they tell you, you will have an incredibly successful career." By following her guidance, I gained a strong sense of what needed to be done to support their ability to provide patient care. I made it a practice to periodically bring donuts or pizzas to the night nurses because I knew from my mother that those were the loneliest and toughest hours. Those casual yet constructive conversations made my job both fun and impactful.

Can you talk about your experience leading the Hurricane Katrina evacuation?

We mobilized a lot of resources very quickly in order to do extraordinary things. The idea inculcated into HCA's DNA is that the welfare of our employees, patients, and patients' families comes first. We had to make instantaneous, instinctive decisions to get people out and supplies in. I wanted my team to feel empowered to create highly inventive plans rather than worry about criticism.

Who is one of your personal heroes?

I admire the leadership of Winston Churchill so much that I have his portrait on my office wall. As a teenager, I became fascinated with him and formed a lot of my own thoughts and writing style through reading his work. His life was amazing in all respects, and his impact has lasted the course of time.

How do you feel your work impacts patients on a daily basis?

As an example, a report was released by the Institute of Medicine some years ago about how many deaths were caused because of errors in hospital treatment. After reviewing this research, my team and I committed to designing a barcode safety system to reduce medication errors. The nurse would scan each patient's wrist band and then their medication to make sure the dosage, time, and prescription matched up. It was similar to having a copilot in the cockpit. After HCA pioneered that system, it was adopted by many other hospitals, and the error rates went down significantly across the United States. It's an amazing feeling to know that because of HCA's technology and expertise we are able to improve the quality of care across the country beyond our own hospitals.

KAREN GIOVENGO, DNP, RN, CNL & HAZEL ANTIOLA, RN

{Director of Medicine/Surgery/Oncology/Pediatrics, *St. Lucie Medical Center* & Charge Nurse and Supervisor, *St. Lucie Medical Center*}

Karen Giovengo and Hazel Antiola, mentor and mentee respectively, believe that delivering quality patient care is directly tied to team camaraderie. By focusing on communication, guidance, and growth as a unit, the pair has set a standard at St. Lucie Medical Center. Their story is one about the power of kinship. Giovengo, Director and Clinical Nurse Leader, is responsible for her hospital's nurse residency program. When she met Antiola, Charge Nurse and Supervisor, they immediately clicked. The confidants' relationship is built upon giving time, trust, and space to one another. Antiola truly blossomed when paired with the right ally. From holding a scared patient's hands to celebrating with a new mother, St. Lucie's nurses create a comforting, restorative environment. Patients trust and have confidence in a team whose members care for each other. Mentorship, similar to the patient experience, is about honoring the individual spirit and letting them know they are not alone.

At what point did you say, *I want to be a nurse?*
Karen: I can't think of any profession better suited to my personality. My lifelong passion, along with nursing, has been to make a difference in people's lives.

Hazel: In my native Philippines, I took care of my grandmother as she was dying. Afterwards, my mother suggested that I study nursing as a profession. In 1994, I came to the U.S. and joined St. Lucie Medical Center, where I've stayed since.

What makes someone a great nurse?
Hazel: The ability to be flexible and truly listen to others. Good communication with patients, their families, and physicians is critical to a positive experience.

Karen: One of my nurses asked me the other day if it was normal to go home and cry. My response was, "Yes, because that means you are bringing your heart to work." Our job is not just about educating or giving medication but rather being present with a patient so they know you care. We are the comforting voice that alleviates their fear and lets them know that they aren't alone.

It must be very overwhelming at times.
Karen: I become very attached to my patients. One of my very first was a dying woman whose husband stood at the bedside and told me the story of their life together. They had been sweethearts since the first grade and married 70-some years. I stayed there with him as he reminisced about their journey together. She was able to peacefully go through her transition, and he told me later on, "I couldn't have made it without you." My heart connected with them as if they were my very own family members.

Hazel: Working in medical oncology, as I do, it's the nurse's job to assist our patients as they go through the stages of dying. I help them to let go of life by listening and being compassionate. Sometimes family members cry on your shoulder and it's very fulfilling to interact with them in such an intimate way.

How did you both find HCA and why have you stayed?
Karen: I first came to HCA as a nursing student and immediately felt like I had come home. Even when I was moved to a non-HCA hospital, I always kept my foot in the door because I missed the supportive environment. When I returned, my CNO encouraged me to go after my bachelor's, master's, and doctorate degrees, which is an example of how HCA sets its staff up for success. The company gave me tuition reimbursement and was also behind me every step of the way. Growth in terms of your career and education is endless at HCA.

Hazel: One month, St. Lucie Medical Center paid for an apartment directly across the street from our hospital. The bridge I crossed every day to return home was closed for maintenance. If they hadn't done that, my commute would have been endless. That action demonstrated HCA's commitment to its employees.

Karen: Everyone at HCA is of equal importance.

How did you two find each other as mentor and mentee?
Karen: When I was an ICU nurse and floating throughout the hospital, I got to know Hazel. Similar to a marriage, we complement one another. While we don't always see eye-to-eye, we are able to express our opinions in a respectful manner. Together, we've been able to take our team to unthinkable levels. It's easy to stay where you are,

which is why I gently try to push Hazel outside of her comfort zone. Watching her grow has been unbelievably gratifying.

Hazel: Karen has an open-door policy which makes me feel comfortable in terms of communication. She is a role model that, similar to a mother hen, pushes our unit to be better. Through our relationship, I've gained confidence and learned to lead. She teaches me that we are all in this together.

What are some of the benefits of mentorship?
Karen: Aside from high employee retention, we all have a lot of fun together. We are known as the party unit because you never know what we'll do for our patients. We dressed up as super nurses for Halloween and created a float for Mardi Gras. We are always thinking of ways that everyone can celebrate together. While we are very serious about our work, we also enjoy being silly to lighten the spirits of our patients.

relate to one another. When she left, she was smiling because of that connection.

Hazel: We can talk about work as well as our personal issues. Also, if someone has an emergency, we are ready to help. We have one another's backs.

Karen: My nurses and I attended a conference recently as colleagues and spent every evening together as friends. Seeing different sides of your coworkers through team-building activities allows you to relate on a personal level.

What about your job boosts your mood every time?
Karen: On my daily nursing rounds, I get to hear patients brag on my staff, which makes me feel like a proud mom. I love hearing that patients sense how wonderfully we all work together.

IT'S EASY TO STAY WHERE YOU ARE, WHICH IS WHY I GENTLY TRY TO PUSH HAZEL OUTSIDE OF HER COMFORT ZONE.

In which ways do you nurture your team?
Karen: As that old saying goes, "The ones who play together stay together." That is why we have monthly outings, from meals to bowling. They bolster our team dynamic so it's even stronger. We recently hosted a luncheon called "Come Grow With Us," in which new nurses could learn about the opportunities available to them. After we realized that the physicians and nurses needed a stronger rapport, we arranged an event so they could build those bridges.

Why has the nurse residency program you developed been so successful?
Karen: The program, which dramatically reduced our turnover rate, helps nurses understand all of the ways in which they can grow at HCA. Some young nurses want instant gratification through constant feedback and position changes. My success has come through learning what the new generation wants and needs. If a nurse has stagnated, I will invite them to a training or educational program. By listening to my nurses, I've increased their satisfaction in the workplace.

Hazel: Karen and I love showing other nurses their potential. As a team, we encourage, champion, and support one another.

Karen: Sharing your own story has a great impact on others. A nurse admitted to me this morning that she felt anxious because she carries her work home with her. I told her that what she is experiencing is normal. She felt comfortable opening up to me because we could

Hazel: One patient cried recently because of how our staff had personalized his stay. He was just so moved by the amount of care they put into his experience. It was incredibly touching.

What is gratifying about mentorship?
Karen: I love seeing how the people I mentor grow, develop, and then help the next generation. I try my hardest to stay in tune with those whom I mentor to understand where they are. I have to be cued into what they're feeling even if they don't feel comfortable enough to vocalize it.

Hazel: Karen always asks for my opinions, which means the world to me because she values them.

What does the HCA mission mean to you?
Karen: I believe HCA represents the future of nursing because the organization revolves around supporting the patient, nurse, and physician. The company realizes that making life easier for us results in better patient experiences and outcomes. My philosophy is that every patient is your father or mother. I hope to pass that level of respect and dedication on to my nursing team.

Hazel: Through HCA's leadership and nursing classes I've been able to increase my knowledge and become a better leader to my staff. That, in turn, results in better patient care. The nurses are there for one another, and HCA is there for us.

JILL FAINTER

{VP of Quality Standards Clinical Service Group (retired), *HCA Healthcare*}

Some people say they were born to be in medicine. Jill Fainter, former Vice President of Quality Standards, admits that her first healthcare job just seemed like a good idea at the time. However, since joining HCA in 1974, Fainter has been instrumental in raising the bar in the industry. As an advocate for healthcare quality who has created change by means of national policy and certification programs, Fainter calls her career at HCA the greatest privilege of her life. Fainter grew up in the pint-sized community of Big Island, Virginia, located on the Blue Ridge Parkway. One day her father came home and told his little brown-eyed daughter that she was to enroll in a new degree program called medical record science. Her response was, "Whatever you want, Pop," and she promptly signed up and graduated with academic honors. Hospital companies, a relatively new concept at the time, intrigued Fainter. Starting out at an HCA hospital in Blacksburg, Virginia, Fainter dreamed of working at HCA's corporate offices in Nashville. Tenacity, a deep devotion to the care of patients, and a drive to learn the intricacies of her industry is how Fainter thrived at HCA. Over the course of her career, Fainter worked across all sectors of HCA, engaging with everyone from board members to the medical and dietary staff. That's why people skills have been fundamental to her success.

How did you obtain your first corporate role at HCA?
HCA was growing at the time and quickly building resources to support the HCA hospitals in patient quality and safety. In late 1975 at work in Blacksburg, Virginia, I received a call from John Hyden, a former Vice President of Quality Assurance, who asked if I'd like to go to Florida the following week to help him consult. I called my mother who was a buyer at a high-end ladies' department store and she responded, "We need to go shopping because you must be dressed properly!" (Laughs) I flew to meet Mr. Hyden, and we proceeded to an HCA hospital to consult regarding accreditation standards, which are the foundational rules similar to a seal of approval. The Joint Commission accreditation has always demonstrated to our communities, shareholders, leadership, and patients that HCA's hospitals meet minimal standards. After teaching me how to consult, Mr. Hyden asked if I wanted to interview for a full-time position in the Quality Standards department. At age 20, I was offered the job and moved to Nashville.

What was it like to leave your small community for a bigger city?
I started work on January 2, 1976, and still remember Mary Greer welcoming me. "Good morning, you must be Jill!" she said. It was the first time I realized how family-oriented HCA is. It was incredibly comforting. I went into my office, and on my desk was a personal letter from Dr. Frist, Sr. welcoming me to the HCA corporate office. What an incredible way to walk into a brand-new job.

What were the first years of your career like?
For the first 25 years, I traveled to do on-site surveys and consult with HCA's hospitals. From the board room to the boiler room, I surveyed the hospitals to help each department raise their level of safety and quality care. Depending upon the facility's needs, I would stay there for days and often weeks.

It must be amazing to have a comprehensive knowledge of your industry.
I've had the honor to watch HCA expand from tiny communities, where often the hospital was the largest employer, to major facilities. It's been amazing to watch the HCA lifecycle. In my career, some of my favorite work has involved initiatives to decrease patient errors and improve clinical safety. It's been a huge honor to help influence national healthcare standards, along with my team, and develop new regulations and policy.

What about the healthcare industry moves your spirit?
There is nothing more sacred than caring for someone who is sick. At HCA, we treat 110,000 patients a day, which is why I'm so passionate about improving outcomes. As Dr. Frist, Sr. would say, "HCA has gotten better, which has caused everyone else to

get better." Those scalable improvements impact the individual, community, competitors, and industry as a whole. It's incredible.

There's something really beautiful about the culture of HCA.

This is a culture where every time a door opens, people are there to support you. Helen K. Cummings, my longtime mentor, worked her way up at HCA to become the first female vice president. I was a young corporate staff member who watched her grow and develop right before my eyes. She inspired me to spend the latter part of my career helping to influence national policy and set health standards. Her world was financial and mine quality; however, she would make sure our paths crossed to put me in the right situations. I was blessed to have her help and guidance. It is an example of Dr. Frist's belief that "Good begets good, success begets success."

My younger sister had a two-month prognosis. After receiving all of her healthcare at HCA's LewisGale, she is now 12 years in remission. My sisters' experiences always remind me that we are all just a few cells away from being hospital patients. The other thing that pleases me is watching people develop and move to the next level in their education and careers. I love seeing others grow and advance. Lastly, it feels absolutely amazing when I can look at a federal healthcare law or standard and think, *I helped contribute to that*.

What is one memory about someone who impacted you?

I had an accident a few years back. When I was wheeled into the ER in a rural Tennessee hospital, a nurse came out and said, "You're Jill Fainter." After I nodded, the nurse continued, "Seventeen years ago you came to this hospital and helped me get through Joint Commission. Because of that survey, I was promot-

THERE IS NOTHING MORE SACRED THAN CONSISTENTLY PROVIDING PATIENTS WITH RESPECT, INTEGRITY, AND TRUST. NOTHING.

What does it feel like to have power in your industry?

One person does very few things, which is why HCA's legacy is in its team efforts. Historically, healthcare has not been forthcoming in terms of sharing when something goes wrong. At HCA, we formulated a disclosure policy, which promises that when something bad happens, we're going to tell the patient or patient's family, apologize, express empathy, commit to investigation, and prevent it from happening to someone else. My department's job was to respond when something serious, egregious, or worrisome happens. I am proud to say that disclosure started at HCA and is now a part of patient safety throughout the country. I love that we impact our industry as a community.

What made you happiest in your career?

The first is when we've done something really great in regards to patient care. Both of my sisters are cancer survivors, which is why I am so passionate about Sarah Cannon's oncology research.

ed and able to raise my son as a single mom all the way through to his recent high school graduation." I had to get the Kleenex out for that one. It's a small world, and the rewards are huge.

What does the HCA mission mean to you?

Over the years, we've recommitted and reaffirmed ourselves, even through some difficult times of the company, to the improvement of human lives. There is nothing more sacred than consistently providing our patients with respect, integrity, and trust. Nothing.

Looking back on your 43 years of service, how do you hope your work has impacted patients?

I hope every patient turns out similar to my sisters. There is nothing more difficult than lying in a hospital bed. Your clothes are gone, you're in an unfamiliar environment, and you feel as though you've lost your dignity. If we do what we promise in our mission statement, then our care system will work. HCA's value system is built upon sacred trust and healing. I've seen it with my own eyes.

MARTY PASLICK

{SVP and CIO, *HCA Healthcare*}

Marty Paslick, Chief Information Officer, gained an even deeper appreciation for hospital IT after being a patient himself. Technology is Paslick's first passion and one he stumbled across as a teenager while tutoring his brother in a software development class. He acquired degrees in business and engineering and was hired more than three decades ago at HCA as a developer. After life changing experiences as a cardiac and cancer survivor, he has worked hard to help his team draw connections between their cubicle jobs and HCA's collective healthcare-inspired cause. In case his employees haven't been patients themselves, Paslick provides ways for them to connect their work beyond code and computer screens. Every month, he arranges for 12 technologists to tour an HCA hospital. Seeing people fighting for their lives, Paslick assures, never fails to elicit an emotional attachment.

How did your upbringing influence your demeanor in the workplace?
I come from a traditional middle-class family. In 1958, my dad's mom left him a small inheritance. Working two jobs with two small children, my parents could have chosen to use the money to simplify their financial situation. But with the support of my mom, Dad decided to go to college and earn his bachelor's degree. That decision changed the future of my family. From that moment on, education was highly prioritized, which is why my brother, two sisters, and I have a collection of undergraduate and master's degrees.

What were you like as a kid?
I was always early. With a little brother only 14 months younger, I began school at age four, which I tease my mom about, saying that she tried to simplify the toddler support challenge at home. Therefore, I graduated from college at age 20 with no idea of what I wanted to do. With no plan, I continued to work as a meat cutter with tough working hours and conditions. But even in that environment, I came to realize that my middle-class work ethic was important and something that differentiated me. Some of my favorite leaders came from this time of my working life. They demonstrated faithfully the ability to place their teams before themselves.

What is an example of this kind of selflessness?
When my bachelor's degree was not enough to elevate me out of the meat-cutting industry, I decided to go back to school to get another undergraduate degree. Halfway through my pursuit of a second degree, I was transferred at work. I was worried that my full-time job requirements would slow my degree efforts. On my first day in my new store, the manager said, "I understand you are going to school. Every semester, you make the best school schedule you can, and we'll work your 40 hours around it." I was blown away by his interest in what was important to me. I would have run through a wall for that guy. I decided right then that if I was ever placed in a leadership role, I wanted to follow his servant leadership style.

How would you define a leader?
A leader is someone who sets the tone while also keeping in mind that this is a team sport. I try to surround myself with individuals who value the same things I do. You build a strong workforce by understanding and taking advantage of your team's strengths. I have always been fortunate to be surrounded by talented leaders.

When did you begin your career with HCA?
I was hired at HCA through the Humana-Galen bloodline along with another guy who I quickly realized was much smarter than me. I went from being thrilled to terrified. My thought was, *How am I going to hold onto it?* That's when I realized that the only way to compete was to work harder. I said to myself, *If it takes him an hour to do something, then I'll put in two or three to be even better.*

Where does that mindset come from?
I've accepted that it's okay to be chronically dissatisfied with our current scenario and have a bit of a chip on our shoulders. I try to continuously motivate myself by creating a voice in my head that says, *They don't think you can do this*. My wife is a 25-year veteran of HCA, and she and my son have always been incredibly supportive of me. Their encouragement has been critical to my success.

How did you work your way from software developer to where you sit right now?
Until I was promoted to CIO, I had never applied for a job in my 32 years at HCA. Opportunities always found me by means of

my supervisors. Through them, I've had chances to start projects from scratch, turn around disappointing situations, and execute organizational transformations. Hard work and creative vision are everything here. I put in my hours and took risks, which caught the right people's attention.

What HCA principles do you share with new hires?
The first thing is that I hope this is the last place they ever work. I hope we create an enriching environment for their careers. The second is that our history and culture are important and that everyone needs to take personal responsibility to maintain and add to it. Finally, I emphasize that we don't make refrigerators here. Our profession has a critical mission, and we want our folks to think of themselves as healthcare professionals first and IT people second.

Why do the small things make a huge difference in healthcare?
As a patient, you sometimes feel like a specimen. It can be dehumanizing, which is why we try to give them some form of control. That, in addition to empathy, is healing.

What mentors looked out for you along your career path at HCA?
As you go through your career, the managers you have can make you feel like you're Goldilocks. One micromanages too much, and the next doesn't care what you're working on. Noel [Williams, former SVP] gave me the autonomy I craved and the constructive criticism that I needed. Without her, my probability of sitting in this seat is zero. The best mentors have the courage to tell you the truth to bring you to the optimal place.

WE WANT OUR FOLKS TO THINK OF THEMSELVES AS HEALTHCARE PROFESSIONALS FIRST AND IT PEOPLE SECOND.

How did your own life-or-death experience change your vision for IT&S?
I want to make life easier for our clinicians and patients. Here's an example: my sister-in-law had cancer, and one weekend, my wife and I visited her. We asked the nurse a question, and she reached into her pocket, grabbed her mobile device, and texted the physician. Three minutes later she says, "They added the fluids because chemotherapy dehydrates her." Before nurses started carrying mobile device, that process would have been much more labor intensive. Seeing technology I've worked on out in the field is rewarding. Streamlining the work of our physicians and nurses so they can get insightful data faster, focus more intensely on the patient, and have better work-life balance is what motivates me.

Is technology magical in a way?
Yes. In the first twenty-plus years of my career, healthcare IT was most concerned about back-office operations. Today we are beginning to create innovative solutions that connect patients with their care through digital platforms like patient portals and improving their hospital stay with technologies like smart televisions.

What does the HCA mission mean to you?
At some companies, mission statements are just words on a wall. At HCA, we believe that taking care of people in their most vulnerable state is the noblest cause anyone could ask for. I would put our persistence for quality patient care against anyone's. To quote Dr. Frist, Sr.: "Don't worry about the bottom line. Put the patient first, and the rest will follow."

How would you like to cement your legacy at HCA?
My worst nightmare is being given a great opportunity and doing nothing with it. I follow several great CIOs who served memorably throughout HCA's history. They set the direction for IT, which is why I see my CIO role as an extension of their work rather than a stand-alone proposition. I hope to look back one day and know that I along with my team changed the IT landscape for HCA and the healthcare industry by significantly improving the way we take care of our patients. I also feel like the IT leadership team is the best in the company's history, and I believe they will continue building our reputation and credibility long after my time ends. If I can leave that legacy in the room, I'll be happy.

JOANN ETTIEN

{COO/ Administrator, *Centennial Women's and Children's*}

Joann Ettien built the Children's Hospital at TriStar Centennial located in Nashville, Tennessee. By asking the right questions, listening, and starting conversations, the Chief Operating Officer learned what resources clinicians needed to do their best work. Ettien, born and raised in Pittsburgh, Pennsylvania, took a bus and streetcar to volunteer as a candy striper when she was a pre-teen. A natural nurturer, she enjoyed the satisfaction that came from asking others, "How can I make your day better?" After working for seven years as a chief nursing officer in Largo, Florida, Ettien was asked by her supervisor if she had one last hospital in her. Soon after, she was promoted to Administrator and Chief Operating Officer of the Women's Hospital at Centennial Medical, the only freestanding Tennessee facility designated for women and babies. When she and her team began conceptualizing the Children's Hospital, they tapped the expertise of local pediatricians and sub-specialists. Connecting with the community is a vital component of her hands-on leadership. Ettien knows that success is sweetest when achieved together, which is why she allows herself to be advised in order to guide. In her 37 years at HCA, her mission has remained the same: make sure patients know they are number one

How did your upbringing shape the way you approach the world?

My father was born in Germany and relocated to the United States at age four. His parents taught themselves English, which I always admired. My grandmother was a housekeeper and my grandfather a gravedigger. Dad was the first child in his family to get a degree, which made me want to do something special with my life. I learned discipline by playing the violin since age seven.

What brought you to the healthcare world, especially at such an early age?

My school facilitated the opportunity, and I sort of stumbled into volunteer work and, eventually, the nursing program that I entered. However, I found the industry to be rewarding the moment I arrived. I've always loved helping people and finding different ways to show respect to them. People are vulnerable in a hospital setting, and the way to ease their minds is by providing compassionate care.

When did you think, *I can turn this extracurricular activity into a career?*

I wanted to do something where I could earn a good living, care for people, and make a difference. Being a teacher particularly appealed to me, and in many ways, I've gotten to do that in my career as a nurse, chief nursing officer, and chief operating officer. I am able to teach others how to be leaders and put the patient first.

How did your career as a nurse prepare you for your current role as COO?

My first job with HCA was at Largo Medical Center. My goal was to work and also be able to take my kids to school and pick them up, which they allowed me to do. One day I went to the Director of Nursing and said, "I would like to give other floating nurses a little guidance about what to do when they go to an unfamiliar floor." At her encouragement, I created a book called *Notes for Floats*, a set of guidelines for that hospital and also the beginning of my leadership potential. HCA empowered me to make a difference, which has continued throughout my tenure with the company.

Do you feel like HCA recognizes its workers as individuals?

I do. HCA rewards and recognizes those who go above and beyond in their role. As a leader, similarly, I never stop learning. To use a golf term, which is my preferred hobby, I always enjoy the game of healthcare whether I'm on the front nine or the back nine. Today, I actually feel more dedicated to mentoring than I did before.

Can you tell me about one of your most moving experiences at HCA?

In Florida, I initiated a program for special needs high school students in which we gave them jobs at our hospital. On my last day of work, the entire staff, volunteers, and group of high school students lined the halls to say their goodbyes. It was the first time I felt that I had really made a difference. I was so moved to see the joy that it brought these kids to be a part of something. To me, it proved that no matter what difficulties God has given you, we are all capable of anything. Building that program was incredibly special.

Do you have any mentors at HCA who helped you believe in yourself?

When I was a nurse manager, the director of nursing came to me one day and said, "I would really like for you to apply for my position."

ANOTHER REASON I LOVE AND AM INSPIRED BY HCA IS THAT THEY GIVE THE INDUSTRY WHAT IS NEEDED, WHICH IS WHY THEY'VE PUT A GREATER FOCUS ON WOMEN AND CHILDREN'S CARE IN RECENT YEARS.

While I had previously led the emergency room and built a chemotherapy program, I wasn't sure if I could take on her role. However, by allowing myself to be mentored, I was able to do so.

I love that you are so open to learning.
If you don't listen, you never learn. I came to Nashville to understand what Centennial had and what we could do to make it better. That came about through conversations with physicians, staff, and managers, during which I reinforced the idea that we are all reliant upon one another. I constantly ask myself, *How can we make our patients feel special? Why would every mother want to come here to have her baby? How can we empower our team to make this a better place?* Fortunately, HCA's leadership training also provides great guidance for engaging with patients every step of the way.

Do you feel genuine connection helps patients heal faster?
The constant attention to progression and individualized care is in itself healing. The most important element of care is consistency. When someone knows you are going to round every hour, they can rest easily and get better faster. Loyalty breeds loyalty.

When you changed careers, how did you tap into that new headspace?
Two years after I arrived at Centennial, we began exploring the idea of a children's hospital. I was always frightened by the idea of taking care of children in a medical setting because I couldn't stand to see them in pain. I also knew if we pursued this idea we'd have to do it right. Once again, the beauty of HCA is the accessibility we have to other hospitals and their leadership teams. Why reinvent the wheel when there is such a wealth of knowledge already in existence? Medical City Dallas and Methodist had very mature children's programs. I spent time with their leaders and asked, "What are your best practices? What would you do differently?" If you can dream it, you can do it.

How did the physicians and administrative staff feel about that?
They were so appreciative because it was the first time anyone had ever asked them for their opinion. Our reverse strategy in which we asked, "How does this program need to look in order for us to serve you best?" was a giant success. We met our goal of getting everyone on the same page in order to give the best service to the child and their family.

Do you feel HCA prioritizes women and children's care?
Absolutely. Another reason I love and am inspired by HCA is that they give the industry what is needed, which is why they've put a greater focus on women and children's care in recent years. We are one of 27 children's hospitals within the company, and Centennial's personal mission is to do everything in our power to keep families together.

How has HCA empowered you as a leader?
I went back to school at age 40 for my bachelor's and master's degrees in healthcare administration and business. Not only did HCA reimburse me for my tuition, but my mentors also provided much needed encouragement. My success at HCA comes from doing the best job that I could and receiving the right recognition and tools.

What has kept you at HCA for 37 years?
In my career, HCA has nurtured me as a leader and allowed me to achieve my professional and personal goals. I've also loved being a part of the bigger picture by working with other women and children's hospitals across our company to make sure we are on the same ethical page. Community involvement is also a great passion of mine, from partnering with local events to sitting on multiple boards.

How has being engaged with your community improved Centennial?
By partnering with local nonprofits, we are able to have double the support for mothers, children, and their families. Being involved in the community allows us to bring in new support services, demonstrate what we do have to our neighbors, and discover new ways in which we can help them.

How would you like your work to impact patients on a daily basis?
I don't ever want to lose anyone on my watch, which is why I hope that everything I do positively impacts patient care. Hopefully I inspire my staff to act the same.

What does HCA's mission mean to you?
People, versus bricks and mortar, make a hospital. From my CEO to our division president and the CEO of HCA, the attitude is consistently about doing what you can for another. While asking, *What could I have done better?* sometimes keeps me up at night, it is also my greatest motivator. We learn from our errors and then keep moving forward. HCA's culture inspires others to be their best and keep the patient at the focus. It's been an absolute honor to work for this company.

RICHARD M. BRACKEN

{Chairman and CEO (retired), *HCA Healthcare*}

Richard Bracken's relationship with HCA started very early in his professional life. Upon joining the company in 1981, the former Chairman and CEO told himself, *This is an organization well-positioned for the future, a perfect place to start a career.* The California native wasn't always interested in working in the healthcare industry. Bracken's love of the outdoors led him to consider studying geology, but a summer job in a hospital, which he found to be an energetic, inspiring, and intellectually engaging environment, swayed him. During graduate school at the Medical College of Virginia, Bracken learned about HCA through conversations with classmates. As a young man, he was attracted to an organization that was still young itself. The pragmatist positioned himself so that he could grow alongside HCA, his company of choice. Over time, he did just that, progressing from an entry-level hospital management position to the top tier of the corporation. "It turned out to be a choice that lasted a full career," Bracken says.

How did you pursue healthcare administration?
I enrolled in a master's of health administration program at the Medical College of Virginia. As a young man, one of the things that drew me to the school was its longstanding record of nearly 100 percent job offers upon graduation. That looked pretty good to me.

What was your first job in healthcare administration?
I worked for a small non-for-profit hospital in Arizona. The limited scale of a single facility confirmed my desire to work for a company like HCA. (Laughs) I wanted to be part of a larger organization where I would have unlimited opportunity. Moving from one organization to another as my career evolved seemed like an inefficient approach, and if one organization had the capacity to accommodate a range of opportunity, so much the better.

What was your first role at HCA?
It was an entry-level administrative position at one of our hospitals in San Diego. I took that job because my wife was about to have our second child and wanted to be closer to her family. From there, I was promoted to my first CEO position at a Los Angeles hospital. It was a troubled facility, staff morale was low, and the assignment was short-term in nature. Needless to say, it had been difficult to fill that post, but I felt differently about it. At 29 years old, I saw it as a great opportunity to enter the CEO ranks and demonstrate that I was willing to take on tough assignments. I figured there was nowhere to go but up. (Laughs)

How did you learn to lead?
By watching others deal with difficult challenges and dealing with them myself. Of course, some characteristics of leadership are instinctive, and we all are who we are, but significant elements of leadership can be learned. And nothing teaches leadership better than actual experience—from both the successes, and more forcefully, from the failures. At HCA, performance matters, and success in difficult situations is recognized. I demonstrated a willingness to take on challenging situations, and over time, I was able to create a successful track record. Rather than leadership per se, I focused on performance and achieving outcomes through a manner in which the company would be proud.

How do you view the HCA culture?
Culture is something that is created and tested every day. The HCA culture reflects the many organizations and individuals who are, and have been, part of the company. The core of the culture is always the same, a strength and integrity that started with our founders. It provided the structure for a truly great organization, but our collective culture has continued to evolve and reflects the positive contributions of thousands and thousands of people.

What did it feel like to transition from hospital to corporate leadership?

I feel very fortunate that the first part of my career was in the direct operation of our hospitals. One of the main differences between working in a hospital and the corporate office was being able to see on a firsthand and real-time basis the effects of your decisions on people, patient care, and strategy. There was always immediate, direct, and unfiltered feedback that was so helpful, even when not favorable. This experience gave me great appreciation for and sensitivity to the jobs our colleagues do every hour of every day. Moving to the corporate office gave me a view of the overall healthcare environment and how, as a collective organization, we could operate within it. Having that operational perspective was foundational, and something on which I always relied in my corporate roles.

What did you learn as a hospital-level leader that you were able to apply to your role as a corporate-level leader?

Working at HCA's hospitals, I learned about the dynamics that make each facility work, which was priceless knowledge as CEO. It was at the hospitals that I got a full appreciation of the challenges our nurses and caregivers were struggling with, the pressures on physicians, the importance of clear and concise communication, and how change actually occurs at the operations level. Those experiences taught me to be visible and available and flexible and fair in executing change.

Why were you so passionate about HCA as an organization?

My passion for HCA grew over time as my respect for my many colleagues grew, and I gained perspective about what our organization could do within the healthcare system. I'm a competitive person, and I wanted HCA to be the best and to set the standard for both clinically effective and operationally efficient healthcare services. I saw a real opportunity for our organization to lead in the industry and wanted to be a part of that.

Succession strategy is a part of HCA's legacy. How are leaders chosen?

While it's important to choose leaders that have adequate technical and business skills, that's really the easy part. Really, it's more critical to understand the essential characteristics of people, their values, decision-making processes (especially under pressure), their work ethic, and how they communicate and represent themselves and the company in public. Those are attributes that are best witnessed over time. It's never an easy decision. We all have strengths and weaknesses, but it's perspective over time that matters.

What do you think is beneficial about staying within one organization?

If it is the right organization with a full range of opportunities, like HCA, career growth within one organization increases your understanding of the company's strengths and weaknesses, how decisions are made, how change is accommodated, and how it responds under pressure—all so important to performance and outcomes. Career growth within one company allows your career to grow in stages without having to relearn everything in a new organizational structure. This depth of knowledge proved to be very powerful in my career.

When did you feel like you hit your stride as a leader?

When I was about 34, I became CEO of Green Hospital at Scripps Clinic and Research Foundation, which was one of the leading medical institutions in America. My predecessor had just passed away, and it was a very emotional time for the organization. I had to lead a grieving team while at the same time drive performance at this facility, a marquis hospital actively involved in leading-edge clinical research and treatment. That was a huge responsibility and an incredible experience, both personally and professionally, and a time I never will forget.

> **I SAW A REAL OPPORTUNITY FOR OUR ORGANIZATION TO LEAD IN THE INDUSTRY AND WANTED TO BE A PART OF THAT.**

Why is the quality agenda important to HCA's legacy?

A very important part of my tenure as CEO was about applying HCA's business logic to the clinical side in order to improve outcomes. I felt the overall positioning of the organization to deal with our clinical quality agenda was underpowered. We needed to bring the same level of resources, personnel, and analytical capability to the clinical side of our business as we did with the financial side. For example, there was a time when if you asked how long it would take to see a doctor in one of our emergency rooms the answer would vary widely depending upon the facility. Every hospital measured its data differently. We decided to standardize the way we defined, measured, and reported that process. Through this approach, we were able to lower the average wait time from over an hour to around 15 minutes. It seems simple in retrospect, but it was an industry-leading concept, and it took two years to get it right. From there, we installed billboards outside each hospital to communicate wait times to the public. Now we have some of the shortest wait times in the industry, and an accurate system that holds us accountable. The pursuit of improved quality of care will

continue to distinguish HCA over time and is a pillar of its legacy. By harnessing our collective thinking, we were able to significantly move the clinical quality agenda and create new and better standards of performance, which translated to better care. I am proud that so many people at HCA played critical roles in making this happen. It was a true team effort.

What do you think is the secret to problem-solving?

It's imperative to take personal responsibility to reach solutions to problems in a timely manner. A leader needs to be able to recognize bad news early and deal with it. It's essential to put the right people in charge of managing the problem and then trust them to execute the solutions. For example, on the quality agenda, I found it was critical to bring in new clinical leadership, clearly set the agenda and related expectations, and give them room to run.

What does the HCA mission mean to you?

The HCA mission is about operating a healthcare organization that is responsible in how it conducts its affairs, whether they are financial or clinical, and bold in terms of introducing new ways of providing quality, efficient, and compassionate healthcare. The crux of this organization's success is its ability to choose good people, to operate consistently with its value system, to be open to change, and to execute at industry-leading levels. That's a great formula for success.

What are you most proud of looking back at your HCA tenure?

Perhaps my best achievement was leaving the company in solid shape and in good hands. I am proud to have led an organization where one's character and moral compass are critical determinants for success. Looking back, I'm incredibly gratified to have navigated a path from hospital administration to CEO of the company, to have played a role in the execution of a leading clinical agenda, and to have helped guide one of the largest IPOs of its time. I'm also pleased to have helped to develop an impressive team of leaders who will take HCA well into the future. And I formed friendships that will last a lifetime.

SHARN BARBARIN, FACHE

{CEO, *Medical City Lewisville*}

Sharn Barbarin, FACHE, believes that everyone has the same chance to advance at HCA. The CEO at Medical City Lewisville, located outside of Dallas, Texas, wants to repay the organization's investment in her career by providing others with the right roles, mentors, and guidance. Many of Barbarin's memories of her upbringing in Baton Rouge, Louisiana, are of being in a hospital setting. The empathetic manner in which the medical staff treated her family influenced her to view every life that comes through her doors as a gift. After earning her master's in health administration, Barbarin began her career with HCA as an administrative fellow at Medical Center Lewisville. In a short period, she was promoted to COO at the Medical City McKinney, and next, worked as COO at Medical City Arlington before taking on her current role as CEO at Lewisville in 2015. Nominated as a Young Healthcare Executive of the Year by the Dallas Fort Worth Hospital Council, Barbarin enjoys championing and bolstering others. She knows that love and compassion, when demonstrated by a leader, have the ability to cascade throughout all levels of an organization.

What drew you initially to healthcare?
Like many, I had a number of family members who worked in the healthcare field, in a variety of roles from transporter to physicians and registration clerk. Also, a number of my family members were severely ill while I was growing up, so I spent a tremendous amount of time in the hospital setting. I wanted to be a part of the healthcare industry because of the support that was given to my family and me. As a child, I was able to see first-hand the impact that compassion can have during the tough and celebratory times.

Can you give me an example of exceptional caretaking?
The first time that my brother had an asthma attack, I was only seven years old and very alarmed to see someone I loved in that state. I'm certain that the clinical care was outstanding, but it was a dietician asking my brother what popsicle flavor he wanted every day that made a huge impact on our mood. Personal connection and compassion make a huge difference in terms of healing.

Do you think HCA places as much emphasis on connection as caretaking?
Absolutely. We pride ourselves on delivering an exceptional patient experience, which involves making sure patients understand that they aren't just a medical record. They are someone's mother, sister, brother, or best friend. It is our expectation that every staff member makes a personal connection with every patient. When I conduct my patient rounds, I ask our physicians and nurses to notate something personal about each individual in addition to their clinical stats.

Does HCA naturally curate a compassionate staff?
The HCA culture is our greatest recruitment tool. Likeminded people tend to attract one another, which is why our team is filled with staff members who are passionate about healing others and delivering excellence. If you enter our hospital with that shared value system, then we can train you to do almost any skill. While I can teach someone how to provide care, I can't teach him or her how to care.

How do you know if you want to hire someone?
In the interview process, we interview for skill and fit. For this reason, we ask questions about what motivates the candidate or ask them to describe a circumstance in which they impacted a patient's life. The responses provide you with meaningful insight on whether he or she has a strong connection to purpose.

You are almost seeking a compassionate depth.
Yes. Treating every individual who enters the doors of our facility with dignity and respect is imperative. We want our staff members to see and engage with their patients in the same way as they would a family member.

Can you speak to what goes into great leadership?
That would be: vision, accountability, a drive for excellence, resolve, humility, and the ability to inspire. What keeps me grounded is doing my employee and patient rounding. Those are opportunities to connect and know, through listening and asking my staff questions, what is happening on every level.

Why do you have such a good read on people?
I got my master's in healthcare administration, but my undergraduate is in psychology with a minor in sociology. I am innately drawn to understanding people, teams, and what motivates them. Whether that is metrics or praise, it is imperative that I know the motivation drivers and connect with that in order to influence our team to do

THE HCA CULTURE IS OUR GREATEST RECRUITMENT TOOL.

their absolute best. For this reason, we also begin every leadership meeting by talking about our purpose, which establishes our collective *why* and aligns our team with a mission to do their best.

How critical has emotional intelligence been to your success?
It is the source of my success. I have always been that person who others freely consult with because I am trustworthy, candid, invested in the organization's and individual's success, and capable of coaching and coming up with solutions. Creating an environment in which you can connect honestly is important to me.

How did your upbringing influence your personality in the workplace?
My parents set very high expectations of me in terms of academic success, being goal-oriented, having a strong sense of community, and serving as a role model for others. It's fortuitous that striving for excellence was expected since birth because that prepared me for HCA.

When you first started at HCA, did you think, *One day I'll be a leader*?
Absolutely. In high school and college I served as a leader in different organizations, and upon joining HCA, my goal was to one day become a CEO. When I first joined the company, my mentor and I met on a monthly basis. During those touch-point sessions he would ask about my goals and eventually accelerated my promotion ahead of my personal timeframe. I was elevated when he felt that I was ready, versus going off a blueprint timeline.

Why do you think HCA's mentorship program is so beneficial?
Establishing a pipeline for staff to be promoted to executive positions is core to HCA's success. For this reason, tremendous emphasis is placed on recognizing talent, assessing an individual's competencies and making sure they are in the right role, acknowledging their career goals, and collaborating to define plans to achieve them. Everyone has the same chance to advance at HCA.

Did you ever think, *I don't know if I can do this?*
Of course, because with leadership comes a significant amount of responsibility. There are individuals counting on you for your guidance, support, and your skill set. My goal is to always approach my team as experts in their field. By saying, "I am here to learn from you and remove any barriers to your team's success," you earn their trust and elevate performance levels.

Can you speak to HCA's inclusive mentality and why this is so important?
HCA knows that we can only provide the best possible care if our employees represent the same diversity of our patients. Our Workforce Diversity and Inclusion Program creates a global community as well as a connection to our patients. At HCA, we champion and value every part of the human race because that is whom we serve.

How has HCA's culture facilitated your own growth?
While I always knew that I had something unique to bring to the healthcare field, HCA was the organization that said, "We choose you." After I was accepted into the graduate program at Tulane University, I ended up being a recipient for a scholarship through HCA, which funded 100 percent of my graduate studies. That is when I knew this company invests in its leaders. I have been privileged to serve at HCA for 20 years but can never repay the organization for my career.

Why is face-to-face connection so important in your job?
Words are powerful; however, emotional connections happen when you can sense someone's energy, body language, and authenticity in person. Emails don't inspire. Connections do. I want my team to know the importance of our relationship, that no topic is off the table, and I am here to serve so they can take care of our patients.

What is the best compliment anyone has ever given you?
I became close to one family whose father was very, very ill and near the end of his life. I let his daughter know that we were here to support their family and give their father and them everything they needed. When their father passed, the daughter contacted me, and I immediately went to the unit to console her and the other family members. After her father's services, she sent me a note thanking me for my presence and saying how powerful it was to know they were loved and supported. I still have that letter because it impacted me on every level.

What does HCA's mission mean to you?
Our mission inspires me each and every day. It is my connection to purpose, and as an executive, it serves as my compass, guiding every decision.

How has your work impacted patients?
Heroism occurs at every level at HCA, which is why my team constantly humbles me. At the end of the day, I would hope that patients who have been cared for in any of my facilities would say that they received compassionate care and love, which led to healing. If I could hope to achieve one-tenth of Dr. Frist's legacy, I would be so happy.

MAURICE "MEL" LAGARDE III

{President, *MidAmerica Division*}

The values of the organization that he joined 38 years ago mirror those of Maurice "Mel" Lagarde III's own civic-minded, fifth-generation New Orleans family. Lagarde's story proves that a solid foundation is key to keeping your cool in the toughest of circumstances. In his early twenties, Lagarde, a graduate of Tulane University's School of Public Health and Tropical Medicine, became acquainted with HCA. The same reasons that drew him to the organization are why he has remained: having the ability to play a role in the bigger picture of healthcare and contribute to an egalitarian culture where everyone, no matter their ranking, is respected. Lagarde's résumé includes titles such as CEO for five HCA hospitals, COO of the Gulf Coast division, and President of HCA's Delta division. Now he serves as the MidAmerica Division President, a role he describes as "the neck of the hourglass." His job allows him to make a difference at a corporate level while also maintaining a personal connection with his hospitals, physicians, employees, and patients. Lagarde served on the ground in his hometown in the wake of Hurricane Katrina, directing the evacuation of Tulane Medical Center. Post-tragedy, Lagarde let no grass grow underneath his feet. As co-chair of the "Bring New Orleans Back" Commission, he and 16 other community leaders passionately guided local and federal governments on how to rebuild the city. Lagarde's allegiance to HCA and New Orleans go hand in hand.

How did you become interested in healthcare administration?
Initially I was interested in attending medical school until one of my Tulane University professors alerted me to a recently launched health systems management program. He was chairman of the department and talked me into applying. I was led to HCA through another one of my professors. After he facilitated a meeting for me at their New Orleans office, I chose our organization and then did my residency program in an HCA hospital in Columbus, Georgia. HCA has always been everything that an employer should be and more. Almost forty years in, I am still amazed by the organization's generosity and loyalty.

What do you feel makes HCA's environment so special?
The character, ethics, and personality of Dr. Frist, Sr. shaped the culture here. He led more with his heart than with his mind. Early on, he took an interest in me. I was 22 and Mr. Nobody. After meeting me on a hospital visit, he continued to write me notes and call to say that he'd been thinking about me. I was always struck by his desire to invest his time in me. I thought, *If I am ever in a position of power, I want to also reach out to people in unexpected ways.* The religion of HCA is about a common bond between fellow human beings. While I've done some remarkable things inside of HCA, I have always received more than I have given. That is certain.

How does the HCA value system mirror that of your own family?
HCA's values are entirely consistent with how I was raised: we are judged by what we do when no one is watching. I hope, no matter how big we get, that ideology never goes away. It has been one of the things I've held onto the most during tough times. I won't let our culture, organization, or family down. I am always trying to make sure that everything I do would have made Dr. Frist, Sr. proud.

How has mentorship played a part in your HCA career?
The mentors I've patterned myself after were all fairly similar individuals. They make up the composite that is my design. I stole great people's personalities along the way, held onto them, and made them my own.

How do you feel about your HCA legacy?
You don't realize the passage of time until something or someone causes you to step back and see all that has happened. That's the only time I think, *Wow it really did work out pretty well.* HCA, similar to my own family's work in the New Orleans community, continuously evolves as an organization to become more relevant, yet it also values continuity. Our culture recognizes and rewards individuals who do their very best. That mentality is what keeps me here.

When I joined HCA, I was just happy to be here. My career path has been a natural evolution that came from doing what was necessary. What HCA offers is a culture of caring. Money can't buy that. Those values are embodied through our employees' daily actions and how we make hard decisions.

WHAT HCA OFFERS IS A CULTURE OF CARING. MONEY CAN'T BUY THAT.

What is one of the top realizations you've had during your time at HCA?
I have worked in a lot of different states, hospitals, and positions because of HCA. Hospital executives have a responsibility to our hospitals and company as well as to our communities as a whole. Being a community leader is very important in my eyes, and therefore, I gradually stepped into that role in order to have the greatest impact and make it my own.

What was it like to witness Hurricane Katrina with your own eyes?
If you compiled every news story, that couldn't even begin to explain what it felt like to watch New Orleans be washed away. We had the clothes on our backs and no place to live. There was no running water, electricity, gas, law, or mail service. You could see every star in the sky because the city was so dark. The city had never faced anything like it before.

At the time, my HCA division included Louisiana, Mississippi, and Austin, Texas, but my command center was at Tulane Hospital in New Orleans. I was responsible for coordinating the disaster planning and allocating resources to all of our hospitals and employees. After Tulane and the city flooded, the depths of the waters made it impossible for us to evacuate the hospital for six days. We were completely alone. There were no resources other than what HCA brought to us by air.

What was most difficult about that tragic time in New Orleans' history?
People were looting, rioting, and you could see dead bodies everywhere. Sounds carried like you were in the country. You could hear the screams of people from their rooftops, crying out to be saved. I really wondered sometimes whether or not I was going to live. We were so far outside the realm of normalcy that anything was possible. A satellite phone was our principle means of communication to the HCA command center. We would give them our status and our needs, and they would send back resources we needed and instructions. It was very difficult to cope and also keep people at Tulane without them eventually rioting.

How did Hurricane Katrina change your perspective on life?
You are really never the same after a situation like Katrina. I was pulled in every direction. I had a responsibility to HCA to take care of our patients and employees. I had a responsibility to my family who now had no home. And I had a responsibility to the community to deal with the crisis at hand and rebuild. To balance that without losing your mind is something else. The support of HCA is how I got through that traumatic time. Our culture is about doing what is necessary to support patients and staff. Hurricane Katrina is one of the definitive moments in our history.

What was the most uplifting epiphany you had during that time?
What is remarkable about humanity is that in times of disaster you see the very best of people. There was a great deal of generosity from the U.S. government, our fellow countrymen, and HCA. All opened up their doors and wallets, which was remarkable and unprecedented. HCA, in particular, did more for our employees than any other New Orleans business. While it was certainly heartbreaking to see some people decompensate during Hurricane Katrina, I also saw others act in incredible ways.

How do you feel that HCA went above and beyond to help the victims of Hurricane Katrina?
What I learned from Katrina is how temporary life is. Anything can be taken away from you in a single moment. You don't think that is possible until it happens. Under the most brutal, high-pressure conditions, HCA handled them masterfully by not putting an emphasis on cost. Rather than money, we wanted to make sure our employees, patients, and the families of New Orleans were safe. Leading during that time was one of the greatest blessings of my life. Afterward, even when I was in a state of shock, I couldn't stop thinking about all that HCA had done for our patients, physicians, and employees. That is the silver lining of a sad situation. What HCA did for my hometown was undeniably heroic.

What does the HCA mission mean to you?
The HCA mission is very much a part of who I am. I've had a small part in defining HCA as a company, but HCA has played a huge part in defining me. As an organization, I hope that our employees know we care about them as individuals and want to create long-term relationships with them. HCA has taught me the gratification of doing meaningful work alongside exceptional individuals. That is what keeps me coming back here every day.

How would you describe the HCA culture?
The reason HCA exists is because of our patients. Every day we try to prove that we are worthy of serving them. Expectations change regularly, like in any industry, but at our core, we want to show our patients and the HCA family that we care. I could not even begin to describe what an honor it has been to work for this organization. It's been one of the greatest blessings of my life.

JENNIFER BUFORD

{Executive Recruiter, *HCA Healthcare*}

Jennifer Buford's candor and common sense are her greatest strengths. As an Executive Recruiter, she prides herself on her ability to slow down and get a good read on the person in front of her. In her ten-year tenure, Buford has vetted potential candidates to see if they have the skills, talent, and character needed to succeed at HCA. Experience may get someone in the door, but they must have drive, authenticity, and the patient-focused perspective that is emblematic of HCA's culture as well. Buford, a Nashville native, is a lifelong learner. After taking a semester off from college, she began her first career as a local bank teller. She worked her way up in banking to the personal and business sector, where she learned the art of customer service and how to develop trusting relationships with her clients. Since entering healthcare, Buford has used her gift to match personalities with the right position.

How did your upbringing influence you?
At age 35, I have lived in Nashville my entire life, which was not the plan but it happened. (Laughs) I grew up in a very traditional family where my mom, a homemaker, greeted my dad at the door every single day. My upbringing was very nurturing—if not a bit sheltered. At Middle Tennessee State University, I decided to study communications and marketing because I love to talk to people. A few semesters in, I took a break and never returned. One day, my brother and I were brainstorming career ideas, and he suggested that I either become a flight attendant or work in banking. The latter struck a chord, which is when I applied for my first teller position at AmSouth.

What did you learn from that first position?
I learned that I really thrived in the banking industry. From there, I applied for a personal banker position at Bank of America. That job eventually led me to commercial and business banking in which I dealt with individual portfolios versus the consumer needs. I learned from my first position in banking that the art of customer service is about building relationships and trust with your clients.

What skills did you acquire in banking that apply to your current role?
How to assess my clients' needs and build bridges of trust between us. I love to learn about people and from those with different opinions and personality types. Similar to in my current job, my goal every day was to understand why my client had entered their industry, what motivated them, and where they wanted to be. All of that information was key to helping the client achieve their desired goal. It is similar to recruiting; you need to understand the hiring manager's need along with the applicant's desired goal in terms of their career to make a successful match.

Going from banking to healthcare is quite an unconventional career path.
To be honest, I had no idea what I wanted to do and somehow stumbled upon the perfect jobs for my personality. I crave challenging conversations and having the freedom to come to my own conclusions. I am a bit rebellious, and HCA has offered me the ability to create my own path. I tell people to this day that I do not know what I want to be when I grow up, but I know the roles I do not want, which I think is a great start. (Laughs)

What brought you to HCA?
A dear high school friend made an introduction to HCA, and it has been the best fix-up I have had to date. The decision to apply at HCA led me to look at what else I wanted to do in my professional life. I love HR because it allows me to talk to people and try to understand their story in a 30-minute or hour-long window. After assessing their personality and background, I decide if they will fit the HCA culture, which is critical to our success.

What is your favorite thing about what you do?
The stories and people I get to meet. I love meeting all kinds of people. One woman I interviewed recently quit her big corporate job to become a truck driver. Another left her graphic design position to take on a role as a funeral director. Hearing those stories is what makes my job fun.

What do you want people to understand about the job interview process?
A résumé is similar to a striking profile picture. It will get you an interview. From that point forward, I seek substance. I have learned to go with my gut in terms of making decisions. I also pay close attention to body language, vernacular, and topics of conversation that people avoid. HCA has one giant culture, and every department has its own

I REALLY FEEL THAT MY ROLE AT HCA IS TO SEEK OUT FUTURE LEADERS FOR OUR ORGANIZATION.

ambiance, so I also take that into account. My process is different from your typical interview, which means there are no trick questions. I also do not put people on the spot. I talk to the applicants and try my best to get to know them in the limited time that we spend together. You can gain a great understanding of someone by just listening and observing their behavior.

What is the most important tool you use to assess a candidate?
I listen and take a huge step back to take in everything that person is saying. Then I look at all of the things that aren't talked about. Similar to social media, interviewees put forth everything they want you to see, but I am looking for authenticity. I love nothing more than when someone is vulnerable enough to say, "I probably shouldn't share this with you but I will." That allows me to get to the real him or her. I don't believe in trick questions but rather figuring out what led each person from one situation to the next. If I can figure out where they've been and where they want to go, then I can place them in the right spot.

How do you view work?
Even if I had a fountain of money I would still work. For one reason or another, I feel the need to prove that I can do anything I put my mind to. Self-education is my thing because if one book helps me to do better at my job then it's worth it. I also believe in hands-on learning because taking things at face value is not my style. If someone tells me the sky is blue, my answer will be, "Let me go check." I view my work as a source of continuous learning. Acquiring knowledge and being challenged is what keeps me motivated on a daily basis.

Why do you think you have a good read on people?
I enjoy getting to know people and taking my time to understand them. There are also certain experiences I've had at HCA that make me love this organization and therefore help me to choose the right candidates. Shortly after my father passed away, I volunteered with the Hurricane Harvey relief in Houston. I will remember my 29 fellow volunteers until I am 90 years old. The bonding experience was incredible. The HCA employees in Houston who had lost everything still came in to work every day. There were nurses who hadn't left the hospital in 13 days. Meeting people who just lost everything but still came in to work to care for our patients put things into perspective for me. Nothing seems to be that bad after experiencing a tragedy like Hurricane Harvey. Today I look for people who are willing to step up in the midst of a crisis. To survive another tragedy—knock on wood—we need people who want to do their part. Those moments exemplify this organization's passion and dedication.

From your perspective, how do you retain a culture that pays it forward?
I ask that question all of the time, specifically because I have eight- and four-year-old daughters who I want to become benevolent individuals. I really feel that my role at HCA is to seek out future leaders for our organization. I think, in a changing landscape, we retain that value system by instilling it in the next generation. I do a summer program for students every year in which they work at a variety of nonprofits. Oftentimes, they comment on what an eye-opening experience it was. Sometimes they will even go on to do more volunteer work beyond our program. That makes me feel as though the community is embracing HCA's philanthropic values and planting a small seed of giving back.

Why do you feel as though you are in the perfect position?
I love that my job offers me autonomy, work-life balance, and the ability to lead. I love finding the right jobs for the right people. Certain jobs take a specific kind of compassion that cannot be taught, and it's inspiring to meet those who have found what they see as their calling.

What should potential applicants know about HCA?
It's a company full of opportunities; however, to prove yourself here, you must work hard and be willing to stay in a position for quite some time before expecting a promotion. HCA is filled with successful people who, after working here for 25 years, are still driven and loyal to the organization. HCA's culture is one built around doing the right thing. We are a family.

What was your father's patient experience at TriStar Summit Medical Center and Centennial Heart?
In my eyes, everyone receives the same treatment that he did. My father was highly critical and not someone to mince words. One of his last requests was for me to write a letter about how exceptional the care was. My dad said, "I want every single person that I came into contact with at TriStar and Centennial Heart to know that they are the closest thing I've ever met to God." I thought he would criticize the staff and embarrass the fire out of me, but all he said was how compassionate they were. The medical staff was able to break through a wall with my father. That is exceptional care, which came about through listening, patience, and caring. To me, that spoke volumes.

Why have you stayed at HCA for a decade?
Everyone's job at HCA is connected to the patient. That purpose is what makes this place special. My reason for being here is to find people who are teachable, hard-working, and want to do the right thing.

What does the HCA mission mean to you?

In my eyes, the HCA mission underscores the exceptional, world-class healthcare that we deliver every single day. In many ways, our mission statement is my personal motto because I believe that actions speak louder than words.

GABRIEL O. PEREZ

{Director Application Development, *East Florida Division*}

Gabriel Perez doesn't take anything at face value. A developer by nature, Perez looks at a piece of paper and sees a paper plane. Every success in the Director of Application Development's life has occurred because of purpose, patience, and presence. When Perez studied computer science in his native Puerto Rico, he realized that he needed to move to the continental United States to absorb the latest and greatest knowledge. After a serious learning curve, during which he studied in his non-native language and absorbed a new culture, he obtained a degree in management information systems and computer science. From there, Perez carried on his family's legacy by asking, *How can I do my job better than those before?* While he has earned five patents during his 14-year HCA tenure, he also knows how to pace himself. The big-picture thinker believes in the perfect time and place to implement his initiatives in order to give them enterprise-wide impact. He pushes himself, as well as his team, to feel the power of the patient experience. HCA presents Perez with a problem and then provides him with enough space to find an innovative solution. Collective knowledge, collaboration, and a connection to his purpose are how he elevates healthcare IT.

How did your upbringing influence your character in the workplace?
I was born and raised in Puerto Rico. My mom is Catholic, which heavily influenced my mindset in terms of helping others. I was a very inquisitive child, obsessed with knowledge and asking, *Why are things like that?* My dad was an electrical engineer with whom I built my first computer at age 11. He and my mother encouraged me to look at the bigger picture and ask, *What else could it be?* They taught me that if the path doesn't exist then you create your own.

How did that mentality help you to flourish?
My mother and father both came from very humble, hardworking backgrounds and taught me that success was never going to just show up. I had to push myself forward and constantly create more opportunities. I attribute my love for figuring out what is behind a certain situation to them. Aside from that, I was very fortunate to have a high school friend who saw my potential. After he invited me to a computer programming competition one day, I was hooked. I loved the challenge of it. Before that, my school told me I should be a plastic surgeon. (Laughs)

What was your experience attending school and working while learning English?
It was an extreme challenge because, while I had studied English as a second language, I wasn't strong in my conversational skills. I had to not only learn computer science but a new culture and language as well. While I struggled internally and questioned myself constantly, I finally realized that I had to shift gears, move forward, and embrace my own learning style. By asking myself, *How can I adapt, do better, and conquer my industry?* I achieved my bachelor's degree in MIS and computer science. Much of the time, I had to learn on my own.

Where did you gain your footing before moving over to HCA?
While attending school, I began working for an IT consulting company who eventually hired me for their spinoff. I absolutely loved my work, which involved ethical hacking and computer investigations, because you never knew what you were going to do. I am not a fan of being told what to do but rather being assigned a challenge on which I can collaborate with others. That role prepared me for my current position at HCA.

Why do you find working with others to be the source of success?
We all have something to contribute, and the combination of different opinions and strengths means you, as a collective, are unstoppable. Like a key to a car, you fit the various grooves together to open a door. Lone rangers who want all of the credit tend to chip away at the success of a collective.

Combining expertise also takes the pressure off of the individual.
Great presidencies come about because of a leader and those who can steer their ideas into the right direction. Just because I'm a director doesn't mean everything I say is right. I respect my team's thoughts because you go so much farther together rather than just checking tasks off a list. In the development department, every innovation starts with a blank sheet of paper. We state the problem, figure out the solution, and fine-tune the process. Rinse and repeat.

How were you introduced to HCA?
After September 11, the government shut the door on many nongovernmental agencies with access to classified information. My

WE PUT TECHNOLOGY IN THE RIGHT HANDS AT THE PERFECT TIME AND PLACE TO SOLVE PROBLEMS.

company folded, and I was out of work for two years. Fortunately, my best friend's mom worked for HCA and suggested that I apply. HCA offered me a position as a tech analyst replacing keyboards, terminals, and fixing computers and printers. I didn't even know that healthcare IT existed at the time.

How did your job gain the purpose that it has today?
The day I became "healthcare-inspired" was when I noticed a sign in the hallway that said, "If you're not directly helping a patient, you are helping someone who is." In that moment, I realized that the printers and terminals I was replacing were a lifeline to each patient. I went from just fixing another paper jam to thinking of each action as a step to help a nurse, physician, or patient. That transition gave my experience in IT a dramatically different impact.

Did becoming present make your daily work much more meaningful?
Yes! And from that point forward, I would ask myself, *What else can I do to help?* That ideology gave birth to the first version of PATRA in 2004, which is a patient transport application I helped invent that logs where each patient is sent within the HCA system. Can you imagine the frustration of being sent to the wrong nursing home? After developing the application and seeing its success, I was inspired to develop more innovative solutions to help physicians and nurses do their jobs better. Another highly influential event was meeting with prior CIO Noel Williams and a number of other team members to consider how we could be more community oriented. On a white board, she drew a circle with a dot in the center and rings orbiting around it. She described the dot in the center as being the patient and the rings around it as the different roles at HCA. The purpose was to value the various roles in healthcare and make us think about how close our work was to helping the patient directly or indirectly.

How did that deepen your own purpose?
My own realization opened the door, and Noel's exercise kicked it open even wider. She helped me to understand that every person at HCA comes together to facilitate the ultimate purpose, which is to help the patient and their caregivers.

Did that experience unlock your creative doors?
Absolutely, and it also was instrumental in me bringing that same mentality to my team as well. Before my team and I began creating Care Assure, an initiative that allows us to detect potential health issues in a patient, I wanted my team to see the impact of this very complex project. I explained to them that by catching ailments, we could collectively save lives. Saving one life through software development is work worth doing and also instills a genuine appreciation.

What is so important about understanding the ripple effects of your work?
If we are all on the same page as far as the value of our job, then the brainstorming sessions become so much more fruitful. We move beyond the agenda to finding the absolute best approaches. Success is a result of collective knowledge.

Do you feel that HCA fosters bringing heart and soul to work?
Absolutely, which is the primary reason I have stayed here for 14 years. I am a developer by nature, which means that I like a challenge and a dynamic work environment. What fuels my brain is walking in and finding a new problem to work on. This organization allows and encourages my team and me to come up with innovative solutions. HCA is on the cutting edge of modern healthcare because we constantly ask, as an organization, how do we get there?

How do you know if an idea is worth pursuing?
We are smart and strategic about what initiatives we implement. The question we ask ourselves is, *Will this be valuable and can we deliver on our promises?* People, process, and technology compose the IT platform of HCA. We put technology in the right hands at the perfect time and place to solve problems.

How has the art of patience served you as a leader?
By coming to the realization that you cannot throw out the latest and greatest technology and expect it to work. Proper timing and pace is the secret to moving an initiative forward. Too much change too fast can hurt adoption from your intended audience.

What are you proudest of during your tenure at HCA?
I'm most proud of the success and positive impact of ER Wait Times and Care Assure and the role they had in inspiring others to innovate. I am honored to work for an organization that recognizes and appreciates its innovative employees. An example of this is the HCA Innovators Awards, which spotlight individuals, bring them forward, and invest in them so they continue to bring their own solutions to the table. HCA understands that in order to make the patient care the best that it can be, you have to value your people. It's amazing to have HCA acknowledge homegrown, locally developed solutions.

What does it feel like to be an example of innovation?
It further fuels my engine to pay my success forward. While HCA is a large organization, the leaders pay attention to the work that people are doing in the field. They see who is contributing, which makes you want to do even more.

What does the HCA mission mean to you?
HCA exemplifies the benefit of valuing your employees and contributing to overall patient care. The leaders look at the real HCA, which is the people, and encourage us to do what we can to save lives and value the patient as an individual. Hopefully those reading this book will aspire to be one of the next 50.

BEVERLY WALLACE

{President (retired), *Parallon*}

Beverly Wallace, former President of Shared Services and Parallon Business Solutions, spent her career jumping the kinds of hurdles that might intimidate others. Hard-wired into her personality is a flexible yet focused way of problem-solving. Growing up in a military family made Wallace open-minded and adaptable. She was excited by the fact that healthcare was always in motion and tended to have a similar melting-pot culture to the one she was raised in. During her 18 years with HCA, Wallace received the right tools, team, and support system to help Shared Services thrive. In between scaling revenue cycles, workforce management solutions, and health information management services, Wallace also became one of the first women in a senior management position. What she didn't realize at the time was that other women were watching. They admired her confident yet grounded demeanor and how she created a consistent HCA culture in various centers across the U.S. By pulling systems, revenue streams, and the right people together, Wallace renovated Shared Services. The healthcare industry has given her a purpose by allowing her to improve the way exceptional care is delivered.

What about healthcare and finance were the perfect marriage?
Accounting and healthcare were my two passions, and I knew that one needed the other in order to be successful. After that discovery, I never looked back.

How did you stay connected to your purpose at all times?
HCA's culture consistently brings your focus and attachment toward the patient, which is our number-one priority. HCA tries to seek out people with that same passion.

What drew you to improving the lives of others through healthcare?
The first time that I did volunteer work in a pediatric cancer unit, I was inspired by the spunk of the patients. They had an inspiring desire to live. I wanted to be a part of their experience. If you are someone who loves people, there is nothing more rewarding than helping someone who is vulnerable and sick. This industry is a part of who I am.

Why do so many leaders spend their entire career at HCA?
HCA creates loyalty through the mission and culture. When people become attached to an organization and their role within it, they want to stay. From day one, I saw the opportunity to grow within the framework of HCA because of how much they supported me. If you hire a team who cares deeply about the welfare of others and surround them with positivity, you will have long-term tenures.

How did the current organization of Shared Services come about?
Before we took this on in the late '90s, no one in the hospital industry had ever effectively created a way to share administrative and business services. We thought that if we created the infrastructure to streamline purchasing, distribution, billing, and collections functions, we could run the organization more efficiently and give our hospitals the ability to fully focus their local resources on patient care. It was a big change for the company and took a lot of communication and planning to consolidate those functions, and in the end, it was worth it. Through Shared Services, we really leverage our scale, expertise, and collective experience.

What is the philosophy of the Shared Services department?
We are "the first, the last, and the right impression" for the patient, and that is an important foundation for our service culture.

What was the secret to making such a massive transition?
As always, within this organization we had the right leaders and team. Jack Bovender, who was CEO at the time, was massively passionate about Shared Services. He instilled in me the confidence to sell the idea to our employees. Some people didn't want to get on

CHRISTINA HUX, RN
{Direct Care Nurse, *Tulane University Hospital and Clinic*}

Christina Hux is the woman on the cover of Leave No One Behind, the nonfiction book that chronicles Hurricane Katrina and the rescue of Tulane Hospital. The image of a distressed nurse carrying a child in her arms has become a symbol of the catastrophic event. Hux, who started and intends to finish her career at Tulane, has a sweet, childlike presence that makes her a perfect fit for pediatrics. Born and raised in New Orleans by a mother who operated a nursery right out of their home, Hux was always drawn to children. As a teenaged babysitter, she recognized her talent for putting this age group at ease. Once she graduated from nursing school in 2003, it was clear to Hux that pediatrics was her domain. There, she could bring into play her youthful personality and compassion. As someone who craves stability for herself, minimizing patients' stress through hugs, smiles, or a simple touch is second nature. Loyal to her practice and the families that she encounters, Hux has used her compassion to help others overcome tragedy.

What is it like to be a pediatric nurse?
There is tragedy, which are the days when you don't want to come back, and lots of successes where you see your kids get better. We get close to the children and their families, which can take an emotional toll when they leave. Dealing with a diversity of age ranges makes my work interesting. Seeing kids hurt is definitely the hardest part.

Do nurses have a special relationship with patients?
We are at the bedside and more hands-on than the physicians, so we do get to know their personalities on a deeper level. I think nurses become more attached. As a mom, it is easy for me to understand children, yet I am also extremely sensitive to their pain. It is especially tough when I have to care for someone who is my daughter's age because you can't help but think, *That could be my kid*. Yet I also fight for them that much harder because I can imagine how the parents must feel.

How do you develop bonds with your patients?
What patients really want is someone to console them. We also try to lift the spirits of parents who have to watch their children cry or scream in pain. I try to do what I can to make the situation better. Understanding where children are coming from is critical. I am constantly asking myself, *What are they seeing or feeling right now?*

Do you think children can sense your compassion?
Absolutely. When you are in a stressful situation, you need someone who can calm it down. We don't want to stick these poor kids with needles or see them in pain. If we can let them know that we have their best interests at heart, then the outcome will always be better. Interestingly enough, there are a lot of similarities between geriatrics and children, which is why we treat them similarly. Older people have a harder time articulating their feelings and have less of a filter.

When was the first time you felt like a nurse?
I still remember being brand new in my unit and finding it odd that the team was so cheerful when we were surrounded by calamity. Slowly, I realized that you have to be positive in order to give the patients hope. Without that, they have nothing. Our job is to give them a happy environment to heal in.

How does optimism promote optimal health?
You have to fight and strive to survive whatever illness you have been given. Without willpower you end up going down. Like anything in life, you have to work for your health, and it must be worth it to you. My special needs nephew, who I took care of from birth, passed away three months ago. From the day he was born, his prognosis was always dismal. If he weren't going to die from one thing, it would be another. I believe that because of our hope he made it to ten years of age. We were privileged to have him with our family for a decade.

How has your profession shaped your perspective on life?
The scariest thing in the world is to lose someone's child on your watch, which is why I am a glass-half-full person. I always think, *We can get past that*. Things can always be so much worse. I feel fortunate to see the worst things in life. However, I try not to judge others if they are petty or uptight, because they don't see what I do every day. That is why there are different fields for everyone. This job has made me a better person and mom.

Does your work make it easier to accept death?
No, but it has made me stronger. I know how to deal with it a bit better. I watched a few young nurses recently experience their first death and felt like I was looking in a mirror. Sometimes I wish I was in a bubble and didn't see half of the things that I do. But I learn

HCA IS AN ORGANIZATION IN WHICH YOU CAN GET THINGS DONE AND DO THEM RIGHT.

the "northbound train" at the time, but today, most admit that they wouldn't go back. Still, we hit stumbling blocks throughout the four-year migration period. Change is a lot for some people, whereas it energizes me.

Do you think creating the right environment is critical to success?
Absolutely. Individual temperament is internal yet also influenced externally. HCA has the best operators in the industry because of our environment. This is an organization in which you can get things done and do them right.

How much did mentorship play into your HCA tenure?
Mentorship has been more formalized in recent years; however, I always tried to observe the coworkers and leaders that I admired. I focused on the way they viewed issues, processed problems, managed, and made decisions. From there, I tried to bring my own personality to the table. A lot of younger women asked me over the years how I progressed into a management role. Regardless of their position, I would mentor them because I feel that support is critical to building your legacy. Mentorship feels natural at HCA because everyone is so close.

What is one piece of advice you continuously gave to others?
Learn through your eyes and keep them open 24/7. You will witness some things you don't admire but far more you do. In the end, you'll be a better person.

Did you ever face and overcome a challenge in your HCA tenure?
When we were building Shared Services, we also decided to rebuild our receivable system. Through hiring outside firms and partnering with IT, we built a brand-new system. One year into it and $120 million dollars later, I realized that we couldn't find the right external people to do the programming and train our internal people. The system was very complex. Finally, I approached Noel [Williams, former IT&S President] and said, "Let's shut it down." Together we told the leadership team, which felt like a huge failure and financial loss. However, they respected us for our honesty and knowing when it was time to call it quits. That speaks volumes to HCA and was an invaluable learning experience.

What was it like to be at the helm of Parallon prior to your retirement?
After building a roster of business services, the question was asked, *Why not sell them?* From there, we grouped our services together (under Parallon) to offer them to others in the marketplace. I am ecstatic that the business is alive and serving HCA and its external clients with top industry performance.

How do you educate others about an entirely new way of doing things?
You rely upon a refined sales program to explain your actions. What I didn't anticipate in terms of Shared Services was that employees were nervous about moving to a different facility and losing the HCA culture. To reassure them, I stayed on the road and traveled to our various centers to maintain that one-on-one contact. Over time, they saw that nothing had changed other than legalities.

Why do you feel face-to-face conversation is so critical?
Being able to look into someone's eyes and read their body language creates a bond. Today, social skills are a bit of a lost art form. A lot of people struggle to make that one-on-one connection. I would choose to visit our facilities any day in order to give that personal touch. Sensing someone's energy is critical to establishing trust in your leaders and maintaining culture across an organization.

Do you think that bond increases attachment to the organization?
Absolutely. When I worked at corporate, I would walk around every day and chat with my colleagues. People need a reason to stay engaged. My job was to motivate our team so they felt rewarded for their contributions.

What does the HCA mission mean to you?
HCA's culture is built upon a feeling of being a part of something bigger than you. Everyone is looking towards the same goal, which is to care for other human beings. Our organization's foundation began with the Frist family and continues because of the leadership. The mission and values keep us true to our core. Everyone feels a sense of ownership and connection to HCA.

CHRISTINA HUX, RN
{Direct Care Nurse, *Tulane University Hospital and Clinic*}

Christina Hux is the woman on the cover of *Leave No One Behind,* the nonfiction book that chronicles Hurricane Katrina and the rescue of Tulane Hospital. The image of a distressed nurse carrying a child in her arms has become a symbol of the catastrophic event. Hux, who started and intends to finish her career at Tulane, has a sweet, childlike presence that makes her a perfect fit for pediatrics. Born and raised in New Orleans by a mother who operated a nursery right out of their home, Hux was always drawn to children. As a teenaged babysitter, she recognized her talent for putting this age group at ease. Once she graduated from nursing school in 2003, it was clear to Hux that pediatrics was her domain. There, she could bring into play her youthful personality and compassion. As someone who craves stability for herself, minimizing patients' stress through hugs, smiles, or a simple touch is second nature. Loyal to her practice and the families that she encounters, Hux has used her compassion to help others overcome tragedy.

What is it like to be a pediatric nurse?
There is tragedy, which are the days when you don't want to come back, and lots of successes where you see your kids get better. We get close to the children and their families, which can take an emotional toll when they leave. Dealing with a diversity of age ranges makes my work interesting. Seeing kids hurt is definitely the hardest part.

Do nurses have a special relationship with patients?
We are at the bedside and more hands-on than the physicians, so we do get to know their personalities on a deeper level. I think nurses become more attached. As a mom, it is easy for me to understand children, yet I am also extremely sensitive to their pain. It is especially tough when I have to care for someone who is my daughter's age because you can't help but think, *That could be my kid.* Yet I also fight for them that much harder because I can imagine how the parents must feel.

How do you develop bonds with your patients?
What patients really want is someone to console them. We also try to lift the spirits of parents who have to watch their children cry or scream in pain. I try to do what I can to make the situation better. Understanding where children are coming from is critical. I am constantly asking myself, *What are they seeing or feeling right now?*

Do you think children can sense your compassion?
Absolutely. When you are in a stressful situation, you need someone who can calm it down. We don't want to stick these poor kids with needles or see them in pain. If we can let them know that we have their best interests at heart, then the outcome will always be better. Interestingly enough, there are a lot of similarities between geriatrics and children, which is why we treat them similarly. Older people have a harder time articulating their feelings and have less of a filter.

When was the first time you felt like a nurse?
I still remember being brand new in my unit and finding it odd that the team was so cheerful when we were surrounded by calamity. Slowly, I realized that you have to be positive in order to give the patients hope. Without that, they have nothing. Our job is to give them a happy environment to heal in.

How does optimism promote optimal health?
You have to fight and strive to survive whatever illness you have been given. Without willpower you end up going down. Like anything in life, you have to work for your health, and it must be worth it to you. My special needs nephew, who I took care of from birth, passed away three months ago. From the day he was born, his prognosis was always dismal. If he weren't going to die from one thing, it would be another. I believe that because of our hope he made it to ten years of age. We were privileged to have him with our family for a decade.

How has your profession shaped your perspective on life?
The scariest thing in the world is to lose someone's child on your watch, which is why I am a glass-half-full person. I always think, *We can get past that.* Things can always be so much worse. I feel fortunate to see the worst things in life. However, I try not to judge others if they are petty or uptight, because they don't see what I do every day. That is why there are different fields for everyone. This job has made me a better person and mom.

Does your work make it easier to accept death?
No, but it has made me stronger. I know how to deal with it a bit better. I watched a few young nurses recently experience their first death and felt like I was looking in a mirror. Sometimes I wish I was in a bubble and didn't see half of the things that I do. But I learn

from every experience, which allows me to better empathize with others. All you can do is remain aware of how you are affected.

How do you care for yourself while caring for others?
I had some back trouble about a year ago; it was a wake-up call that I had to take care of myself. That was the moment that I realized I am not indestructible and must find time for myself. If you don't take care of yourself, then you can't take care of others. I am trying to get better at prioritizing myself.

What was it like to be a nurse during Hurricane Katrina?
I was born and raised in New Orleans and grew up having hurricane parties. Of course, Katrina was a lot scarier than usual because my hometown was entirely under water. I remember thinking, *This is real and not just a rainstorm passing by*. We had babies on breathing machines that we had to manually operate, and we almost ran out of medication at one point. I didn't know where my family was because there was no way to communicate. When they started setting up evacuations, I had no idea where I was going. The photo on the cover of *Leave No One Behind* was taken in Alexandria, Louisiana, where the staff was so welcoming and willing to do anything they could to assist. That was the moment I realized how caring of an organization HCA is.

How did you put aside your own emotions to step into action?
At Tulane, there was a heart transplant patient whose machine was being manually operated. When I would get scared, I would think about that teenager and how he must have felt. If he could get through it, then I could too.

What did it feel like to see your face all over CNN and on a book cover?
I felt a little guilty because lot of my coworkers went through much worse trauma than I did. I did what I could to encourage the media to document their stories. I think the photo is so powerful because I am holding a baby and look distressed. What I felt most honored by was when HCA's Jack Bovender, the CEO at the time, came down to New Orleans just to shake my hand. I felt like a genuine, valuable part of this massive organization.

Was it scary and surreal to watch your hometown be destroyed?
All that goes on in your head is, *How can this be happening?* I am not easily frightened, but it was terrifying to think that you could lose everything in an instant. At the same time, things could always be so much worse. One of my coworkers lost her mom in the storm, and others experienced more devastation than me.

What has it been like to spend your life caring for others?
I used to see a phrase around Tulane that said, "Wherever you are, wherever you'll be, you will always be important because you played a role in a child's life." If I was able to help a child and their family, even just a little bit, then I know that I did my job. That is what brings me back and keeps me going.

Do you have any advice for other nurses?
Think of someone who is true to you whether that's your child or grandmother. Then see the patient as that person. You would want your relative to receive the best possible care. Sometimes you click with a patient and other times you don't; however, that all gets put to the side. A nurse should give 150 percent.

UNDERSTANDING WHERE CHILDREN ARE COMING FROM IS CRITICAL. I AM CONSTANTLY ASKING MYSELF, *WHAT ARE THEY SEEING OR FEELING RIGHT NOW?*

Is there any accomplishment you are proudest of?
Being a part of my nephew's healthcare. I had to combine being a nurse with being his aunt, which was tough because I couldn't allow my emotions to blindside me. Remaining clear and focused was a challenge, but I am so happy that I was there.

Could you describe the teamwork that exists in the nursing field?
You never throw your coworker under the bus. We all support one another and try to bring out the best in one another's personalities. To give the best care, nurses must be a united front. Our job is intense, and therefore we have a special bond. When you deal with horrific situations that are deeply upsetting, you grow a lot closer. We are there to soothe and connect with patients on a personal level, which only comes from real conversations.

Do you have any hobbies outside of nursing?
I grew up dancing, which I believe is why I am a determined, disciplined person. Dancing taught me to be a fighter and never give up. Despite having short legs, I have continued to dance my entire life. Having the odds stacked against me is why I appreciate my successes more. I would call myself a survivor.

What does the HCA mission mean to you?
Our ultimate goal is to provide the best patient care. Every company standard comes from the corporate level because they set the standard. I love that HCA encourages growth and allows people to transfer between different facilities. The organization is safe, secure, and supportive, both emotionally and financially. They know how to show their employees respect, which creates loyalty towards the organization. I, like many of my coworkers, feel valued here.

MARCUS THOMAS

{EVS Supervisor, *Sunrise Hospital and Medical Center*}

Marcus Thomas, Environmental Services Supervisor at Sunrise Medical Center, has become a legend at the Las Vegas facility over the 17 years he's worked there. Walking down the hospital's hallway, Thomas is similar to the town mayor: everyone who crosses his path receives a handshake, smile, or hug. His contentment comes from giving others a lift when they are down and out. Thomas's humility and compassion stem from growing up in less-than-ideal circumstances on Chicago's South Side. Now, during his graveyard shifts, the supervisor aims to bring a sense of control to what can be a chaotic environment. In a world where the unexpected too often happens, a hospital in tip-top shape can be reassuring to patients. When Sunrise treated hundreds of victims of the 2017 Las Vegas mass shooting, Thomas calmly and efficiently guided his team to keep the facility clean through a fast-paced, tough situation. He exudes gratitude for HCA as an organization that has always encouraged him to exercise his natural leadership skills. His story is proof that housekeeping is a crucial part of every hospital's team.

How did you end up at Sunrise Medical Center?
I moved from Chicago to Las Vegas in 2001 to take care of my auntie who was sick at the time. That summer, I filled out a job application at Sunrise Hospital and have been here ever since. All my life I wanted to work at a hospital.

Why do you value making others feel good?
I am an outgoing guy who loves learning from my fellow man through talking. I believe that I am respected at Sunrise because I don't try to act like anyone but me. I would give my coworkers my last dime if they needed it.

Why do you see everyone the same?
I realized as a child that a few members of my own family were racist. One day my uncle took me out on his paper route, which was the first time I had ever been around white people. They treated me so well that I went home and told my grandmother that she was wrong. Ever since, I've always treated people the way I want to be treated. That technique still works and maintains my morale.

How would you describe what you do in your own words?
When I first started here, I had to go around the whole roller coaster ride, which meant doing everything from biohazard duties to replenishing linens. My current duties as a supervisor are to make sure everyone is in the right spot, checkouts are done on time, and the hospital is clean from the time I arrive to when I clock out. That means every inch because I don't play around. (Laughs) I am known around Sunrise as the guy who notices every speck of dust on the carpet.

What did it feel like to have someone see your leadership skills?
My manager's support made me feel amazing, and once I had that confidence, all I wanted to do was give it to the next person. They noticed that I was taking the initiative to improve my department and therefore helped me to get further than I was before. I thank them for believing in me because, by God, I've been able to make progress ever since. If the entire world tried to uplift one another instead of put each other down, we wouldn't have as many problems. If others want to see me sad, I give them a handshake and a smile versus that satisfaction.

How do you feel about the Las Vegas mass shooting?
It was the first of its kind and an overwhelming experience. I had to gather my strength, team, and leadership skills to assist the medical team however they needed. When I returned home, I shed a few tears and hugged my girlfriend, two teenagers, and three-year-old daughter. Life is precious and no one should ever have to experience what our patients did that day.

Despite your hospital's disaster drills, how do you react in the moment?
The reason I want to retire at Sunrise is because our team feels like a family. Vegas is a perfect instance in which we came together stronger than before. Our communication has also improved tremendously because we want to be solid if anything like that were to ever happen again. And I pray that it doesn't.

How do you get over your fears in order to be fearless?
I am human just like everyone else, but when it's time to take care of business, that's what we're focusing on. Emotionally I am strong just like my father. Before he passed away he told me, "One day, son, you might change the world." Those words meant nothing until last year. As I get older and see the reality of life more clearly, my fears have started to die out bit by bit.

THE REASON I WANT TO RETIRE AT SUNRISE IS BECAUSE OUR TEAM FEELS LIKE A FAMILY.

Why do you think you are a natural leader?
I have always felt a great sense of responsibility for others. I am the person who thinks to buy life insurance for my family members. If the hammer were to come down, I want to be mentally prepared. At work, I am always the one who organizes potlucks or secret Santas because I think we should still have fun from time to time. Looking after others can be exhausting, but it is who I am.

Do you think your coworkers appreciate this?
Yes. I can tell when something is wrong with my employees, and I always make it known that they can talk to me at any point in time. Nine times out of ten they will. They know that I will help them to solve their problems—even if they can't fix mine. (Laughs) Being good with people is my gift and one I'm grateful for.

What is it like working the graveyard shift?
I love making a good impression on my superiors. When they walk into their office, I want them to think, *I can eat food off this floor*. Being depended on to get the job done is a really good feeling and one I don't take lightly.

What do you think is so comforting about a tidy environment?
When I was coming up in the Robert Taylor projects on Chicago's South Side, there were many days where we didn't know if we could eat. When I finally earned enough money to rent my own place, I absolutely loved coming home to a spick-and-span, good-smelling apartment. Cleanliness is the only way.

Could you speak to the importance of communication in your job?
What I tell my team is that you can fall out without communication. It's best to talk your issues through. Some of the nurses, I had never talked to before the Vegas incident, and now we chat all of the time. The ability to talk openly and honestly keeps us from being caught off-guard during catastrophic events. The night of the shooting, people were coming in so rapidly that it felt like a drive thru. The whole ER was packed with patients and family members who were concerned about their loved ones. That night was both unreal and beyond real, yet because of strong communication skills, we were in the clear.

How did that experience change your perspective on life?
Be humble and take nothing for granted. We have no idea what can happen from one second to the next. Ever since that experience, I've had a greater desire to learn from my fellow brothers and sisters. If they like politics, that's what we'll talk about. If history is their interest, then let's jump on that train. Through learning about their lives, I gain a better understanding of my own. I'm no better than you and you're no better than me, which is why I always try to look at the individual. By not feeding into stereotypes, I have made some of my very best friends.

How did that experience change your perspective on your work?
Historically, Environmental Services may have been looked at as the bottom of the totem pole. Today, I tell my team we are number one. Without a clean hospital, no doctor or nurse can do his or her work. I think the hospital staff realizes this as well.

How would you like to touch the healthcare industry?
I hope that I can touch others simply by being myself. Let me give you a scenario. One day a patient kept complaining that her room had not been cleaned. Even though I knew it had, I finally knocked on her door. She was lonely and wanted acknowledgment. Patient satisfaction is most important. Through word of mouth, eventually the entire community knows that they will be taken care of at Sunrise—from the cleaning crew to the physicians.

What advice would you give to others?
As long as you recognize your own beauty, then nothing else matters. I've given this advice to everyone from a coworker who opened up to me recently about her domestic violence situation to a quadriplegic patient who my girlfriend cares for at another hospital. I love uplifting people. No one should ever take your pride.

Do you feel like the more good you give the more comes back?
Absolutely. Many of my blessings have come after situations in which I did something kind for someone else. Perhaps I found money on the floor or someone took care of my restaurant bill. The reward may have varied, yet it was all related to karma. If we could all keep that in mind, there might be peace.

How would you describe the culture at Sunrise Medical Center?
Everyone who works here is on the right page. Our number-one goal is patient satisfaction, which my team does by ensuring cleanliness, comfort, and safety. The patient should feel as if they are in their own home.

How has HCA helped to facilitate your personal and professional growth?
HCA gives everyone a chance and meets you halfway there. You can easily go after the big goals because they will support you however possible, whether it's through a flexible work schedule or daycare services. I work at the best hospital in the world, hands down. In return, I hope the entire Sunrise team knows that as long as I'm breathing this place will be spotless. I promise you that.

MARY GREER

{IT&S Voice Services Supervisor, *HCA Healthcare*}

Mary Greer, IT&S Voice Services Supervisor and unofficial historian, has worked for HCA from the beginning. While Greer loves to look at how far the company has come, she never dreamed she'd be sitting here 50 years later. Greer, who went straight from high school to working in clinics, still remembers hiring day. She was determined to make sure no one took her slot as an insurance clerk at Park View Hospital. The Nashville native, whose father was employed by an auto dealership and whose mother worked in a restaurant and grocery store chain, knows the smallest details about HCA. Greer has experienced a great deal of firsts with the company, from flying on airplanes to meeting movie stars. Yet she is most grateful for the moral compass that HCA has instilled in her. Greer believes everything positive in her life is a product of the people of HCA. She wouldn't have it any other way.

How were you first introduced to HCA?
After high school, I worked as an outpatient clinic coordinator at General Hospital and became acquainted with the Chairman of the Board, Dr. Thomas F. Frist, Sr. Immediately I embraced his compassionate philosophy of putting the patient first. When I heard Dr. Frist and his partners were building Park View Hospital, I knew that I wanted to work there. Initially hired as secretary to the administrator, I was fortunate to see HCA become a reality from the very first planning sessions.

What was it like working at Park View Hospital from day one?
It was amazing to work with a team who helped build the private hospital which would later serve as the pilot for HCA. As I told the Drs. Frist and Mr. Jack Massey, "I knew HCA was going to be something special." Even when we didn't know what would happen, my intuition said to stick with the company. Looking back, it is clear that the caliber of leadership was a critical factor to HCA's success then and now.

What is it about healthcare that you love?
The fact that the corporate culture has remained consistent as it has grown from the original 11 hospitals to an international giant. There is an equal respect for the patient and the employee. As Dr. Frist, Sr. always said, "Give the highest quality healthcare possible at the most affordable prices."

What do you like best about being a connector?
I am privy to the overall picture of HCA's progress. I get to interact with every hospital, help patients, insurance companies, and all genres of healthcare to negotiate the system. It's exciting to meet new employees and see what departments are expanding. I love having the best seat in the house, which is to view the overall picture of what is happening at HCA at all times.

In what ways do others rely upon your role?
Our response is always, "Yes, sir or ma'am, we can take care of that!" Our job is to get them where they need to go. Doctors, nurses, and employees call for information and guidance in a variety of situations. When that phone rings, the most important thing is to get your mind in gear to process the information quickly and take care of whatever that person needs. It is critical that we are fast on our feet.

Where does your caregiver nature come from?
I just love HCA as a company as well as its community, which I consider my family. I am enthused when I come here every day and so grateful for the opportunity to constantly be inspired.

Why do you think people succeed so swiftly and gracefully at HCA?
HCA places trust and confidence into each employee, allowing individuals to grow to their greatest potential. You will definitely succeed if you do your job well and honor the high ethical and moral standards intrinsic to our company. Next, they surround every employee with mentors, which is why the sky is the limit to advance within the company. You always feel nurtured. Even when someone has occasionally left, they always regret their decision and say, "They don't treat their employees the same as HCA does." I tell my own story of a girl right out of high school with a few business course credits who was given the opportunity to learn, grow, and contribute. Here I am today, 50 years later, honored to be recognized as a member of this great team.

Tell me more about your HCA family.
I still have friends who I met 50 years ago whom I see almost every week. We've gone through everything together. In 2005, I decided to get some original HCA employees together for dinner, and 256 people showed up. After arriving, they never moved from the front door. Everyone was hugging, crying, and talking. Who does that except for people with very fond memories of their time together at HCA? It was a remarkable experience that represents our devotion to HCA.

Do you think, at age 78, your passion for this company keeps you young?
Absolutely. My passion for this company and exercise keeps me energized and enthusiastic to come to work every day. Working at HCA is a great incentive to live a healthy lifestyle. I also try to find the humor in situations. Even if someone is rushing you or being ugly, I don't take it personally. I try to take him or her seriously and communicate in as kind a way as possible.

AS I TOLD THE DRS. FRIST AND MR. JACK MASSEY, "I KNEW HCA WAS GOING TO BE SOMETHING SPECIAL."

How do you continue to create, grow, and learn within your role?
I cross-reference every day between different departments and buildings. Trust me, my job is a lot more complex now than it was back then. (Laughs) Since we have so many divisions, I'm similar to an investigator trying to make all the puzzle pieces fit together as speedily as possible.

What is something you would tell new hires about HCA?
For a girl who has a high school diploma and some college credits and who booked airline tickets to Saudi Arabia when I couldn't even spell the name of the country—this company gave me the opportunity to grow with it. HCA puts confidence into everyone they hire. As long as you do your job well and follow the moral standards, you will succeed at this company.

What have you learned at HCA that helped you in your life outside of work?
Because of the philanthropic example set by HCA's management leadership, I learned the importance of giving back through United Way and the HCA Hope Fund. I tried to instill in my sons, Tyler and Chad, this concept of sharing, and now they both have their own volunteer commitments. I am sure they would tell you I continually preached to them what I saw played out by both the Drs. Frist.

Can you give me an example of the moral compass HCA demonstrates?
Dr. Frist, Sr. lived by the theory that you should never judge anyone else, because you don't know how you'd act in that same situation. He was always ready to give people a second chance. That stayed with me when I would start to judge.

What is your favorite thing about HCA?
I love the people here and the happy environment. It's been an honor to see the main objective of Dr. Frist, Sr. come true, which was to leave the world a better place than he found it. My favorite memories are of the picnics at his home where we played ping-pong, went on pony rides, and hit golf balls. You can't find that closeness at any other company. Since 1968, HCA has created a positive environment for workers and patients. While the company and industry have changed dramatically, our core mission and commitment to quality is the same.

What does HCA's mission mean to you?
Over 50 years, it's been incredible to see the many spinoffs formed by employees who got their start, knowledge, and education at HCA. HCA continues its goal of delivering the highest quality healthcare while building better communities. I am so grateful to this company. I hope to alleviate stress and make the tough times easier for patients, their loved ones, and my HCA family.

DR. THOMAS FRIST, JR.

{Co-founder, *HCA Healthcare*}

A true legacy comes from devoting your life to others. By taking the focus away from himself, Dr. Thomas "Tommy" Frist, Jr.—creative thinker, giver, and goal setter, has created an organization that provides top-quality healthcare to millions of patients. For 50 years he has nurtured HCA from a single hospital to a multidisciplinary healthcare company by following the guiding principle often stated by Thomas Frist, Sr.: "Good people beget good people." That philosophy remains the same despite the diversity and complexity of the industry. The physician, philanthropist, and entrepreneur understands that encouraging others is the secret to a company's success. His openness to taking risks has sparked innovation at HCA. Frist had the idea of merging his passion for healthcare with a hotel chain business model. Through this out-of-the-box thinking, HCA was born. He saw it as the ultimate opportunity to use his talents, medical degree, and business instincts. Frist's innovation combined his three passions of healthcare, business, and aviation into one spectacular career. He credits his parents for his strong sense of ethics and family values, both of which are reflected in the culture of HCA. He attributes HCA's success to his father, the heart and soul of the company, and Jack Massey, whose belief in him made it all possible. Since 1968, HCA's secret edge has come from its deep company culture, a devotion to putting patient care and human connection at the forefront of every endeavor. The right environment, resources, and values allow team members to be their best. Yet while Frist's career has been remarkable, his quiet philanthropic work provides his deepest satisfaction.

What has it been like to be Dr. Thomas "Tommy" Frist, Jr.?
My life has been good—no, great. I will be 80 years old this August. If I could change places with one of my grandchildren, I would not. I would be afraid it would not turn out as great the next time around.

How did your upbringing influence your demeanor in the workplace?
I was blessed to have two great parents who devoted their entire lives to helping others. I could not have had better role models. From my earliest memories, I remember them as a caring, compassionate team. They influenced me tremendously by giving others joy. They would always put the needs of others before their own. And they would do so with grace and humility.

When did you know that you wanted to study medicine?
It never occurred to me to do anything other than be a physician. From early childhood I wanted to be a doctor like my father. He loved his patients and their families. He enjoyed his association with other physicians, nurses, and especially the hospital employees.

What did it feel like to stumble upon your dream career?
To find HCA was a dream come true. It enabled me to combine my love for medicine with a strong interest in business and a passion for aviation. All three provided me a long, happy career. Having said that, I must admit that changing my healthcare career caused me to have a healthy dose of anxiety. The success of HCA was far from assured. I still keep my medical license up to date just in case things at HCA don't go so well. (Laughs) While there was a lot of nervousness in regards to not pursuing a path of becoming an open-heart surgeon, the rewards were such that I took the risk and never looked back. For me, HCA was always a lifetime commitment.

Making a commitment of that size and scale is a lot of responsibility.
Everything is relative. With 13 hospitals, HCA's reported earnings in 1969 were $3,400,000. That seemed like a lot back then, but in hindsight it was quite small. Not only has HCA made quantum gains in size over the past five decades, it has increased even more in the complexity and quality of care we can provide to our patients.

Some folks I've interviewed said they knew HCA was going to be big. Did you?

No! While I always knew HCA had vast potential, no one could possibly have foreseen what it has become. I was 29 years old when we founded HCA. After a two- to three-year start-up survival stage, we transitioned to a growth phase in which we set a goal to have 100 hospitals within 10 years. However, we always had a commitment to quality before quantity. Fortunately, HCA achieved both.

What about your partnership with your father and Mr. Massey was successful?

The right people came together at the right place and right time. My father, Dr. Thomas Frist, Sr., was a prominent cardiologist who was active on local, state, and federal committees addressing healthcare issues. Jack C. Massey was owner and operator for over 30 years of Massey Surgical Supply before buying and successfully operating KFC. And I was a 28-year-old United States Air Force flight surgeon whose surgical residency had been interrupted by the Vietnam War. All three of us lived in Nashville, Tennessee, located in the fast-growing southeastern United States.

We came together with a common vision for a multi-hospital company that would address the rapidly growing needs for modern new hospitals in the Sun Belt states. We saw the opportunity to apply tools and technology used in other sectors of the economy that would improve efficiency and patient care. And all three of us brought different strengths to the new company.

My father brought his reputation and wide-spread contacts within the medical community. He also was key to our acquiring our first hospital, Park View Hospital, which he, along with several other physicians, had designed, built, and operated in the 1960s.

Even more important than Jack Massey's friendships and connections with many physicians and hospital administrators was how he was recognized as one of the top entrepreneurs in the United States. His success with growing and taking KFC (then known as Kentucky Fried Chicken) public was legendary within the U.S. capital markets.

My contributions were being a young, energetic, goal-oriented physician with an idea for addressing a rapidly growing societal need for more innovation and capacity within the hospital sector of healthcare. While I was the only one of the founders who would actually be on the payroll at HCA, I truly can say there would be no HCA today if Dr. Thomas Frist, Sr. and Jack C. Massey had not given so unselfishly of their time and energy.

What is the greatest lesson your father and mother taught you?

That would be my core values. These are the basis for the beliefs we have passed down from generation to generation at HCA. They include such important beliefs as trust, integrity, caring, hard work, going the extra mile, and putting the needs of other people before yourself. These along with other beliefs were learned at home. I attribute all of my success to my parents.

Why did you decide to run your business with a family mentality?

I simply wanted my fellow employees to know how much I value and appreciate their many contributions. As a healthcare company, we believe a humanistic approach to management is more likely to be successful over the long term. We do not manufacture a product but rather deliver a service.

What about that environment helps people thrive?

It's a nice feeling for HCA employees to know at the end of the day that they are part of making the world a better place for others. At HCA, we try to be equally sensitive to our patients, the families of patients, and our employees. Living and breathing the mission brings us back to who we are and what we're about in this corporate family we call HCA.

What drives you most in life?

After my family, it is finding ways to make the world a better place for others.

How has the city of Nashville bolstered your success?

Nashville is a wonderful city. It is located in the Sun Belt with two-thirds of the U.S. population within a 600-mile radius. It has excellent intrastate highways as well as airline, river, and rail connections. With two medical schools and numerous universities, it has enabled HCA to attract and retain a highly motivated, highly educated workforce. Importantly, Nashville has built a metropolitan government that, with fair taxation and appropriate regulation, has understood the merits of public-private partnerships. A favorable labor and government market along with access to a supportive financial community were certainly contributors to HCA's success. In a labor-intensive, capital-intensive, and government-regulated industry, it is hard to beat Nashville for its corporate offices.

FOR ME, HCA WAS ALWAYS A LIFETIME COMMITMENT.

How did you know someone was capable of a leadership role?

One of the hallmarks of this company is that we've had the stability, strength, and success to develop leaders from within. The risks are less and rewards are far greater. When you work with people day in and out, you learn their strengths and weaknesses, you see how they perform in a variety of situations, and you make sure they share your company's values. At the core of HCA's success in development of leaders is the oft-quoted truism "Good people beget good people."

Why do you think HCA has such a strong company culture?

Everything begins at the top. It's very important that our leaders translate the mission statement through their actions. They must lead by example. The recent way our physicians and employees so heroically responded to Hurricanes Harvey and Irma or the Las Vegas tragedy are good examples of the best of HCA.

Why is a philanthropic mentality so important at HCA?

My belief is that HCA has been given the right to serve the public. Only if we are good corporate citizens will we maintain that privilege. One of the most effective ways HCA can make significant contributions to the community we serve is to make, encourage, and support its greatest asset, its employees, to become involved in meaningful philanthropic and civic activities. A give-back mindset is an important contribution to the remarkable HCA success story.

Why do you have the ability to always find another way?

I like to think I have an innate entrepreneurial spirit. A key part of that spirit is to have dreams and a discipline of setting aggressive goals to make them a reality. The thrill of the chase can be exciting and, when achieved or exceeded, exhilarating. Much of the success of HCA over its first half-century has been because of a culture of appropriate risk taking. The creation of the annual HCA Innovators Award encourages and recognizes the amazing entrepreneurial activity within our company. The sharing of these best practices is powerful for HCA and the U.S. healthcare system.

Looking back, how would you hope that your work has impacted patients?

I hope every day when thousands of people come into contact with our employees, their lives are extended, enriched, and made more comfortable. I hope the world is a little better because we started HCA 50 years ago. By providing the very best healthcare and an organization run by great leaders, I hope that HCA serves as a benchmark for the entire industry.

What is one last thing you'd like us to know about the HCA legacy?

Today the HCA family is building the legacy for the next 50 years. I am sure it will exceed all of my dreams and expectations.

Improving life. Making history.